Historical Dictionary

of the

EUROPEAN

COMMUNITY

by

DESMOND DINAN

International Organizations Series, No. 1

The Scarecrow Press, Inc.
Metuchen, N.J., & London
1993

British Library Cataloguing-in-Publication data available

Library of Congress Cataloging-in-Publication Data

Dinan, Desmond, 1957-
    Historical dictionary of the European Community / by Desmond
Dinan.
        p.   cm. -- (International organizations series ; no. 1)
    Includes bibliographical references.
    ISBN 0-8108-2666-6 (alk. paper)
    1. European communities--Dictionaries. I. Title. II. Series:
International organizations series (Metuchen, N.J.) ; no. 1.
JN 15.D56 1993
341.24'2--dc20   93-2871

For Conor, our Euro-Baby
Born in Brussels on March 17, 1992

CONTENTS

EDITOR'S FOREWORD

What better way to launch this new series of historical dictionaries than with a volume on the European Community? More than an international organization, this unique supranational entity is an integral part of the emerging "New Europe." Its influence is felt ever more broadly as it expands its coverage from sector to sector and extends its authority over more and more countries. Yet the EC is extremely difficult to comprehend. Just which institution does what, and how, is a puzzle not only for most outsiders but also for many Europeans themselves. Because the EC is constantly evolving, it is imperative to understand its origins as well as its present structure while pausing to consider its future.

This *Historical Dictionary of the European Community* is an excellent guide for all. It explains and analyzes the EC's development, institutions, and policies. It focuses on the role of crucial people, from the historic founders to today's political leaders and prominent commissioners. How the EC has grown is traced in a series of maps and a lengthy chronology. The alphabet soup of acronyms is clarified by a special listing. And, for those who want to know more, there is a comprehensive bibliography.

This volume was written by Desmond Dinan, Director of George Mason University's Center for European Community Studies. A native of Ireland, he studied at the National Institute for Higher Education in Limerick, University College in Cork, and Georgetown University in Washington, D.C. Aside from this book, Dr. Dinan has written extensively on the EC's political development and also on Anglo-French diplomatic relations.

Jon Woronoff
Series Editor

PREFACE

This book contains brief descriptive and analytical entries on the most important people (prominent politicians and statesmen, Commission presidents, and other leading commissioners), institutions, organizations, events, and developments in the history of the European Community. There are also short pieces on each of the Community's member states. An introductory essay assesses the Community's historical development by examining the related issues of enlargement, agenda, and decision making. The book should be useful to students, researchers, and interested lay readers. A comprehensive bibliography serves as a guide to further reading. In the text, items in bold indicate separate dictionary entries.

ACKNOWLEDGMENTS

I am extremely grateful to my friends and colleagues at the Center for European Community Studies who helped me with this project: Jamie Coniglio, our European Community documentation librarian, who provided essential documentation and reference information; Greg Ransom, who produced the maps, tables, and graphs; Caroll Vasquez, who labored on the bibliography; and, especially, Adrian Murcia, my research assistant, who tracked down obscure information, fed me a steady diet of data, wrote the dictionary entries on Felipe González and Spain, and prepared the manuscript for publication. I am also grateful to Susan Wallace, who proofread the text.

This project was made possible in part by a generous research grant from the Delegation of the Commission of the European Communities in Washington, D.C.

ABBREVIATIONS AND ACRONYMS

ACP	African, Caribbean, and Pacific countries party to the Lomé Convention
Benelux	An acronyn formed from Belgium, The Netherlands, and Luxembourg
BRITE	Basic research in industrial technologies for Europe
CAP	Common Agricultural Policy
CFSP	Common Foreign and Security Policy
COREPER	Comité des Représentants Permanents de la CEE (Committee of Permanent Representatives)
CSCE	Conference on Security and Cooperation in Europe
DG	Directorate-General
EBRD	European Bank for Reconstruction and Development
EC	European Community
ECB	European Central Bank
ECSC	European Coal and Steel Community
ECU	European currency unit
EDC	European Defense Community
EEA	European Economic Area
EEC	European Economic Community
EFTA	European Free Trade Association
EIB	European Investment Bank
EMS	European Monetary System
EMU	European Monetary Union
EP	European Parliament
EPC	European Political Cooperation
EPU	European Political Union
ERDF	European Regional Development Fund
ERM	Exchange rate mechanism
ESC	Economic and Social Committee

ESPRIT	European strategic program for research and development in information technology
EU	European Union
Euratom	European Atomic Energy Community
EUREKA	European Research Coordination Agency
G-7	Annual summit meeting of the leaders of the world's seven most industrialized countries, plus the president of the European Commission
GATT	General Agreement on Tariffs and Trade
IGC	Intergovernmental conference
IMF	International Monetary Fund
JESSI	Joint European Submicron Silicon
MEP	Member of the European Parliament
NACC	North Atlantic Cooperation Council
NATO	North Atlantic Treaty Organization
OECD	Organization for Economic Cooperation and Development
OEEC	Organization for European Economic Cooperation
R&D	Research and development
RACE	Research and development in advanced communications technologies for Europe
SEA	Single European Act
STAR	Special Telecommunications Action for Regional Development
UN	United Nations
VAT	Value-added tax
WEU	Western European Union

LIST OF DICTIONARY ENTRIES*

Acheson, Dean
Action Committee for a United States of Europe
Adenauer, Konrad
Andriessen, Frans
Atlantic Alliance
Atomic Energy Community
Bangemann, Martin
Belgium
Benelux
Berlaymont
Brandt, Willy
Bremen Summit
Breydel
Brittan, Leon
Brussels
Brussels Treaty
Cassis de Dijon
Cecchini Report
Churchill, Winston
Clappier, Bernard
Coal and Steel Community
Cockfield, Arthur
Cohesion
Cold War
Commission
Common Agricultural Policy
Common Foreign and Security Policy

---

*Dictionary entries are also indicated in bold throughout the text.

Membership of the European Community

The Original Six

(France, Germany, Italy, Belgium
The Netherlands, and Luxembourg launch
the Coal and Steel Community in 1952;
the Atomic Energy and Economic
Communities in 1958)

The Nine

(Accession of Denmark, Ireland

and the United Kingdom in 1973)

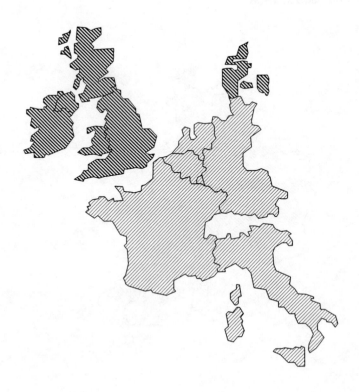

Membership of the European Community

The Ten

(Accession of Greece in 1981)

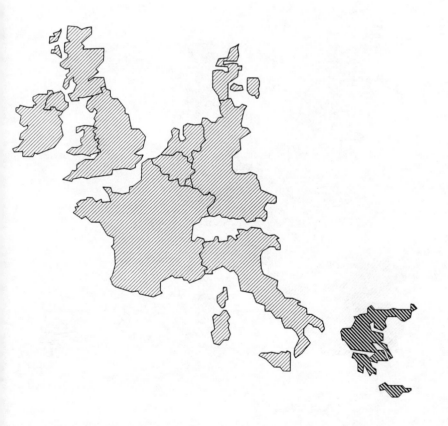

Membership of the European Community

The Twelve
(Accession of Spain and Portugal in 1986)

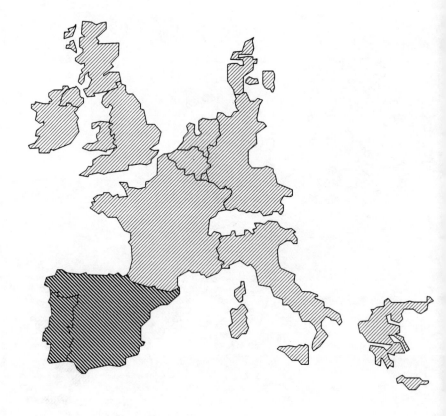

German Unification
(absorption of the former German

Democratic Republic in 1990)

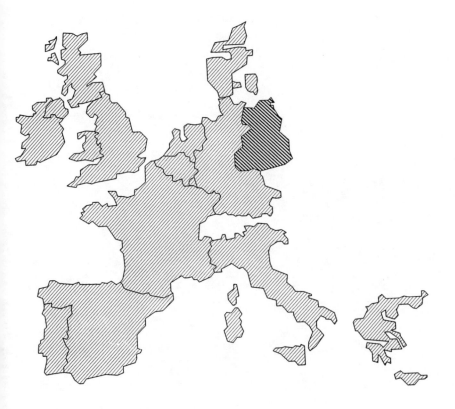

INTRODUCTION

Names and Dates

The nomenclature of European integration can be confusing. Used colloquially or formally, words like **"Common Market,"** **"Community,"** and "Union" often have different meanings. This imprecision is due largely to the incremental nature of European integration and to uncertainty about where such integration will ultimately lead. Thus **European Union** is a destination of uncertain definition. Will it be a United States of Europe, along the lines of the United States of America? Undoubtedly federalism is an appropriate model, although the definitive European Union will be a unique political entity.

In the meantime, the **Maastricht Treaty**, signed in February 1992, officially establishes a European Union as a way-station to the final destination. In the vernacular current during the negotiations that culminated in the Maastricht Treaty, the European Union is a "temple" supported by three "pillars." These consist of the revised **European Communities** (the **European Coal and Steel Community,** the **European Atomic Energy Community,** and the **European Economic Community**), a **Common Foreign and Security Policy,** and cooperation on justice and home affairs. A protocol attached to the treaty implements a **Social Charter,** using **Community** institutions but operating outside the European Union.

The first pillar of the European Union incorporates three Communities, often referred to collectively as the **European Community** (EC). Increasingly, the name "European Community" referred specifically to the European Economic Community, the most important of the three Communities. By deleting the word "Economic," the abbreviated title emphasizes the Community's gradual encroachment into "high-policy" areas. The Maastricht

1

Treaty formalized that usage by stipulating that the term "European Community" would replace the term "European Economic Community."

The "Common Market" is a popular name by which the European Community was known, especially in its early days. Strictly speaking, a common market (now called the single or internal market) is one of the Community's key objectives, eventually due to be achieved on December 31, 1992. But in its "low-policy" epoch the Community became closely identified with the goal of a common market, and the terms grew interchangeable. In the U.K., the practice of calling the European Community the "Common Market" persists, not least because most Britons distrust the Community's high-policy agenda and want it to stick to low-policy issues.

Some citizens of the European Union--principally in Britain--may have wished otherwise, but in the late 1980s and early 1990s the Community came of age politically. The Maastricht Treaty marked the zenith of the Community's development during a busy period that began with the launch of the **single market program** in 1985. "1992," the target date set by the Community for implementing the single market (i.e., completing the common market), became synonymous with the revitalization of Western Europe and the attainment of economic integration. Events in the intervening years, from revolution in Eastern Europe to civil war in Yugoslavia, have pushed the Community to the forefront of international affairs. At a time of spectacular change on the Continent, with old ideas and institutions disappearing daily, the Community seemed singularly stable and self-assured.

Completion of the single market program, leadership of the Eastern European aid effort, and involvement (however controversial) in the Yugoslavian conflict emphasized the Community's new-found confidence and determination. By the same token, they exaggerated the discontinuity between the EC's present and past achievements. The **Cold War** may have ended abruptly and the Soviet Union collapsed unexpectedly, but underlying shifts in the international system stretch far back into the postwar period. Similarly, the single market program that grabbed public attention in the late 1980s could not have come about without the profound ideological, political, and commercial changes of the previous decade. In short, the Mikhail Gorbachev and **Jacques Delors** phenomena should not obscure deep-seated forces and influences that have shaped contemporary Europe.

Thus a proper understanding of the Community's current position is possible only by comprehending its overall development. Precisely because of historical continuity, that development is difficult to compartmentalize chronologically. In 1989, on the eve of the Cold War's collapse, Peter Ludlow divided the Community's history into two parts.[1] The first, from the early 1950s to the early 1970s, saw a "low-policy" Community thrive in the rigid Cold War climate of unquestioned U.S. hegemony, German diplomatic diffidence, relatively stable exchange rates, and unprecedented prosperity in the member states. The second, from that time onward, saw the Community gradually acquire a "high-policy" profile in the changing circumstances of fluctuating superpower relations, marked American decline, growing German assertiveness, oscillating exchange rates, and widely uneven economic performance among the member states.

An alternative, but by no means contradictory, division identifies four stages in the Community's development. The first, from the Monnet Plan for French reconstruction (1946) to the **Treaty of Rome** (1957), covers the Community's emergence out of the postwar enthusiasm for European integration and concern about German revival. The second, from the Treaty of Rome to the **Hague Summit** of Community leaders (1969), involves President **Charles de Gaulle's** "veto" of Britain's membership application, challenge to supranationalism, and assertion of intergovernmentalism. The third, from the Hague Summit to the **Fontainebleau Summit** (1984), includes the Community's first and second enlargements, the relaunch of European integration, and the subsequent economic setbacks and disputes over budgetary contributions and resource allocation. And the fourth, from Fontainebleau to the **Maastricht Summit** (1991), charts the third enlargement, the constitutional reforms contained in the **Single European Act** (SEA), the successful single market program, and the Community's reaction to revolution in the East, culminating in the **Treaty on European Union.**

---

[1]Peter Ludlow, *Beyond 1992: Europe and Its World Partners* (Brussels: Center for European Policy Studies, 1989).

Instead of adopting one or other of these chronological approaches, this introductory essay will analyze the European Community's development by exploring a number of important topics and themes that dominate the Community's history. The first concerns the Community's geopolitical boundaries, including previous and prospective enlargements. The second traces the impact on the Community's agenda of political, economic, and systemic changes, in Europe and beyond, during the postwar period. The third deals with institutional issues and decision-making processes, as the Community adapted to incremental integration over the past forty years. These topics and themes are by no means exclusive or exhaustive. But their exploration helps to place the Community in a proper historical perspective.

Setting the Boundaries

At his famous press conference on May 9, 1950, in which he proposed pooling Franco-German coal and steel production, French Foreign Minister **Robert Schuman** declared that the new international authority would be "open to the participation of the other countries of Europe."[2] Schuman's statement suggests an inclusiveness that, in reality, his proposal plainly lacked. Although the ensuing organization had the word "European" in its title, membership in the European Coal and Steel Community was effectively confined to the West. Schuman and **Jean Monnet**, the brains behind the coal and steel proposal and the architect of European integration, never intended the countries of Eastern Europe to respond to their initiative. By 1950 the Cold War was at its height, and the Eastern European countries were firmly in the Soviet orbit. In his memoirs Monnet claims to have advocated the European Community as a "third way," partly as an attempt to break

---

[2]Quoted in Jean Monnet, *Memoirs* (Garden City: Doubleday, 1978), p. 46.

the bipolar mold.[3] In fact, Monnet expected the Community not only to operate within but also to augment the existing international system. Monnet was too close to the American political establishment to have thought otherwise. For their part, American leaders would not have championed European integration had they suspected that the Community would some day challenge the postwar bipolar order, in which the U.S., after all, had Western hegemony.

Even within the West, the Community was effectively limited to "Little Europe" of the Six: France, Germany, Italy, Belgium, The Netherlands, and Luxembourg. Monnet knew that the geographically peripheral countries to the north, south, and west of "Little Europe" would remain outside the Community but for radically different reasons. To the south, Spain was an international pariah, a legacy of its wartime sympathy and support for the Axis. To the north, the Scandinavian countries had demonstrated, during the negotiations that led to the launching of the **Council of Europe** in 1949, their reluctance to share national sovereignty. To the west, the United Kingdom, an economically and politically much more important country than its Scandinavian or Iberian counterparts, had displayed an even greater loathing of supranationalism. Moreover, in the run-up to the Treaty of Rome Britain had attempted to abort the European Economic Community by proposing instead a broader, looser free trade area. When the Six went on to establish the Community anyway, Britain formed the rival **European Free Trade Area** (EFTA) with Austria, Denmark, Norway, Portugal, Switzerland, and Sweden.

No wonder that Monnet initially conceived of the "European" Community as a select group of countries centered on France and Germany. His government did not even inform London much in advance of the historic **Schuman Declaration**. Of course, the new Community did not preclude the possibility of enlargement. On the contrary, the little countries of Little Europe especially wanted Britain to join, if only to dilute Franco-German domination of the Community. But a consensus existed in the Community that new member states would have to subscribe to the fundamental principle

---

[3]Monnet, *Memoirs*, p. 92.

of shared sovereignty, as a means of achieving the essential objectives of managing a resurgent Germany and promoting general prosperity.[4]

Although completely in sympathy with the Community's political and economic objectives, the United Kingdom never became fully reconciled to supranationalism. Yet Britain was the first country to ask for membership in the new Community. The reason for Britain's application was not only economic--a marked redirection of trade toward the Continent in the late 1950s and early 1960s--but also strategic--an awareness of the growing importance of the Community within the Western Cold War system. It was the latter point, and especially America's advocacy of it, that motivated de Gaulle to keep Britain out. De Gaulle's "veto" delayed the first enlargement of the Community until after his departure, when Britain and its economically dependent neighbors, Ireland and Denmark, finally joined in 1973.[5]

The second and third enlargements--Greece in 1981, and Spain and Portugal in 1986--amounted geopolitically to little more than tying up loose ends. Emerging from right-wing dictatorships in the mid-1970s, all three countries saw membership in the Community as the key to economic development and political stability. Greece applied first, playing the trump card of cultural affinity and democratic heritage. Disregarding an unfavorable **Commission**

---

[4]For the early history of the European Community, see John Gillingham, *Coal, Steel and the Rebirth of Europe, 1945-55* (Cambridge: Cambridge University Press, 1991); Michael Hogan, *The Marshall Plan: America, Britain and the Reconstruction of Europe, 1947-1952* (Cambridge: Cambridge University Press, 1987); Walter Lipgens, *History of European Integration*, vols. I and II (London: Oxford University Press, 1981 and 1986); Alan Milward, *The Reconstruction of Western Europe, 1945-51* (London: Methuen, 1983); and Peter Stirk and David Willis, eds., *Shaping Postwar Europe: European Unity and Diversity, 1945-57* (New York: St. Martin's, 1991).

[5]See Stephen George, *An Awkward Partner: Britain in the European Community* (Oxford: Clarendon Press, 1990).

opinion, the **Council of Ministers** endorsed the Greek request. It is a decision that some member states now regret, not only because the Greek Socialist government in the 1980s obstructed the Community's development but also, in the early 1990s, because of Greece's persistent economic problems and political difficulty in recognizing the breakaway Yugoslav republic of Macedonia. Spain and Portugal, by contrast, acceded to the Treaty of Rome after difficult and protracted negotiations and pride themselves today on being model Community countries, while tenaciously advocating their special interests.[6]

By contrast, in the 1970s and early 1980s the remaining EFTA countries were content to remain outside the Community. All were democratically sound, economically prosperous, and, with the exceptions of Norway (which had narrowly voted against EC membership in 1972) and Iceland, strategically neutral. After Britain and Denmark joined the Community, the remaining EFTA members negotiated individual trade agreements with **Brussels**. Given the relatively low level of economic integration attained by the Community in the 1970s, a level thought unlikely to be surpassed for some time, there was little incentive for the EFTA countries to seek another arrangement.[7]

Thus, by the early 1980s the Community's boundaries seemed permanently set around the soon-to-be **Twelve** member states. Turkey was the "odd man out," the only anomaly in an otherwise coherent Western system. Apart from Norway, Turkey was the sole continental European NATO country outside the Community. Unlike Norway, however, Turkey was both unwanted in the

---

[6]See Frances Nicholson and Roger East, *From the Six to the Twelve: The Enlargement of the European Communities* (Harlow, England: Longman, 1987).

[7]See Helen Wallace, *The Wider Western Europe: Reshaping the EC-EFTA Relationship* (London: RIIA, 1991).

Community and desperate to join.[8] After a troubled relationship with the Community, exacerbated by the invasion of Cyprus in 1974 as well as political and human rights violations at home in succeeding years, Turkey applied for membership in 1987. Turkey's performance in the Gulf crisis in 1990 and 1991 won American support for Ankara's application and seemed to strengthen the country's case for membership. By that time, however, the end of the Cold War had eradicated the systemic imperative for Turkish participation. Paradoxically, the dramatic changes of the last three years have, on the one hand, made it less likely that the Community will admit Turkey as a member and, on the other hand, opened the Pandora's box of the Community's boundaries to the East.

Even before events in Eastern Europe began to speed up in the late 1980s, the Community's commercial and institutional revitalization in the immediately preceding years had reopened the enlargement question. Responding to both sets of circumstances, Austria reviewed its relationship with the Community and applied for membership in 1989. Sweden followed suit in 1991; Finland and Switzerland in 1992. In an effort to respond to the EFTA countries' concerns about exclusion from the single European market, and to ward off a rush of membership applications, the Community sought to establish a joint EC-EFTA "European Economic Area" (EEA). Negotiations almost faltered over three contested issues: fishing rights, Alpine trucking rights, and a "cohesion" fund for the Community's poorer members to compensate for better EFTA access to EC markets. Agreement was eventually reached in October 1991, only to be rejected by the EC's **Court of Justice** two months later, on the grounds that the proposed EC-EFTA tribunal to adjudicate EEA-related disputes was incompatible with the Treaty of Rome. Apart from this legal obstacle to implementing the EEA,

---

[8]Bernard Burrows, "A Community of Thirteen? The Question of Turkish Membership of the European Community," *Journal of Common Market Studies* 17, no. 2 (1977): 143-150.

the earlier Austrian and Swedish applications suggest that an EC agreement with EFTA is unlikely in any event to delay for long membership applications from that direction.[9]

By repeating the rhetoric of the architects of European integration and citing the later examples of Greek, Spanish, and Portuguese accession, the new democracies of Eastern Europe can make a compelling case for membership. When Vaclav Havel spoke about Czechoslovakia and Poland rejoining "Europe,"[10] it would have been disingenuous for the Community to pretend that, to Eastern European ears, Europe was no longer synonymous with the Community. But the prospect of numerous applications from the East greatly bothers Brussels, especially with the single market program not entirely implemented and **Economic and Monetary Union** (EMU) and **European Political Union** (EPU) still on shaky ground. Just as the Community has attempted to delay membership applications from the EFTA countries, so too has Brussels sought to discourage the Eastern European countries from attempting to join. The exception, of course, is East Germany, which entered the Community by default following German unification in October 1990. For the rest, Commission President Jacques Delors envisioned a New Europe of "concentric circles."[11] Not surprisingly, the **Twelve** would form the inner circle, surrounded by the EFTA and Eastern European countries, with North Africa on the outer rim. A network of association and cooperation agreements would bind the circles together.

Czechoslovakia, Hungary, and Poland, the three most economically developed countries in Eastern Europe, have the closest relationship with the Community. But strong protectionist impulses in the member states, especially in France, held up the Community's

---

[9]Council of the European Communities General Secretariat, Press Release, 10323/91.

[10]Quoted in the *Guardian*, 26 January 1990.

[11]See Marinella Neri Gauldesi, "The European Community and Its Twelve Member States," *International Spectator* 25, no. 4 (1990): 236-250.

efforts to assist these countries economically. The Community finally signed separate **"European Agreements"** with Czechoslovakia, Hungary, and Poland in December 1991,[12] as a means of promoting reform and putting off for as long as possible the inevitable accession applications. Brussels hopes eventually to conclude similar agreements with Bulgaria and Romania by the end of 1992. In the meantime, the Baltic states, Albania, the former Soviet republics, Croatia, and Slovenia all seek to cultivate closer contacts with the Community. None is apt to apply to join for some time, although most undoubtedly aspire to membership.

Thus the Community's boundaries are unlikely to stay set for long. As it is, the contemporary Community context bears little resemblance to the world in which Monnet operated, and the Community's size will soon be equally out of proportion to his original conception. By itself, the single market program acted as a catalyst for new applications, although from countries firmly within Western Europe and close to the Franco-German core. Unforeseen developments elsewhere in Europe and the erstwhile Soviet Union now raise the possibility of applications from prospective member states far to the East. With the Cold War over and a new international order emerging, future enlargements will raise fundamental questions not of the usual systemic sort but of a more intractable kind. Specifically, where does Europe end? Which "Europe" is "Community Europe"? And how can a Community of fifteen, or twenty, or twenty-five member states be managed?[13]

Defining the Agenda

As the previous section suggests, the issues of enlargement and agenda are intrinsically linked. Despite the oft-declared, definitive

---

[12]Council of the European Communities General Secretariat, Press Release, 10324/91.

[13]For some interesting answers to the first two of these questions, see William Wallace, *The Transformation of Western Europe* (London: RIIA, 1990).

objective of "European Union," for most of its history the Community had a relatively restricted agenda of sectoral economic integration. Yet the Community's first enlargement in the early 1970s led to a decision to broaden the agenda to include economic and monetary union and foreign policy coordination. The single market program in the mid-1980s acted like a magnet to attract new members from EFTA. Conversely, the collapse of communism in Eastern Europe and the prospect of membership applications from the countries of the former Soviet bloc compelled the Community to consolidate the single market initiative, revisit the question of economic and monetary union, and explore the feasibility of political union.

The external political and economic environment, a range of domestic internal issues, and the changing dynamic of relations between the member states help to set the Community's agenda. Less visible, more mundane factors are also important. Thus the day-to-day functioning of the Community's institutions and bureaucratic behavior in Brussels affect the Community's competence to an appreciable extent. For instance, the Community gradually extended its involvement in a whole range of issues (environmental, educational, cultural, etc.) not formally included in the Treaty of Rome but subsequently incorporated in the SEA and the Maastricht Treaty.

The Community confined itself initially to coal and steel because, for all their rhetoric about integration, the then-member states could agree to share sovereignty only in a relatively restricted area. For Paris, the European Coal and Steel Community (ECSC) provided a means of harnessing Germany's industrial recovery and salvaging the postwar French modernization plan. For Bonn, the Community pointed the way to rapid economic recovery and international political rehabilitation. Germany was more than willing to widen the agenda of integration, but the French parliament's refusal to ratify the **European Defense Community** (EDC) in 1954 ensured that supranationalism would be confined to sectoral economic issues.[14]

A Dutch proposal during the EDC debate, to go beyond functional cooperation and establish a full customs union, laid the

----

[14]See the sources cited in footnote 5.

basis for negotiations in the mid-1950s about rekindling the Community. Monnet thought the proposal too ambitious and suggested instead an atomic energy organization along the lines of the existing Coal and Steel Community. A reaction in France against the EDC debacle and against the excessive nationalism exhibited in the 1956 Suez crisis enhanced the political prospects for further economic integration. The ensuing **Messina Conference** eventually produced treaties for a European Economic Community (EEC) and a European Atomic Community (Euratom). Both came into operation on January 1, 1958, with a membership identical to that of the ECSC.[15]

At French insistence the new Economic Community encompassed agriculture in the proposed common market. Just as the last governments of the French Fourth Republic had insisted, against opposition from some of the other member states, that provision for a **Common Agricultural Policy** (CAP) be included in the Community, de Gaulle's government in the new Fifth Republic struggled equally tenaciously to bring the CAP into being. By linking progress on the CAP to implementing the industrial common market, which Germany especially sought, de Gaulle eventually prevailed. As a result, by the mid-1960s, a time of unprecedented economic progress, the Community was well on course.

Sustained economic setbacks would soon plunge the Community into rough seas. In the meantime, Britain's impending accession posed a challenge of a different sort. The **Hague Summit** meeting of Community leaders in 1969 responded with a call for "completion and deepening" to complement enlargement. Completion meant finalizing the common market and, especially, the CAP; deepening meant entering the "high-policy" areas of monetary and political union. Other external factors convinced President **Georges Pompidou**, Chancellor **Willy Brandt**, and Prime Minister **Edward Heath** to extend the Community's agenda. International financial instability, culminating in America's decision in August 1971 to float the dollar, and the corresponding erosion of American leadership

---

[15]See Hanns-Juergen Küsters, "The Treaties of Rome (1955-57)," in Roy Pryce, ed., *The Dynamics of European Union* (London: Croom Helm, 1987), pp. 78-104.

within the Alliance gave added impetus to new EC initiatives. Two Community reports, the **Werner Plan** on monetary union and the **Davignon Report** on foreign policy coordination, pointed the way. At the **Paris Summit** of October 1972, the Community set 1980 as the target date for EMU. Earlier, the member states had endorsed Davignon's findings and launched **European Political Cooperation** (EPC).[16]

The worsening international climate, especially in the aftermath of the 1973 oil embargo, almost submerged the Community. Not only was the new objective of EMU unattainable, but the customs union itself seemed jeopardized. Huge divergences in member states' economic performances made monetary union impossible to achieve. More important, member states' separate, rather than collective, responses to the economic downturn undermined the political will for further integration. Coping with falling productivity, rising unemployment, and soaring inflation, the member states reversed the achievements of the previous decade by championing national manufacturers and reinforcing nontariff barriers. By the end of the 1970s, especially in light of the second oil shock, "Eurosclerosis" had set in.

Given the seriousness of this situation it seems remarkable that, less than a decade later, the Community had revitalized and recharged. The rise of "Europhoria" and the recasting of the EC agenda were due to a combination of interrelated economic, political, and ideological developments, both inside and outside the Community. Together they led to a conviction that, unless the eighties were to be as recessionary as the seventies, the Community would have to return to first principles. Simultaneously, the Community's southern enlargement diversified the EC's agenda by stressing the importance of regional policies and highlighting the issue of resource redistribution.

Technological innovations in the 1970s and early 1980s provided a strong impetus for change in the Community. New technologies demonstrated the drawbacks of a fragmented European market, while growing competition from the U.S. and Japan forced

---

[16]See Christian Franck, "New Ambitions: From The Hague to Paris Summits (1969-72)," in Pryce, *Dynamics*, pp. 130-148.

European manufacturers to take the initiative. At the same time, an ideological shift toward deregulation and market forces, even in countries with surviving social democratic governments, led to a surge of political support for a "borderless Europe." Realizing that decisive action would have to be taken at the Community level, industrialists and entrepreneurs forged strategic links with Brussels. The Commission, or at least a few farsighted Commissioners, reciprocated. Industry-Commission collaboration resulted in a number of diverse high-technology ventures: ESPRIT, BRITE, RACE, STAR, JESSI, and, to a different degree, EUREKA.[17]

Early experiences of private-public partnership, together with demands for unfettered competition and greater market access, created a climate in which the Delors Commission flourished. In 1985, Commission Vice-President **Arthur Cockfield** produced the celebrated **"White Paper,"** a detailed description of the steps necessary to achieve a single market.[18] Ironically, as far as the Community's agenda is concerned, the single market program represented a reversion to one of the Community's original objectives rather than a bold assertion of a major new initiative. However, unrelated internal and external developments in the early 1980s had launched the Community on an unprecedented constitutional debate. Although the results of that debate proved disappointing, at least they provided a timetable and a decision-making framework in which the single market program could be implemented.

The first direct elections to the **European Parliament,** held in June 1979, were an important element in reopening the constitutional question. **Altiero Spinelli,** one of the newly elected MEPs, a former Commissioner, and a veteran advocate of European integration, saw the directly elected parliament as a constituent assembly charged with drafting a new treaty for the Community.

---

[17]See Margaret Sharp and Claire Shearman, *European Technological Cooperation* (London: RIIA, 1987).

[18]Commission of the European Communities, *Completing the Internal Market* (Luxembourg: Office for Official Publications of the European Communities, 1985).

His colorfully named "Crocodile Group" of like-minded MEPs eventually produced a **"Draft Treaty on European Union."** The European Parliament's overwhelming approval of the Draft Treaty, in February 1984, challenged the member states to widen the Community agenda by encompassing security, defense, monetary, and macroeconomic issues. Aware that the Draft Treaty might easily be dismissed as the work of irresponsible, over-exuberant MEPs, Spinelli purposefully presented a reasonable blueprint for a greater sharing of sovereignty.[19]

The member states would probably have ignored the Draft Treaty in any case but for their renewed interest in European integration. For one thing, the recent accession of Greece and the impending entry of Spain and Portugal gave the Community cogent reasons to consider constitutional reform. For another, rising U.S.-EC friction over how best to cope with a sudden renewal of Cold War tension and EPC's limitations in the aftermath of the Soviet invasion of Afghanistan added to the momentum. In November 1981, **Hans-Dietrich Genscher** and Emilio Colombo, the German and Italian foreign ministers, launched a joint initiative to revitalize the EC. Although it resulted only in a **"Solemn Declaration on European Union,"** adopted by the **Ten** at the **Stuttgart Summit** in July 1983, the **"Genscher-Colombo Proposals"** nonetheless fueled the impetus for a radical revision of the Treaty of Rome.[20]

---

[19]See Roland Bieber, et al., *An Ever-Closer Union: A Critical Analysis of the Draft Treaty Establishing the European Union*, European Perspectives (Luxembourg: Office for Official Publications of the European Communities, 1985); Francesco Capotorti, et al., *The European Union Treaty: Commentary on the Draft Adopted by the European Parliament on 14 February 1984* (Oxford: Clarendon Press, 1986); and Juliet Lodge, ed., *European Union: The European Community in Search of a Future* (London: Macmillan, 1986).

[20]Gianni Bonvicini, "The Genscher-Colombo Plan and the 'Solemn Declaration on European Union' (1981-83)," in Pryce, *Dynamics*, pp. 174-187.

Conflicting attitudes in the member states about how closely to cooperate, especially in sensitive areas like security and defense, contributed to the failure of the Genscher-Colombo proposal and continue to inhibit European integration to this day. In the early 1980s, however, a number of unresolved disputes in the Community also impeded initiatives for a greater sharing of sovereignty. Most notable were the persistent and related problems of Britain's financial contribution and the Common Agricultural Policy's bloated budget. The member states settled both issues at the Fontainebleau Summit in June 1984. Reform of the CAP and resolution of the British budgetary problem relieved the Community's pent-up frustration. Newly available energy soon found an outlet in the much larger question of the Community's future agenda.

Also at the Fontainebleau Summit the member states decided to establish an "Ad Hoc Committee on Institutional Affairs" to consider the Community's response to internal and external change. Known by the name of its chairman, the **"Dooge Committee"** drew on the recent Genscher-Colombo and European Parliament initiatives and "attempted to translate a wide range of existing views on the nature of European integration into politically acceptable reform."[21] The Committee's report, dealing with a variety of institutional issues and a plethora of policy options from technology to political cooperation and the internal market, generated an intense discussion of European integration at the **Milan Summit** in June 1985. As a result, and based on a majority vote of the heads of state and government, the Ten decided to convene an intergovernmental conference (IGC) similar to the one that recently ended in Maastricht to propose treaty amendments.

Despite the initial opposition and continued skepticism of Britain, Denmark, and Greece, the IGC proceeded remarkably quickly. By February 1986 the Ten had approved the Single European Act, although full ratification was delayed until the following year. The SEA strengthened procedures for political cooperation and brought EPC, the environment, research and development, and regional

---

[21]Patrick Keatinge and Anna Murphy, "The European Council's Ad Hoc Committee on Institutional Affairs (1984-85)," in Pryce, *Dynamics*, p. 218.

policy explicitly within the treaty framework. Principally, however, the SEA endorsed the internal market program and set the target date of 1992 for its completion.[22] More hard negotiating followed, in 1987 and 1988, before the program was successfully launched. But the SEA's institutional provisions ensured at least that most of the single market program would be enacted in Brussels, regardless of implementation by member states. With a secure legislative base "1992" soon took off. Confident that fiscal, physical, and technical barriers would indeed be eradicated in the Community, business people behaved accordingly. Regardless of increasing productivity and employment, mergers and acquisitions certainly abounded.

But in terms of advancing the Community's agenda, the SEA was a disappointment. Earlier expectations of a radical treaty revision proved unfounded. Yet the launch of the single market program, in which the SEA played a pivotal part, promoted three important areas of Community competence. First, neglect of workers' rights in the initial single market relaunch led to a debate in the Community about the so-called Social Charter[23] and ultimately to the controversial inclusion of a "Social Chapter" in the draft Maastricht Treaty on Political Union. Second, poorer member states' concerns about the program's lopsided economic impact led, in 1988, to a renewed emphasis on regional policy and a massive redeployment of resources from the "core" to the "periphery."

---

[22]See Jean de Ruyt, *L'Acte Unique Européen* (Brussels: Editions de l'Université de Bruxelles, 1987); Andrew Moravcsik, "Negotiating the SEA: National Interests and Conventional Statecraft in the European Community," *International Organization* 45, no. 1 (1991): 19-55; Wayne Sandholtz and John Zystman, "1992: Recasting the European Bargain," *World Politics* 42, no. 1 (1989): 95-128; and David Cameron, "The 1992 Initiative: Causes and Consequences," in Alberta Sbragia, ed., *Euro-Politics: Institutions and Policymaking in the "New" European Community* (Washington, DC: Brookings Institution, 1992), pp. 23-74.

[23]On the origins and politics of the social dimension, see Beverly Springer, *The Social Dimension of 1992: Europe Faces a New EC* (New York: Greenwood, 1992).

Third, the success of "1992" inevitably forced the Community to confront again the complementary question of a single currency and a coordinated macroeconomic policy.

Commission President Delors was more than happy to reopen discussion in the Community about **Economic and Monetary Union** (EMU). He eagerly set about exploring the issue and produced, in April 1989, the **"Delors Plan,"** a three-stage proposal to promote economic convergence, establish a **European Central Bank** (ECB), and ultimately create a single currency.[24] The Spanish government, then in the six-month rotating EC presidency, strongly supported Delors' initiative. At the Madrid Summit, in June 1989, the Twelve agreed that the Delors Plan provided a blueprint for EMU and decided to launch the first stage by July 1, 1991. Mindful of the Community's commitment in 1972 to achieve EMU by 1980 and aware of deep differences over how best to proceed beyond the first stage, the member states refrained at Madrid from setting a target date for a single currency.

Addressing the European Parliament on July 9, 1991, the foreign minister of The Netherlands declared that "the Dutch (EC) Presidency regards the internal market as its absolute priority...without it there would be no monetary union, and without monetary union there would be no political union."[25] This statement and the momentum generated by the Delors Plan suggest that the single market program was the sole reason for subsequent efforts to achieve European Union. Undoubtedly there is a causal connection between a single market and monetary integration; the point is made in the original Treaty of Rome. Yet even the enthusiasm surrounding the single market program was insufficient, by itself, to overcome the deep-rooted reluctance of some member states to go beyond the first tentative steps to establish EMU.

---

[24]Commission of the European Communities, *Report on Economic and Monetary Union in the European Community* (Luxembourg: Office for Official Publications of the European Communities, 1989).

[25]*Financial Times*, 10 July 1991.

Moreover, the single market program might never have been launched but for an earlier initiative in the monetary sphere. Acting on the idea of Commission President **Roy Jenkins**, German Chancellor **Helmut Schmidt** and French President **Valéry Giscard d'Estaing** proposed a **European Monetary System** (EMS) in 1978. Concerned about persistent exchange rate fluctuations and the supposed abnegation of American responsibility in that regard, Schmidt and Giscard sought a zone of monetary stability in Western Europe.[26] Begun in 1979, the EMS exceeded its authors' expectations by quickly acquiring the characteristics of a fixed exchange rate regime, with the German mark playing the part of a reference currency. The consequent fall in inflation and stabilization of prices among the participating states brought the Community back to where it had been in the 1960s, before the collapse of the Bretton Woods system. That, in turn, permitted the Community to turn its attention to the unfinished business of the single market. "In a sense, the creation of the EMS...represented a necessary precondition for the free flow of goods, services and capital within the Community. Thus it is understandable that the **European Council** would not consider [completing] an internal market until the EMS had been formed but that, once formed, attention would immediately turn" in that direction.[27]

Once off the ground, however, the single market program could not automatically ensure a further push toward EMU. Instead, it was the contemporaneous collapse of communism in Eastern Europe and the revolutions there in 1989 that maintained the momentum of the Delors Plan and clinched the imminent completion not only of EMU but also of EPU. Delors rapidly realized that what he called the "acceleration of history"[28] in Eastern Europe, culminating at the end of the year in the fall of the

---

[26]See Peter Ludlow, *The Making of the European Monetary System: A Case Study of the Politics of the European Community* (London: Butterworths, 1982).

[27]Cameron, "1992," in Sbragia, *Euro-Politics*, pp. 47-48.

[28]*Financial Times*, 13 September 1989.

Berlin Wall and the rush for German unification, threatened not
only to derail the single market program but also to undermine the
entire Community system. Events in the East forced the Community
to revisit its political agenda and to expedite EMU. The other
member states' consent to German unification was the bargain on
which the Community's future hinged.

The deal was struck at the Strasbourg Summit in December 1989.
An exuberant **Helmut Kohl** sought to allay his partners' anxieties
about German unification and especially to overcome deep French
suspicion. At the end of the historic meeting, the other member
states acknowledged Germany's right to self-determination, but only
in the context of European integration and unification. In concrete
terms, that meant an end to German foot-dragging over EMU and
a commitment to proceed on EPU. Thus "by linking German
unification to political union, and by making the latter conditional
upon monetary union, [the Twelve] drew the lines along which the
ensuing debate [on the Community's future] was to be
conducted."[29]

The prospect of German unification nevertheless continued to
cause strains within the Community, notably between Paris and
Bonn. Only after the decisive East German elections of March
1990, when German unification appeared unstoppable, did France
accept the inevitable and attempt to implement the agreement
reached at Strasbourg. A famous Franco-German letter followed,
endorsing European Union and calling for "fundamental reforms--
economic and monetary union as well as political union--[to] come
into force on January 1, 1993."[30] This proved the starting point for
two years of frenetic discussions among the member states and the
Commission about the nature, scope, and competence of the
proposed European Union.

EMU, at least, was easy to conceptualize. The Delors Plan
already existed as an acceptable blueprint. At the Rome Summit in

---

[29]Panos Tsakaloyannis, "The 'Acceleration of History' and the
Reopening of the Political Debate in the European Community,"
Journal of European Integration 14, nos. 2-3 (1991): 88.

[30]*Financial Times*, 20 April 1990.

October 1990, **Margaret Thatcher** was isolated and outmaneuvered in her opposition to further monetary integration, contributing to her political downfall at home some weeks later. Thereafter the Twelve, including a more compliant United Kingdom, began to tackle the plan's most pressing particulars, notably convergence criteria, composition of the European Central Bank, and the ECB's relationship to other EC institutions and the member state governments. Negotiations ebbed and flowed during the specially convened intergovernmental conference on EMU that began in Rome in December 1991 and ended in Maastricht a year later. At Maastricht, the "member states in effect adopted the Delors Plan,"[31] setting the definitive date of 1999 for a single currency in the Community.

By contrast, the parallel intergovernmental conference on EPU lacked focus and direction. Negotiations covered a wide range of issues, including institutional reform, the Social Charter, and foreign and security policy. Political cooperation had always been an enigmatic issue in the Community. Defining a "security identity" and developing a **Common Foreign and Security Policy** proved especially arduous for the Twelve. The Gulf crisis highlighted once again the limitations of EPC, while demonstrating the difficulty of coordinating the member states' defense policies. On the one hand the U.S. cheerfully cited the Community's response to the Gulf crisis as proof of the EC's feebleness. On the other hand, discussions in the Community about acquiring a military capability provoked an intemperate American response, with warnings from Washington about the dangers of undermining NATO.

In any event, the Maastricht agreement gave the future European Union a defense dimension in addition to a common foreign policy but within a framework that soothed Washington's sensitivities. The **Western European Union** (WEU) was the means chosen to satisfy both requirements. Formed in 1955 to bring Germany into NATO following the failure of the European Defense Community, the WEU will now be called upon to keep the EC's emerging defense identity compatible with the **Atlantic Alliance**. More likely, the

---

[31]John T. Wooley, "Policy Credibility and European Monetary Institutions," in Sbragia, *Euro-Politics*, p. 157.

WEU will be the midwife for a future EC army, conceived at the time of the Cold War's collapse but apt to endure a lengthy gestation, probably until the end of the 1990s.

The Maastricht Summit, the culmination of the intergovernmental conferences, addressed a wide range of issues encompassed by the contemporary Community. The ensuing Treaty on European Union brought a number of new items formally within the Community's confines. But Maastricht by no means represents the end of formal agenda setting in the EC. The dynamic of European integration, unlikely to diminish in the decade ahead, ensures that the Community's official agenda will continue to change. The next intergovernmental conference on treaty reform is due to take place in 1996 but could well be convened earlier.

Making the Decisions

Decisions in the Community are made at a number of levels. The most visible is that of the European Council, the biannual meetings and occasional extraordinary sessions of the heads of state (in the case of France) and government of the Twelve, together with the Commission president. The European Council ponders the Community's most controversial political and economic problems and tackles issues incapable of resolution at lower decision-making levels. The Maastricht Summit is a striking example of the European Council in action. It took two days of hard bargaining to conclude the work of the intergovernmental conferences and resolve the outstanding particulars of EMU and EPU. Only the Community's highest political leaders had the necessary authority to endorse a single currency by 1999, strike a deal on the Social Chapter, and define a common foreign policy with a defense dimension.

The European Council is a relatively new institution. It emerged out of the occasional meetings of heads of state and government held during the Community's early years. In 1974 President Giscard d'Estaing proposed that such meetings take place regularly to conduct Community business. Giscard's initiative owed something to his predilection for intimate, high-level gatherings--he also proposed annual meetings of the industrialized world's top leaders (now the G7)--and to his frustration with the Community's inertia in the mid-1970s. The European Council proved its worth four years later when Giscard and Schmidt used it as a forum to launch the European Monetary System. Subsequently, some meetings of the European Council have become synonymous with breakthroughs in the Community's agenda, although others have failed spectacularly.[32]

The EMS initiative, and the institutional environment in which it flourished, revealed Giscard's and Schmidt's suspicion of established Community organs and approaches. Both leaders disliked the Commission and distrusted the Brussels bureaucracy. They advocated intergovernmentalism as a means to get the Community going again. Although the European Council soon became an invaluable institution, its mere existence was not enough to end the decision-making deadlock that gripped the Community at the time.

The main problem, as Jacques Delors later declared, was "the ball and chain of unanimity that bedevils the whole Community system."[33] In 1965, General de Gaulle had exacerbated a bitter conflict in the Community over budgetary reform (the so-called **Empty Chair Crisis**) by trying to prevent a provision of the Rome Treaty on qualified-majority voting in the Council of Ministers from coming into force. The others refused to renegotiate one of the Community's key supranational provisions. Faced with united opposition, and chastened by a surprisingly difficult victory over **Francois Mitterrand** in the December 1965 presidential election, de Gaulle sued for a settlement. The crisis ended with the "**Luxembourg Compromise**" of January 1966, an agreement to disagree over the question of qualified-majority voting. Although the treaty's provision stood, the other member states noted France's

---

[32]On the role of the European Council in launching the EMS, see Ludlow, *EMS*; for an analysis of the evolution and impact of the European Council, see Simon Bulmer and Wolfgang Wessels, *The European Council: Decision-Making in European Politics* (London: Macmillan, 1986); and Annette Morgan, *From Summit to Council: Evolution in the EEC* (London: RIIA, 1976).

[33]Quoted in Marina Gazzo, ed., *Towards European Union*, vol. 2 (Brussels: Agence Europe, 1986), p. 26.

consideration that "when very important issues are at stake, discussion must be continued until unanimous agreement is reached."[34]

The Luxembourg Compromise left a mixed legacy. On the one hand, it impeded effective decision making in the Community for a long time to come. De Gaulle's insistence on unanimity heightened the member states' awareness of each others' special interests and increased their reluctance to call a vote in the Council. For the next fifteen years or so, the Council made no decisions by majority vote on important issues (with the notable exception of the budget), even when national sensitivities were unruffled. But on the other hand, the intergovernmentalism that de Gaulle so bluntly asserted during the 1965 crisis laid a foundation for the Community's survival in the 1970s and reinvigoration in the 1980s, as epitomized by the European Council.

By the early 1980s, evidence emerged of the member states' willingness finally to question the norm of unanimity and, for the first time in fifteen years, to use majority voting. At the same time, enthusiasm for the single market initiative and the need to revise decision-making procedures before an impending enlargement convinced the member states to modify key provisions of the Treaty of Rome. The ensuing Single European Act extended majority voting to cover the bulk of the internal market program, while the political will to implement "1992" ensured that, if necessary, decisions would be put to the vote.

The Commission's role in the decision-making process has fluctuated with the Community's fortunes. In 1965 the Commission provoked the Empty Chair Crisis by proposing greater legislative power for itself and the European Parliament, in the full knowledge of de Gaulle's inevitable negative reaction. **Robert Marjolin**, a Commission vice-president, warned his colleagues not to persist with their proposal. Apart from its probable political repercussion, the proposal violated the Commission's "golden rule" of not taking any initiative "likely to encounter any outright veto [by a member state]

---

[34]The text of the Luxembourg Compromise and a good account of the crisis that preceded it can be found in John Lambert, "The Constitutional Crisis of 1965-66," *Journal of Common Market Studies* 6, no. 2 (1966): 195-228.

that would have left no room for negotiation."[35]   As Marjolin feared, the crisis resulted in a boost for intergovernmentalism, a setback for supranationalism, and a calamity for the Commission. Thereafter, the Commission refrained from asserting itself until the Jenkins' presidency in the late 1970s.

The Commission has once again regained its confidence, not only because of the inspired leadership of Jacques Delors but also because of the altered political and economic environment of the 1980s, which gave rise to the single market program.   The Commission is more likely once again to make bold proposals, although not if a single member state is apt to be isolated on issues still subject to unanimity. The European Parliament, which also suffered a setback at de Gaulle's hands in 1966, has similarly reasserted itself. Subsequent budgetary agreements strengthened Parliament's hold over the Community's purse strings, while direct elections have bolstered the assembly's self-confidence. But the EP acquired little additional legislative power under the Single European Act and did not fare much better in the European Union Treaty. The EP has undoubtedly become a key player in the Community's decision-making process, but its role cannot yet be compared to that of a legislature in a liberal-democratic state.[36]

At the level below the European Council, decision making involves continuous interaction between government ministers, Commission officials, key MEPs on relevant Parliamentary Committees, member states' civil servants based either in the national capitals or in their country's permanent representations in Brussels, and officials of the Council Secretariat. As the Community's agenda increased over the years, the number of actors and the complexity of the decision-making process grew proportionately. More and more participants at the less politicized, and therefore less visible, levels--below that of the Council of Ministers--make some of the most important decisions and continually push the Community's parameters. Thus "progress

---

[35]Robert Marjolin, *Architect of European Union: Memoirs, 1911-1986* (London: Weidenfeld & Nicholson, 1989), p. 314.

[36]See Francis Jacobs and Richard Corbett, *The European Parliament* (Boulder, CO: Westview, 1990).

toward supranationalism seems possible when manifestly political institutions are confined to the mere enregisterment of decisions made elsewhere...The institutions of the European Community have not achieved that bureaucratized state perfectly, but they do permit substantial policymaking activity by bureaucracies before political officials ever see the prospective decisions."[37]

Decision making in the EC, therefore, has evolved into a complex system of intergovernmental negotiating and intrabureaucratic bargaining. Throughout, national and transnational interest groups play a vigorous part, lobbying government and Community officials at all levels and lobbying elected representatives both in Brussels, where MEPs hold committee meetings, and in the national capitals, at critical points of the member states' political processes. Treaty revisions such as the Single European Act and the Maastricht agreement help to elucidate and streamline decision-making procedures but have not unraveled the Community's intricate legislative system.

Conclusion

In his opening speech at the intergovernmental conference preceding the Single European Act, Jacques Delors remarked that "conferences like this one are not convened every five or ten years. There may not be another between now and the year 2000."[38] Little did Delors realize that not one but *two* intergovernmental conferences leading to far greater revisions of the Treaty of Rome would begin in 1990. The latest IGCs took place so soon after the previous one because the success of the single market program and revolution in Eastern Europe had abruptly pushed the pace of integration. But milestones like accession treaties, new Commission investitures, or intergovernmental conferences should not obscure the reality of incremental integration in the European Community.

---

[37]B. Guy Peters, "Bureaucratic Politics and the Institutions of the European Community," in Sbragia, *Euro-Politics*, p. 82.

[38]Quoted in Gazzo, *European Union*, vol. 2, p. 23.

Institutional evolution, economic undercurrents, and long-term political trends have arguably been equally important in the Community's history as dramatic, newsworthy events. Thus the contemporary Community is a compound of constitutional construction, institutional design, and accumulated operational experience. As for its policy-making persona, it is difficult to dispute Stanley Hoffmann's ironic observation that the EC today is "an improbable, yet not ineffectual, blend of de Gaulle and Monnet."[39]

---

[39]Stanley Hoffmann, review of *De Gaulle: The Rebel, 1890-1944*, by Jean Lacouture, in the *New Republic*, 17 December 1990, p. 34.

THE DICTIONARY

ACHESON, DEAN (1893-1971)   The title of Dean Acheson's autobiography, *Present at the Creation*, refers not only to the U.S. secretary of state's key role in the inception of the **North Atlantic Treaty Organization** (NATO) but also to his participation in the launching of the **European Coal and Steel Community**.   By chance, Dean Acheson arrived in Paris on May 7, 1950, when **Jean Monnet** and **Robert Schuman** were busily preparing their radical proposal to pool French and German production of coal and steel.   Taking advantage of the secretary of state's unexpected appearance, Monnet and Schuman quickly took him into their confidence.   Grasping the importance of the proposal, Acheson endorsed the **Schuman Plan** and drafted a statement of support for President Truman to release once the plan became public on May 9.

In view of America's influence on European affairs in the immediate postwar years, Acheson would have received advance notice in any case of the Schuman Plan.   But his presence in Paris just as the plan was being formulated ensured its favorable reception in Washington.   Moreover, Acheson's enthusiastic response was due in large measure to his close friendship with Monnet, whom he first met in Washington during the war. Within a month of the famous May 9 declaration, Acheson set up a special "Working Group on the Schuman Proposal," in the Paris Embassy, staffed by young officers who fully supported the goal of European integration.

ACTION COMMITTEE FOR A UNITED STATES OF EUROPE
In 1954, when he announced his decision to resign as president of the **Coal and Steel Community's High Authority**, **Jean Monnet** began to form the Action Committee for a United States of

Europe, a small, powerful pressure group to lobby for greater European integration. The invited membership consisted of political party and trade union leaders from the **Community's** member states. The Action Committee remains in existence, with the same membership profile and objectives, although it is far less prominent than in Monnet's day.

ADENAUER, KONRAD (1876-1967) Konrad Adenauer was the first chancellor (1949-1963) of the Federal Republic of Germany and the architect of his country's postwar revival under the aegis of European integration. Early on the morning of May 9, 1950, **Robert Schuman** sent Adenauer a confidential copy of **Jean Monnet's** proposal to pool French and German production of coal and steel. The German chancellor responded enthusiastically. Like Schuman, Adenauer had a strong personal yearning for Franco-German reconciliation. Moreover, keenly aware of the depth of French distrust toward the new Federal Republic, Adenauer realized that shared sovereignty pointed the way to Germany's international rehabilitation. Only by integrating closely with neighboring European countries could Germany hope to remove the remaining controls on its domestic and foreign policy. Thus Adenauer fully endorsed the **Schuman Declaration**, which the French government released on the afternoon of May 9. Two years later, the **Coal and Steel Community** came into operation. Under Adenauer's leadership, Germany also participated enthusiastically in the negotiations that led to the signing of the **Treaty of Rome** in 1957, establishing the **European Economic Community** and the **Atomic Energy Community**. In the meantime, Adenauer had achieved his objective of German remilitarization, although not through participation in the **European Defense Community** (EDC), which Monnet had proposed in October 1950 in response to American and British pressure for German rearmament. The proposed Defense Community collapsed when the French parliament rejected the EDC treaty in 1954. This development threatened the future of European integration. If shared sovereignty was good enough for German industry, Adenauer wondered, why was it not also acceptable for German rearmament? Consequently, the U.K. proposed the **Western European Union** (WEU) as a suitable vehicle for German rearmament and membership in the **North Atlantic Treaty Organization** (NATO).

For Adenauer, harmonious relations with France were the guiding principle of German foreign policy and held the key to the success of European integration. An exceptionally close relationship between Adenauer and French President **Charles de Gaulle** cemented the Franco-German entente. They met for the first time on September 14-15, 1958, when Adenauer paid a highly successful visit to de Gaulle's country residence at Colombey-les-deux-Eglises, and immediately became firm friends. During the remaining years of Adenauer's chancellorship neither leader would allow other issues to come between France and Germany. Yet Adenauer's closeness to de Gaulle ultimately proved the chancellor's undoing. Members of Adenauer's own political party, not to mention the opposition Social Democrats, resented the chancellor's acquiescence in de Gaulle's rejection of Britain's EC application, in January 1963. More important, most of Adenauer's cabinet colleagues feared that the chancellor's friendship with de Gaulle, noted for his hostility toward Washington, would strain U.S.-German relations. Germany's security dependence on the United States--a fact of life during the **Cold War**--was too important to be jeopardized by a special personal relationship between Adenauer and de Gaulle.

Two Gaullist initiatives especially fueled German concern and undermined the chancellor's domestic position. The first was the **Fouchet Plan** to establish an institutional framework for regular consultations between the Six on security questions. This was in keeping with de Gaulle's idea for a "Union of States," incorporating the six **Community** countries but involving inter-governmentalism rather than supranationalism. Apart from Adenauer, the other Community leaders opposed de Gaulle's proposal because of its likely negative impact on NATO, although most agreed in principle with closer foreign policy cooperation. They also disliked the Fouchet Plan because of its obvious incompatibility with European integration as understood in the Community. A series of acrimonious meetings of Community member state representatives in early 1962 caused the Fouchet Plan to collapse. Later that summer, de Gaulle abandoned his grandiose scheme for a "Union of States."

But de Gaulle and Adenauer at least salvaged an institutionalized Franco-German alliance from the Fouchet wreckage. By contrast with the indifference and hostility of his smaller European partners, Adenauer had resolutely backed the Fouchet Plan. With Adenauer's political and temporal life obviously drawing to an end (the chancellor was then eighty-seven years old), de Gaulle borrowed the Fouchet Plan's infrastructure to cement Franco-German rapprochement. Thus de Gaulle proposed regular meetings of the French president and the German chancellor, with their relevant ministers, to discuss cultural, economic, educational, and international issues. De Gaulle and Adenauer signed the ensuing **Elysée Treaty** in January 1963.

The Elysée Treaty was the pinnacle of Adenauer's international achievements, symbolizing as it did reconciliation between France and Germany. But bitter political controversy in Germany came to a head during the ratification debate in May 1963, robbing the treaty of much of its value for de Gaulle. Alarmed by Adenauer's apparent acquiescence in de Gaulle's idiosyncratic European initiatives, a majority within the chancellor's own Christian Democratic Party joined with the parliamentary opposition to attach a crippling codicil to the treaty. A new preamble, inserted at the insistence of a majority in the Bundestag, asserted Germany's primary commitment to existing alliance obligations. Over the objections of Chancellor Adenauer, the Bundestag solemnly subordinated the Franco-German entente to Germany's multilateral obligations to the **Atlantic Alliance**, the EEC, and even the GATT.

Adenauer's humiliation over the Elysée Treaty made the chancellor's position untenable. An earlier controversy over an American proposal to establish a multi-lateral (nuclear) force (MLF) had helped to isolate and undermine Adenauer and the so-called German Gaullists in Bonn. Increasingly enfeebled by age and dogged by a domestic political scandal, Adenauer resigned in April 1963. His successor, Ludwig Erhard, was a steadfast Atlanticist and an avowed adversary of de Gaulle's. As a result, a period of steady deterioration in Franco-German relations followed, which Adenauer witnessed until his death in 1967.

ANDRIESSEN, FRANS (1929-) Frans Andriessen served in the **European Commission** first under **Gaston Thorn** (1981-1985), and then under **Jacques Delors** (1985-1992). In the Thorn Commission, Andriessen was competition commissioner; in the Delors Commission, he was agriculture commissioner until 1989 and then external relations commissioner. Andriessen's seniority and experience before coming to **Brussels** (he was The Netherlands' finance minister between 1977 and 1980) and his weighty portfolios in the Commission made him a key figure in the **Community**'s contemporary development. Coming from The Netherlands, Adriessen was an avowed free trader. This conviction often caused him to clash with his protectionist colleagues in the Commission, in particular with Commission President Delors over agricultural subsidies in the Uruguay Round of the **General Agreement on Tariffs and Trade** (GATT). Also in the context of the GATT, Andriessen was a key interlocutor in the Community's dealings with the U.S. and Japan.

ATLANTIC ALLIANCE A colloquial name for the **North Atlantic Treaty Organization** (NATO).

ATOMIC ENERGY COMMUNITY see **European Atomic Energy Community** (Euratom)

-B-

BANGEMANN, MARTIN (1934-) In 1989 Martin Bangemann became commissioner for the internal market, industry, and relations with the **European Parliament**. Before moving to **Brussels**, Bangemann was finance minister in Bonn (1984-88), a member of the European Parliament (1979-84), a prominent German politician, and leader of the Free Democratic Party. As Germany's senior commissioner, with responsibility for the internal market and industrial affairs, Bangemann was expected to wield considerable influence in Brussels.

Yet Bangemann's performance as a commissioner has been disappointing. Known for his humor, charm, and passion for philosophy, Bangemann showed little interest in the glamourless

duties of his Directorates-General (DGs).   Bangemann's
inclination to subsidize EC industries alarmed advocates of free
trade and set him on a collision course with **Leon Brittan,** the
competition commissioner.   Bangemann and Brittan clashed
publicly in 1991 over Brittan's successful effort to block France's
Aerospatiale and Italy's Alenia from taking over de Havilland, a
Canadian aircraft manufacturer.   Subsequently, **Commission**
President **Jacques Delors** sided with Bangemann and changed
procedures in the Commission, obliging Brittan to consult his
colleagues more often on merger cases.   After the de Havilland
case, Bangemann used every opportunity to attack the legal
"ayatollahs" of national and EC merger authorities, notably
Brittan's competition DG.

Partly because of his protectionist impulses, Bangemann also
clashed with **Frans Andriessen,** the commissioner for external
relations.   Moreover, Bangemann's dabbling in diplomacy and
penchant for making important policy pronouncements abroad
understandably angered the external relations commissioner.
Nevertheless, Bangemann continues to enjoy Delors' support.
That, together with his status as Germany's senior commissioner,
and the weight of the industry portfolio, ensures that Martin
Bangemann is a key player in the Brussels bureaucracy.

BELGIUM   Belgium is one of the most enthusiastic advocates of
integration and supranationalism in contemporary Europe.
Having been invaded and occupied during both World Wars,
Belgium immediately grasped the importance and potential of
economic and political integration for future peace in Europe.
Moreover, as a relatively new, decentralized country with strong
regional identities (people in Flanders and Wallonia speak
different languages), nationalism has never been a barrier in
Belgium to closer international cooperation and shared
sovereignty.   Finally, as host to the **Community**'s major
institutions, **Brussels,** the capital of Belgium, has benefited
enormously--culturally as well as economically--from Community
membership.

Throughout the Community's history, Belgian politicians and
diplomats have consistently promoted supranationalism and
encouraged closer integration.   In the mid-1950s **Paul-Henri**

Spaak led the intergovernmental conference that shook the member states out of a depression induced by the failure of the European Defense Community and forged a consensus on the establishment of the **European Economic Community** and the **European Atomic Energy Community.** A decade later Spaak confronted French President **Charles de Gaulle** over the "**Empty Chair Crisis**" and helped to negotiate the January 1966 "**Luxembourg Compromise.**"

Although the Luxembourg Compromise got the Community going again, it soon strangled the legislative process by making unanimity the rule rather than the exception. Belgium steadfastly opposed unanimity and, true to its pro-integration tradition, espoused qualified majority voting. In the 1970s, Belgian Prime Minister **Leo Tindemans** produced a famous report on the Community's future that, among other things, argued for curbs on unanimity and a return to majority voting. But the political climate at the time was not conducive to such a radical step. It was only in the early 1980s, when the extent of the legislative malaise became fully apparent, that member states began to consider seriously the prospect of reform. Belgium led the way: during its Community presidency in the first half of 1982, Belgium called for a vote in the **Council of Ministers** on annual farm prices. Britain, the sole country disputing the proposed agreement, insisted on unanimity and opposed a vote. Belgium's decision to go ahead regardless effectively buried the Luxembourg Compromise.

In the three intergovernmental conferences (IGCs) that prepared the Community's constitutional changes in the mid-1980s and early 1990s--the 1985 IGC leading to the **Single European Act** and the 1991 IGCs on **Economic and Monetary Union** and **Political Union** leading to the **Maastricht Treaty**--Belgium sought to increase the tempo of integration. However, the outcome of each IGC disappointed Belgium. In particular, Belgium hoped for greater progress in the Political Union IGC on foreign policy coordination. After all, **Etienne Davignon**, the author of **European Political Cooperation**, was a Belgian diplomat. The **Common Foreign and Security Policy** proposed in the Maastricht Treaty does not go as far as Belgium would like in squarely embracing military and defense issues. Thus, as far as Belgium is concerned, the agenda of European integration remains unfinished.

BENELUX Benelux is the collective name for Belgium (BE), The Netherlands (NE), and Luxembourg (LUX). **Paul-Henri Spaak**, the Belgian foreign minister, and Jonkheer van Kleffens, the Dutch foreign minister, conceived the idea while in exile in London during World War II. The Benelux Economic Union finally came into existence in 1948, and a new treaty of economic union was ratified in 1960. Benelux is a customs union that survives within the **European Economic Community** because the **Treaty of Rome** permits such internal regional groupings as long as they are compatible with the EEC's objectives.

BERLAYMONT The Berlaymont is the distinctive star-shaped glass and steel building in central **Brussels** that housed most of the **European Commission**. In 1992 the Berlaymont was evacuated for lengthy renovations to remove asbestos used in the original construction. The Commission then moved into a number of adjacent buildings, with the commissioners themselves relocating to the **Breydel** building. Despite this temporary arrangement, the word "Berlaymont" remains synonymous with the Commission, so that people who mention the Berlaymont mostly mean either the seventeen commissioners or the Commission's civil service usually housed there.

BRANDT, WILLY (1913-1992) As leader of the Social Democratic-Free Democratic coalition that came to power in Germany in September 1969, Willy Brandt launched *Ostpolitik*, a policy of openness toward the East. The Christian Democrats, in opposition for the first time in the history of the Federal Republic, denounced Ostpolitik as a sell-out of German interests in the East and a threat to Germany's alliance ties in the West. The ensuing domestic controversy fueled an equally contentious debate in the **Atlantic Alliance** and the **European Community** and gave rise to the specter for Germany's allies of a rootless, neutralist Federal Republic loosening its moorings in the West. Allied and internal Christian Democratic concern about Ostpolitik obliged Brandt to emphasize his support for European integration, which in any event he genuinely espoused. Moreover, Brandt stressed the importance of British accession as a means of reassuring those Community member states that feared Germany's resurgence. Brandt supported British membership in the Community for other reasons also and pushed at the **Hague Summit** in December 1969 for French acceptance of enlargement. He endorsed French President **Georges Pompidou's** call at The Hague for "completion" and "deepening" as well as enlargement but resented the other member states' presumption that Germany would foot the bill. The contrast in style and temperament between Brandt and Pompidou, clearly evident at The Hague Summit, exacerbated the political differences between them. Pompidou especially resented Brandt's repeated criticism of the CAP's bloated budget. Later, in the first year of British membership, Brandt opposed the proposed Regional Fund, which looked too much like an exercise in pork-barrel politics. Brandt's unwillingness to lavish money on the Community may have angered his fellow heads of state and government, but it won solid domestic support.

Secure in office, Brandt seemed set to lead the Federal Republic well into the 1970s. But in early 1974 Brandt was seriously embarrassed by the arrest of his personal assistant on charges of spying for East Germany. In April of that year, two weeks after Pompidou's death, Brandt resigned from the chancellorship.

BREMEN SUMMIT   The July 1978 Bremen Summit marked a decisive stage in the gestation of the **European Monetary System (EMS)**. German Chancellor **Helmut Schmidt's** forceful chairmanship contributed to a general acceptance of a Franco-German proposal, which appeared virtually unchanged in the summit communiqué, calling for an exchange rate mechanism (ERM) using a parity grid and a divergence indicator based on the European currency unit (ECU). Although still open to amendment, the Bremen proposal became the basis of the EMS, which the member states implemented in March 1979. Yet it was also at the Bremen Summit that Britain first balked at the EMS, and the country's unwillingness to participate in the future system became obvious.

BREYDEL   This is the building in **Brussels** to which the commissioners and their immediate staff temporarily moved in 1992 while the Berlaymont was being cleared of the asbestos used in its original construction.

BRITTAN, LEON (1939-   )   Sir Leon Brittan is the highly successful competition commissioner in **Jacques Delors'** second **Commission** (1989-92). A fierce free trader, Brittan has been tenacious--some say overzealous--in ferreting out unfair subsidies to industry and creating a level playing field for manufacturing in the **Community**. Brittan's championing of open competition caused constant conflict with his colleague **Martin Bangemann**, the industry commissioner. Brittan and Bangemann clashed publicly in 1991 over Brittan's successful effort to block France's Aerospatiale and Italy's Alenia from taking over de Havilland, a Canadian aircraft manufacturer.

   Brittan's enforcement of competition rules also caused friction with Delors, who increasingly sided with Bangemann. Apart from ideological or political differences, however, the relationship between Brittan and Delors was bound to be abrasive because of their personal backgrounds and characteristics.   Both are dynamic, forceful, and strong-willed.   Brittan is one of the few commissioners who will stand up to Delors at the weekly Commission meetings.   Moreover, both have well-organized, highly efficient *cabinets* (private offices), which dominate Commission business and more than adequately reflect their leaders' interests.

   Brittan came to Brussels from the U.K., where he was a senior Conservative politician and, between 1979 and 1986, a government minister.   Brittan left government over a policy difference with Prime Minister **Margaret Thatcher**, who nevertheless rewarded his undoubted ability and devotion to free market doctrine by appointing him the U.K.'s senior commissioner in 1989.

BRUSSELS   In the mid-1950s, during the intergovernmental conference that led to the establishment of the **European Economic Community** and the **Atomic Energy Community**, **Jean Monnet** revived his earlier proposal to locate the institutions of the new Communities in a specially designated "European District." Monnet's proposal again failed to win any support, although Luxembourg, then home of the **Coal and Steel Community**, refused to host additional Community institutions. Accordingly, the new Communities located instead in Brussels, where the intergovernmental conference was taking place. As in the case of the ECSC Assembly, however, plenary sessions of the joint Assembly for the three Communities took place in **Strasbourg**. Thus Brussels is the site of the **European Commission**, the **Council of Ministers** Secretariat, and the **Economic and Social Committee**. Brussels also contains offices and conference rooms for the peripatetic **European Parliament**, which may eventually move there entirely. Because of the large number of EC institutions located in the city, Brussels is a popular synonym for the Community itself.

BRUSSELS TREATY   Britain, France, Italy, Belgium, The Netherlands, and Luxembourg signed the Brussels Treaty in 1948 to provide mutual defense. Originally the treaty was directed at a future resurgent Germany. From the outset, however, the **Cold War** shifted the treaty's focus from Germany to the Soviet Union. Yet the signatories' weakness vis-à-vis the Soviet Union led Britain to pressure the U.S. to join. A year later the U.S. made a formal pledge to defend Western Europe and established the **North Atlantic Treaty Organization** (NATO). In 1954, after the failure of the French parliament to ratify the **European Defense Community**, Britain proposed modifying the Brussels Treaty to establish the **Western European Union** as a means of bringing Germany into the **Atlantic Alliance**.

-C-

CASSIS DE DIJON This is the popular name for a landmark Court of Justice decision that facilitated completion of the **Community's** internal market. In February 1979 the court struck down a German prohibition on imports of Cassis de Dijon, a French liqueur. Germany had based its case on a law that prohibited the sale of imported drinks that did not meet minimum alcoholic content requirements. But the court held that Germany could not discriminate against Community products that met the standards set in member states where they were manufactured. Based on the court's decision, the **Commission** developed the principle of mutual recognition, thus avoiding the otherwise impossible process of harmonizing in detail the member states' diverse product standards.

CECCHINI REPORT In 1986 and 1987 Paolo Cecchini, an Italian economist, led a group of researchers in a huge, **Community**-funded project on the "costs of non-Europe." The purpose of the project was to quantify the cost to the Community of maintaining a fragmented market. Based on data from the four largest member states, Cecchini's team of independent consultants assessed the costs and benefits of maintaining the status quo by analyzing the impact of market barriers and by comparing the Community with North America. Cecchini looked at the financial costs to firms of the administrative procedures and of the delays associated with compliance with customs formalities; the opportunity costs of lost trade; and the costs to national governments of customs controls. In early 1988 Cecchini's team produced its findings in a massive, sixteen-volume publication, popularly called the Cecchini Report. The gist of the report was that existing physical, technical, and fiscal barriers to trade cost the Community 3% to 6% of GDP, or a total of $250 billion, annually. Also in 1988 Cecchini published a one-volume version of his report in a book called *The European Challenge: 1992.*

CHURCHILL, WINSTON (1874-1965) Winston Churchill, the great British statesman, played a prominent part in the post-World War II **European movement**. Undoubtedly Churchill's most famous contribution to European integration was his Zurich speech in September 1946, in which he called for a "United States of Europe." Given Churchill's stature as Britain's wartime leader, his rousing speech in favor of closer integration had a huge impact on European public and political opinion.

But Churchill never envisioned British participation in this putative United States of Europe. In view of the cultural, political, and historical differences between Britain and its continental neighbors, Churchill thought that the U.K. should remain aloof from a future **European Community** and instead act as a transatlantic bridge between the continental countries and the U.S. Hence Churchill's opposition at the **Hague Congress** in 1948 to continental European efforts to craft a **Council of Europe** with an assembly that would draft a constitution for the United States of Europe. Had the Council of Europe emerged in that form, Britain would not have participated in it.

Churchill's support for continental European integration and his determination to preserve British sovereignty and independence shaped British attitudes toward the Community in the decades ahead. Thus **Margaret Thatcher's** opposition to British involvement in closer European integration is sometimes characterized as Churchillian.

CLAPPIER, BERNARD (1913-) Bernard Clappier was a French economist and senior civil servant who played an important behind-the-scenes role in the early years of European integration. In the late 1940s Clappier was head of French Foreign Minister **Robert Schuman's** private office at the time of the profound change in French foreign policy that led to the **Schuman Declaration.** Between 1951 and 1954 Clappier was director of external economic relations in the Ministry of Economic Affairs. In that pivotal position Clappier was one of **Robert Marjolin's** key supporters during the negotiations leading to the **Treaty of Rome;** he and Marjolin together helped to convince skeptical French politicians and civil servants of the virtues of the proposed **European Economic Community.** In 1962 Clappier chaired the first enlargement negotiations that French President **Charles de Gaulle** ended abruptly the following year. In 1964 Clappier joined the Bank of France, serving first as deputy governor and then (1974-79) as governor.

COAL AND STEEL COMMUNITY see **European Coal and Steel Community** (ECSC)

COCKFIELD, ARTHUR (1916-) Lord Cockfield was a vice-president of the **Commission**, with responsibility for the internal market, between 1985 and 1988. In June 1985 Cockfield authored the Commission **White Paper** that outlined the steps necessary to bring about the free movement of people, capital, goods, and services in the **Community**. The White Paper was the basis of the spectacularly successful **single market program** that revived the Community's fortunes in the late 1980s.

By that time Cockfield, a former Conservative government minister, was back in London. Although Prime Minister **Thatcher** had appointed Cockfield Britain's senior commissioner in 1985, she refused to reappoint him in 1988 because of the pronounced pro-integrationism that he had acquired in **Brussels** in the meantime. Thatcher supported the single market program but not the attendant policies and programs that sought to promote supranationalism. Cockfield was sorry to leave the Commission. Despite the ideological and social differences between them, he and Commission President **Jacques Delors** had become close colleagues and collaborators.

COHESION Cohesion is a **Community** policy to close the gap between the rich and poor member states and between rich and poor regions within the member states. Generally, the rich/poor divide in the Community runs along north/south lines, with Ireland included as an honorary "southern" member state. Cohesion has always been a Community objective, with initial efforts focused on helping the impoverished south of Italy. Cohesion became increasingly important as the Community enlarged first in the early 1970s and then in the early and mid-1980s. The accession of underdeveloped states such as Ireland, Greece, Portugal, and Spain exacerbated the Community's economic divide.

Cohesion received added emphasis with the launch of the single market program, lest completion of the internal market further widen the gap between north and south. Increased economic and social cohesion was one of the six objectives--according to the **Commission**'s program for 1988, it was "the fundamental objective"--of the **Single European Act** (SEA). Indeed, the SEA and the **single market program** nearly foundered because of the rich countries' unwillingness to endorse the **Delors I** budgetary proposals and double the so-called structural funds--the funds through which the Community promotes cohesion--in 1987. The issue was finally resolved at the February 1988 special **summit** in **Brussels**, where German Chancellor **Helmut Kohl**, representing the northern countries, struck a deal with Spanish Prime Minister **Felipe González**, representing the southern countries, that amounted to "a second **Marshall Plan** for Europe."

In the run-up to the **Maastricht Summit** cohesion similarly became a central issue when Spain, as the standard bearer for the Community's "poor four," insisted that any plans for **Economic and Monetary Union** (EMU) should include provisions for a cohesion fund. Scoring a diplomatic coup, Spain successfully lobbied its fellow member states. The **Maastricht Treaty** calls for the establishment, by the end of 1993 at the latest, of a cohesion fund to help the poor countries finance environmental and infrastructural projects.

As in 1987 after the SEA, so also in 1992 after the Maastricht Treaty, Commission President **Jacques Delors** prepared a budgetary package (**Delors II**) that included a generous provision to increase the structural funds (including the new cohesion fund) from roughly ECU 19 billion to ECU 29 billion. The issue was to have been decided at the June 1992 Lisbon Summit, but the northern countries, again unofficially led by Chancellor Kohl, balked at contributing substantially more money to the Community budget. Apart from popular concern in Germany about the costs of Community membership, fueled by ill-feeling over the substitution of the deutsche mark by the ECU at the end of the decade, Kohl opposed Delors II because German unification continued to absorb huge amounts of money, leaving little available for additional Community contributions.

COLD WAR The Cold War between the Western powers and the former Soviet Union provided the international political and security background for the first four decades of the **European Community's** existence. The movement for European integration and the European Community to which it gave rise were not a response to the Cold War but inevitably were profoundly affected by it. Most obviously, the Cold War ensured that the movement for European integration became, in effect, a movement for *Western* European integration. In the rhetoric of Western

European statesmen and European Community officials, "Europe" and the "European Community" became synonymous. Thus it is understandable that in 1989 and 1990, when leaders of the newly liberated countries of Eastern Europe demanded the right to rejoin "Europe," they meant the right to join the European Community.

Moreover, the Cold War affected the Community's development in a number of specific ways. One was its impact on American support for European integration. More than likely the U.S. would have supported European integration in any case, but the outbreak of the Cold War guaranteed that outcome. For the U.S. saw European integration as a means of strengthening postwar Europe economically and politically, thereby undermining indigenous support for communism and enhancing the region's military capability in the event of a Soviet invasion. This was a powerful motivation for the **Marshall Plan**, which played a decisive part in the history of European integration.

Fear of the Soviet Union also encouraged Western European countries to integrate more closely, apart from American urging to do so. Specific concern about German rearmament, which became an issue in the early 1950s because of the Cold War, caused the countries then attempting to form a **Coal and Steel Community** to explore also a **European Defense Community** (EDC). The proposed EDC eventually foundered in the French parliament, although Germany quickly rearmed and regained full sovereignty under the aegis of the **Western European Union**.

America's domination of the **North Atlantic Treaty Organization** (NATO), itself a creature of the Cold War, gradually gave rise to Western European efforts to use the Community as a vehicle to strengthen the so-called European pillar of the alliance. To a great extent, **European Political Cooperation** (EPC), the Community's foreign policy coordination procedure that emerged in the 1970s, was a response by the member states to the bipolarity of the Cold War international system. By "speaking with one voice" and asserting internationally their collective political identity, the member states hoped to exploit a temporary thaw in the Cold War and promote East-West détente. When the Cold War resumed in earnest in the early 1980s, the Community's member states redoubled their efforts to strengthen foreign policy cooperation and embrace a security and defense dimension in EPC, resulting in such initiatives as the **Genscher-Colombo Proposals** and the attempt to incorporate a security commitment in the **Single European Act**.

These efforts failed not only because of the difficulty of getting agreement among the member states themselves but also because of American opposition. Having dominated the **Atlantic Alliance** since its inception, the U.S. was not about to allow the bulk of NATO's European members to adopt common positions on security and defense issues independent of Washington. America's obvious displeasure with moves by the Community's member states toward security and defense cooperation was sufficient during the Cold War to restrict EPC to coordination of the political and economic aspects of security. Once the Cold War collapsed, however, American objections lost their persuasiveness, if not their persistence. Thus, during the 1991 intergovernmental conference on **European Political Union**, the Community's member states were far less susceptible to American pressure to refrain from developing a security and defense dimension than they had been at any time during the Cold War. The moderate **Common Foreign and Security Policy** (CFSP) that emerged in the **Maastricht Treaty** disappointed many proponents of European integration but could not have come into existence during the Cold War, when the U.S. used the Soviet threat to thwart Western European moves toward an independent security and defense identity.

COMMISSION Unlike the **Council of Ministers** or the **European Parliament**, which have counterparts in the **Community's** member states, the Commission is a unique institution. It epitomizes supranationalism and European integration. Commissioners take an oath of independence from their national governments and agree to act in the interests of the Community as a whole. To a great extent, the Commission embodies the spirit of the Community. A strong Commission (for instance, since 1985) means a strong Community; a weak Commission (for instance, throughout the 1970s) means a weak Community.

The **High Authority** of the **European Coal and Steel Community** (ECSC) was the Commission's forerunner. **Jean**

Monnet intended the High Authority to be the engine of supranationalism in the coal and steel sectors. The other negotiators' insistence on a Council of Ministers to represent the member states' interests curbed Monnet's federalist ambitions. The Council of Ministers immediately acted as a brake on the High Authority, as it sometimes continues to do today in relation to the Commission. Yet the Council of Ministers and the Commission have a singular relationship. When the tension between them is creative, the Community prospers; when it is destructive, the Community declines.

The Commission is sometimes described as the Community's "executive." Indeed, the Commission executes Community decisions, although usually in close association with the member states' much larger bureaucracies. However, the Commission does not resemble the executive branch of government. Its functions are to originate proposals on the basis of the Community's competence, to implement Community legislation, to negotiate international agreements on behalf of the Community (for instance, the **General Agreement on Tariffs and Trade**), and to "guard" the treaties (if necessary, by bringing recalcitrant member states before the **Court of Justice**).

The Commission consists of a college of commissioners and a bureaucracy. The number of commissioners has increased with each Community enlargement. At present it stands at seventeen: two each from France, Germany, Italy, Britain, and Spain and one each from the remaining member states. The heads of state and government select a Commission president approximately six months before an incumbent's term expires. Each government then nominates its own commissioner or commissioners (minus the Commission president). A Commission president's term lasts two years, a commissioner's four years. However, under the **Maastricht Treaty** the terms are being increased to five years, to coincide with the European Parliament's term in office.

Walter Hallstein, a former German state secretary for foreign affairs and an early collaborator of Jean Monnet's, presided over the first Commission. With nine members (two each from Germany, France, and Italy and one each from the other member states), the Commission spent the first few months of its existence settling into temporary quarters in **Brussels**, allocating responsibilities and portfolios among its members, and organizing the necessary staff and services. Commission officials came from the ECSC in Luxembourg, from the member states' civil services, or from academia and the private sector. Setting an important precedent, the first Commission recruited a bureaucracy that struck a national and regional balance.

The Commission bureaucracy has also fluctuated in size over the years, although it remains small compared both to national bureaucracies and to its workload. Currently the Commission employs a total of approximately 16,000 people, of whom about half are "A-level" professionals, the rest being either interpreters or other support staff. The Commission is organized into "Directorates-General" (DGs), the equivalent of departments or agencies in a national government. As the Commission's role has expanded throughout the Community's history, so too has the number of its DGs grown. There are now twenty-three DGs, with responsibility for such issues as external relations (DGI); agriculture (DGVI); information, communication, and culture (DGX); and energy policy (DGXVII). Each DG is broken down into directorates and below that into divisions.

At the top of the career service, directors-general head the various DGs. They report to a commissioner, each of whom has responsibility for one or more DGs. The allocation of DGs among incoming commissioners is based not on merit but on national prerogative. The large countries claim the important portfolios, although small countries can sometimes get a juicy morsel (for instance, between 1989 and 1992 **Ray MacSharry** from Ireland was commissioner for agriculture, which accounts for over 50% of Community expenditure). External relations, competition, industry, agriculture, and the internal market are among the most sought-after portfolios.

Commissioners meet as a college every Wednesday to coordinate their work and discuss draft proposals to the Council of Ministers. Decisions are taken by simple majority vote. Despite their supposed independence of national governments, commissioners are susceptible to political pressure from the member states. For instance, business people and politicians from a country involved in an important competition case will lobby the Commission, including individual commissioners.

Commissioners hoping to return to politics at the national level are especially sensitive to national pressure.

The Commission president plays a vital role. Although one of seventeen supposedly coequal colleagues, in fact he is primus inter pares. "Activist" presidents tend to shape the direction for years ahead not only of the Commission but also of the Community itself. **Walter Hallstein** is a classic example. However, Hallstein went too far in attempting to increase the Community's supranational authority and alienated French President **Charles de Gaulle**. The ensuing "**Empty Chair Crisis**" and "**Luxembourg Compromise**" set the Community--and particularly the Commission--back for nearly two decades.

Jacques Delors is the most successful president in the Commission's history. Delors came to Brussels at exactly the right time (in 1985, at the beginning of the **single market program**); was surrounded by a number of outstanding commissioners with responsibility for key portfolios (notably **Arthur Cockfield** covering the internal market); and had ideal qualities (dynamism, vision, and workaholism), qualifications (in economics), experience (as French finance minister), and contacts (he was close to **Francois Mitterrand** and **Helmut Kohl**) to excel. Soon, Delors personified the success of the single market program and the Community's rejuvenation in the late 1980s. His adroit handling of the Community's response to revolution in Eastern Europe and German unification further enhanced his reputation. The heads of state and government reappointed Delors for an unprecedented fifth two-year term at the Lisbon **Summit** in June 1992.

The **Maastricht Treaty** ratification crisis in 1992 seriously dented the Commission's authority. Paradoxically, the Commission neither played a prominent part in the 1991 treaty negotiations nor benefited much from their outcome. Yet the popular and political backlash against Maastricht was directed more at the Commission in general, and Delors in particular, than at any other institution or individual. Well before the treaty negotiations and the ensuing ratification crisis, Delors and the Commission had developed the idea of **subsidiarity**--that the Commission should take action only if a specific task or policy area could best be undertaken by the Community. For the

Commission's many critics, subsidiarity became a code word for clipping Brussels' wings; for the Commission's few supporters, it became synonymous with political survival.

COMMON AGRICULTURAL POLICY (CAP)   The Common Agricultural Policy (CAP) is the oldest and most controversial **Community** policy.   It was controversial even before the **European Economic Community** (EEC) came into existence. During the intergovernmental conference that resulted in the **Treaty of Rome**, the French government insisted, against opposition from some of the other participants, that agriculture be included in the new Community.   Apart from the overall economic importance of agriculture, France saw a Community-wide CAP as the best means to modernize and finance its huge agricultural sector.

The objectives of the CAP, as stated in the treaty, are to:
* increase agricultural productivity;
* ensure a fair standard of living for farmers;
* stabilize agricultural markets;
* guarantee regular supplies of food (a critical concern after World War II); and
* ensure reasonable supplies for consumers.

Charles de Gaulle, who became president of France in 1958, fought hard to formulate and implement the CAP.   In view of the relatively vast size of French agriculture, some other member states fought equally hard to limit the CAP.   In effect, de Gaulle wanted his Community colleagues, especially the Germans, to prop up French agriculture.   His quid pro quo was Germany's expected profit from the lowering and ultimate abandonment of industrial tariffs between the **Six**.

Apart from French concerns, agriculture was a controversial and problematical point for a number of reasons.   The importance of peasant proprietorship in Western European political culture and the persistence of a disproportionately influential farmers' lobby alerted governments to the potential pitfalls of agricultural issues.   A Community-wide decline in the economic importance of the primary sector and a corresponding drop in income for Europe's relatively few remaining farmers raised the political stakes.   By the mid-twentieth century agriculture had become a heavily protected and subsidized sector. In order to be politically acceptable, therefore, the CAP had to replace individual member states' systems of customs duties, quotas, and minimum prices with a Community-wide system of guaranteed prices and export subsidies. **Sicco Mansholt**, vice-president of the **Commission**with responsibility for agriculture, became the CAP's chief architect. He convened a conference of Commission officials, member state delegates, and representatives of farmers' groups in Stressa in July 1958 to draw up the blueprints. Detailed discussions on the CAP's fundamental points and procedures followed, including a series of complex and rancorous negotiations that preoccupied the Community in the early 1960s. It was several years before the Commission and the member states thrashed out the precise means by which the CAP would operate.

As finally agreed by the **Council of Ministers**, the CAP is based on three principles:
*   A Single Market: agricultural produce should be able to move freely throughout the Community;
*   Community Preference: priority should be given to EC produce over that of other countries;
*   Financial Solidarity: the cost of the policy should be borne by the Community rather than by the individual member states.

The CAP operates through instruments that vary from commodity to commodity. These instruments include:
*   guaranteed prices with intervention purchasing of produce in surplus supply;
*   quotas, levies, and tariffs on imports to prevent external supplies from undercutting Community produce; and
*   support for Community exports, mainly by refunds, to allow them to compete on world markets.

The CAP's problems inside and outside the Community are inherent in these instruments:
*   guaranteed prices bear no relation to demand and encourage overproduction;
*   surplus produce has to be stored in "intervention," at additional cost to Community taxpayers;
*   quotas, levies, and tariffs are protectionist measures that inhibit global market liberalization;

      *   export price supports distort world prices and undercut other exporters, leading to trade disputes.

The problems of overproduction, intervention, excessive protectionism, and international trade distortion became apparent early in the CAP's existence. At the end of the 1960s, Sicco Mansholt tried to rectify some of the CAP's most obvious excesses, but to no avail. By that time vested business and political interests had a firm grip on the CAP and resisted any reform. It was only in the early 1980s, when overproduction had reached obscene levels and the CAP was virtually bankrupting the Community--**Brussels** spent over 70% of its income on the CAP-- that the member states turned their attention to the issue. They were encouraged to do so by British Prime Minister **Margaret Thatcher**'s linkage of a settlement of Britain's budgetary dispute with curtailment of the CAP's excessive expenditure.

As part of an overall budgetary agreement at the **Fontainebleau Summit** in June 1984, the heads of state and government decided to reform the CAP. The Commission subsequently introduced proposals to bring production under control, diversify support to farmers (including the provision of direct income support), promote rural development, achieve a more effective distribution of support, and facilitate reciprocal arrangements with other world producers. The last point was critical in view of the recently launched **Uruguay Round** of the **General Agreement on Tariffs and Trade** (GATT). Attempts to reform the CAP proved equally contentious inside and outside the Community. Member states with large agricultural sectors or powerful agricultural lobbies--notably Germany, France, and Ireland--strongly resisted the Commission's proposals. The Council of Ministers finally endorsed the Commission's most recent reform effort, the so-called MacSharry Plan (named after the current agriculture commissioner, **Ray MacSharry**), in early 1992. In so doing, the Council hoped not only to curb the CAP but also to pave the way for a GATT agreement, which had hitherto eluded negotiators largely because of conflict over Community agricultural export subsidies. But the member states and the Commission misjudged the extent of international hostility toward the CAP. Other agricultural producers and exporters bitterly resent the Community's export subsidy program and continue to demand more extensive change than the Community is willing to make. For its part, the Community is offended because other agricultural trading countries, most of which are also protectionist, fail to appreciate or acknowledge the extent of Brussels' reforms. As a result of the impasse, a GATT agreement is long overdue, and the Community is acquiring an unfavorable image internationally.

COMMON FOREIGN AND SECURITY POLICY (CFSP) The Common Foreign and Security Policy (CFSP) is the successor to **European Political Cooperation** (EPC). CFSP is an integral part of the **European Union** established in the **Maastricht Treaty** at the end of the 1991 intergovernmental conferences. EPC had served the **Community** well but was an inadequate instrument for closer foreign and security cooperation, the need for which became glaringly obvious during the Gulf War and the outbreak of the Yugoslav conflict--events that took place while the intergovernmental conferences were in session.

The CFSP obliges member states to inform and consult each other in the **Council of Ministers** on foreign and security policy. Where necessary, the Council may define a "common position." On the basis of general guidelines from the **European Council**, the Council of Ministers may go beyond a common position and decide that a certain issue should be subject to "joint action." If so, the Council of Ministers may take decisions, by qualified majority, to which the member states are bound.

The CFSP includes "the eventual framing of a common defense policy, which might in time lead to a common defense." In the meantime, the CFSP will rely on the **Western European Union** (WEU) to take actions that have defense implications on behalf of the newly established European Union. Accordingly, the WEU's member states invited Ireland, Denmark, and Greece, the three EC countries not in the WEU, to join the organization or at least become observers. They also decided to move the WEU's secretariat to **Brussels,** close to the EC **Commission** and the **North Atlantic Treaty Organization** (NATO) headquarters.

It is too early to say how the CFSP will operate in practice. It is a cumbersome procedure replete with potential operational problems. For instance, the treaty stipulates that the Council presidency "shall represent the Union in matters coming within the common foreign and security policy." That raises the possibility of a non-WEU member state being in the Union presidency at a time when the WEU was acting on behalf of the Union. Apart from procedural issues, the CFSP presupposes a predisposition on the part of member states to work closely together. But the Yugoslav conflict has shown the difficulty of coordinating member states' positions. The most dramatic example was French President **Mitterrand's** gesture of flying to Bosnia in June 1992, immediately after the Lisbon **Summit**. Despite a commitment at Lisbon to coordinate the member states' foreign policies more closely, Mitterrand did not inform his fellow Community leaders of his impending initiative.

COMMON MARKET   The **Treaty of Rome** identified the establishment of a common market as one of the key objectives of the **European Economic Community** (EEC). In Britain, where a minimalist view of the **Community** prevails, the term "Common Market" is synonymous with the EEC and more generally with the EC itself.

The most immediate and tangible step on the road to a common market was to build a customs union. Thanks to French financial and economic reforms, the first intra-EC tariff reductions took place, on schedule, on January 1, 1959, and the customs union came into existence ahead of schedule on July 1, 1968. But the member states never implemented other steps necessary to achieve a real common market. Only in the mid-1980s, with the launch of the **single market program**, did they return to first principles and set out to complete the common market. To that extent, **"1992"** should have happened by 1972 or at least by 1982.

COMMUNITY   see **European Community**

CONFERENCE ON SECURITY AND COOPERATION IN EUROPE (CSCE)   The Conference on Security and Cooperation in Europe (CSCE) originated in a Soviet proposal, in the mid-1950s, to convene a conference of European countries to discuss such interests and concerns of the Warsaw Pact countries as

secure national borders, military security, and economic
cooperation with the West. The proposal, revived periodically by
the Soviet Union, languished largely because the Soviets refused
to allow Western Europe's North American allies to participate.
Only when the Soviets lifted their objection did a conference
begin in the early 1970s. It resulted in the signing in Helsinki, in
August 1975, by the heads of state and government of the thirty-
five participating countries (all European countries except
Albania, plus the U.S. and Canada), of the Final Act of the
Conference on Security and Cooperation in Europe. The Final
Act was not an international treaty but a statement of political
intent and commitment to bring about peaceful change, to
minimize the dangers of miscalculation, and to manage crises and
controversies in East-West relations. In three "baskets," or
categories of commitments, the accord covered political,
economic, cultural, humanitarian, information, and military
confidence-building issues.

The **European Community** member states, meeting in
European Political Cooperation, played a prominent part in the
negotiations leading to the CSCE's Final Act and in its numerous
follow-up meetings (Belgrade, 1977-1978; Madrid, 1980-1983;
Vienna, 1986-1989; and Helsinki, 1992-) and in occasional
special meetings and conferences. During the renewal of **Cold
War** hostilities in the late 1970s and early 1980s, the CSCE
proved invaluable at least in keeping the protagonists at the
negotiating table. Moreover, although the CSCE had resulted
from a Soviet initiative, it soon rebounded on the U.S.S.R.
because of the emphasis in "Basket III" on human rights. Citing
Basket III, Western countries and dissident groups in the Warsaw
Pact countries pressured the Soviet Union and its allies to curb
human rights abuses and set international standards of behavior.
Such pressure contributed imperceptibly but enormously to the
revolution in Eastern Europe in 1989.

Because the CSCE was a creature of the Cold War there was
much speculation in the late 1980s about its ability to survive in
the post-Cold War world. The U.S. had never liked the CSCE,
but the European participants saw its potential for peacemaking
in a new international system likely to be dominated by
nationalist struggles in the East. In a famous speech in Berlin in

December 1989, U.S. Secretary of State Baker identified the CSCE as a pillar of the "New Europe." That set the tone for negotiations culminating in the "Charter of Paris for a New Europe," signed in November 1990. The charter marked a watershed for the CSCE: by creating CSCE institutions, it shifted the focus of subsequent CSCE meetings from setting domestic and international standards of conduct to monitoring their implementation.

The disintegration of Yugoslavia and the Soviet Union resulted in a huge increase in CSCE membership as the newly independent republics applied to join. From a membership of thirty-five in 1990, the CSCE had swollen to forty-eight by 1992. Events in Eastern Europe also tested the CSCE's capacity to resolve conflict and mediate disputes. But perhaps the greatest threat to the CSCE's future lies in continuing U.S. ambivalence toward it, which is best exemplified by the establishment of the **North Atlantic Cooperation Council** (NACC). Although supposedly complementary organizations, the CSCE and the NACC, with similar memberships and functions, are potential rivals.

COPENHAGEN SUMMIT The Copenhagen Summit of heads of state and government took place on December 14-15, 1973. The summit was to have set the recently relaunched **Community** on course for the decade ahead. Instead it marked the Community's imminent demise in the face of soaring inflation, rising unemployment, yawning trade deficits, and a worsening oil crisis. To make matters worse, the October 1973 Middle East war and the ensuing oil crisis compounded the member states' existing economic and monetary problems and put the Community under enormous pressure. The Copenhagen Summit turned into a disaster: Denmark, then in the Community presidency, had a caretaker government and an acting prime minister; a group of Arab foreign ministers arrived in Copenhagen on the eve of the summit to lecture their Community counterparts on Middle East history and politics; British efforts to establish a regional fund ran into strong German opposition; and French President **Georges Pompidou** and German Chancellor **Willy Brandt** bickered incessantly about the best way forward.

COUDENHOVE-KALERGI, COUNT RICHARD NICOLAUS (1894-1972) In the interwar years Coudenhove-Kalergi championed the cause of European integration. Proud of his internationalism--the Coudenhoves were Flemish nobles, the Kalergis were Greek, and his mother was Japanese--in 1923 Coudenhove-Kalergi wrote *Pan-Europa*, a political tract advocating European unification, and subsequently launched a pressure group of the same name. Coudenhove-Kalergi spent World War II in the U.S., mostly teaching at New York University. He returned to Europe after the war but was not in the mainstream of the **European movement**. Instead he served as secretary-general of the European Parliamentary Union and later campaigned to turn the **European Economic Community** into a political organization.

COUNCIL see **Council of Ministers**

COUNCIL OF EUROPE The Council of Europe emerged out of the deliberations of several hundred influential Europeans at the **Hague Congress** in May 1948. The purpose of the Congress was to plan a strategy for European unity. However a sharp difference of opinion between "unionists" and "federalists" made agreement difficult to reach. The former, personified by **Winston Churchill**, advocated intergovernmental cooperation while the latter, personified by **Altiero Spinelli**, espoused supranationalism. But both agreed on the desirability of European unity and on the need to institutionalize that ideal by establishing an international organization with a parliamentary body. For the "unionists" that body would be merely a consultative assembly, bound to defer to an intergovernmental ministerial committee. For the "federalists," by contrast, the parliamentary body would be a constituent assembly charged with drafting a constitution for the United States of Europe.

What emerged from the acrimonious Hague Congress and from follow-up negotiations in late 1948 and early 1949 had the appearance of a compromise, but was a capitulation to the minimalist "unionist" position. The ensuing Council of Europe was a far cry from what the federalists had initially wanted. Although pledged "to achieve a closer union between its members in order to protect and promote the ideals and principles which constitute their common heritage and to further their economic and social progress," the Council of Europe did little more than exchange ideas and information on social, legal, and cultural matters. Only in one area, that of human rights, did the Council of Europe really distinguish itself. The Council's Court of Human Rights, often confused with the **European Community's Court of Justice,** is today an extremely important means of protecting and promoting civil liberties throughout Europe. Apart from its human rights agenda, the Council enjoyed a brief resurgence in 1989 during the revolution in Eastern Europe, when public attention once again focused, as it had forty years earlier, on the possibility of establishing pan-European institutions.

In addition to its role in the early history of European integration, the Council of Europe influenced the European Community's development in at least two unexpected ways. First, the decision of the Council of Europe's founding members to locate its assembly in **Strasbourg** convinced the **Six** to locate the European Community's parliament there also. Second, the Council of Europe's assembly socialized an entire generation of European politicians, particularly British parliamentarians who had had little exposure during the war to the intellectual ferment of the resistance movement. This was especially true of British Labour politicians, who were traditionally hostile to the European Community.

COUNCIL OF MINISTERS The Council of Ministers is the **European Community's** decision-making body. It consists of a government minister from each of the member states and a European commissioner. Foreign affairs ministers and the commissioner for external relations comprise the General Affairs Council, which decides politically important issues and technical questions that other ministers (e.g., agriculture, trade, transport, etc.) are unable to decide in the technical councils. The **European Council** can also constitute the Council of Ministers, although mostly it meets as a separate entity.

In the negotiations leading up to the **European Coal and Steel Community** (ECSC), the contracting countries persuaded **Jean Monnet,** against his better judgment, to include a Council of

Ministers in the ECSC's institutional framework. Monnet resisted because he feared that the Council would monopolize the ECSC's organizational structure, which it duly did. As the representative of member states' interests, the Council is inherently anti-supranational. The **Commission**, representing the "Community's" interests, is the Council's institutional antithesis. Tension between the Council and the Commission has been occasionally creative but often destructive. Thus the progressive strengthening of the Council of Ministers, at the expense of the Commission, has slowed down the pace of European integration.

The **Treaty of Rome** not only maintained the Council of Ministers as a Community institution but also strengthened its power vis-à-vis the ECSC Treaty. However, to prevent a single member state or a small group of member states from obstructing Community decision making, the Treaty of Rome stipulated that, after a transitional period, decisions in the Council could be taken on a wide range of issues by qualified-majority vote. Based on its size, each country has a certain number of votes; in order to become law a proposal must win a qualified majority (approximately 75%) rather than an absolute majority (50% plus one vote).

Qualified-majority voting was to have come into operation in January 1966, but French obstructionism during the so-called **Empty Chair Crisis**--when France withdrew from the Council of Ministers for a seven-month period beginning in July 1965--obliged the other member states to temporize. Under the terms of the January 1966 **"Luxembourg Compromise,"** the member states agreed to disagree on majority voting. While insisting on the validity of majority voting as outlined in the Treaty of Rome, they conceded France's point that a member state's special national interest ought to be respected. As a result, the member states avoided majority voting out of extreme sensitivity to each other's concerns and instead maintained unanimity. For the next twenty years, until pressure for reform finally forced the Council to abandon unanimity, the legislative process became clogged up with proposals on which the member states could not agree.

The **Single European Act** brought about a dramatic change. The Council's poor legislative record, the improbability of reaching unanimity on anything in an enlarged Community (Spain and Portugal were due to join in 1986), and the urgency of the **single market program** forced the member states to insist on majority voting for the bulk of the **"1992"** directives. That stipulation, together with moral pressure on the member states not to resort to unanimity in other areas, considerably improved Community decision making.

The Council has a small permanent secretariat, located in **Brussels**. Most Council meetings take place in Brussels, although a few are held annually in Luxembourg. A committee comprising the ambassadors (called "permanent representatives") of the member states assists the Council in its work. Known by its French acronym "COREPER," the permanent representatives' committee meets weekly to prepare Council meetings, discuss the legislative agenda, and liaise with the Commission. Given the enormity of Council business, COREPER has become extremely powerful during the Community's history. To a great extent it is in COREPER that the Community's day-to-day decisions are made.

The work of COREPER and the Council takes place in secret. There are numerous media reports and leaks, but outsiders cannot attend meetings. Consequently the Community's legislative process is closed to public scrutiny. Criticism that important decisions are being taken secretly in COREPER by a group of bureaucrats has fueled debate in the Community over the so-called democratic deficit. In their defense the member states retort that the Council is responsible for COREPER's actions, and the Council consists of elected politicians. The limited legislative role of the **European Parliament** is another dimension of the democratic deficit debate. The Council's relations with Parliament are frosty. The "cooperation procedure," introduced in the Single European Act to give the EP some decision-making power, has not worked out well in practice. The **Maastricht Treaty** increases the Parliament's decision-making power by extending "cooperation" and introducing "co-decision." It is too early to say how co-decision will work in practice, but the history of Council-Parliament relations suggests that conflict between both institutions will persist.

The Council enjoys a more harmonious relationship with the Commission, with which it must deal responsibly on a daily basis.

Nor can the Council make decisions unless the Commission has presented proposals. For its part, after the bitter experience of the Empty Chair Crisis, the Commission will not present a proposal likely to embarrass or incur opposition from any member state. A host of working groups and groups of national civil servants discuss Commission proposals and try to work out any potential problems. Day-to-day liaison between the Council and the Commission takes place through COREPER's contacts with the *cabinets*, or private offices, of each commissioner.

Presidency (chairmanship) of the Council rotates among the member states every six months in alphabetical order, according to each country's native language. Countries holding the presidency are expected to play a conciliatory role and not to press their own agendas. Nevertheless each country has a certain number of objectives that it attempts to promote during its presidency. During the British presidency in the second half of 1992, for instance, London hoped to complete the single market program, ratify the Maastricht Treaty throughout the Community, reach a settlement on the "**Delors II**" budgetary package, and begin enlargement "pre-negotiations."

The Council presidency is a politically challenging and logistically burdensome job. Large countries tend to fare better logistically because of their greater resources. But not all large countries meet the political challenge or at least not during each of their presidencies. France, for instance, performed abysmally in the Council presidency in the first half of 1979 but brilliantly in the first half of 1984. The difference lay in the level of commitment at the top: in 1979 President **Valéry Giscard d'Estaing** was bored and irritated with the Community; in 1984 President **Francois Mitterrand** was enthusiastic about it. Small countries generally try to compensate for their limited resources by bringing political goodwill and fewer vested interests to their presidencies. The Portuguese presidency, in the first half of 1992, is a case in point. In its first-ever presidency, during a period of turmoil in the Community caused by the rich countries' refusal to fund the Delors II package and Denmark's rejection of the Maastricht Treaty, Portugal performed extremely well.

The Community's likely enlargement in the near future has already raised the question of the rotating presidency's future.

The system is inherently fair but inefficient. In a Community of fifteen, twenty, or twenty-five member states, countries would be out of the presidency for periods of eight, eleven, or thirteen years. But restricting the presidency to large member states is not politically feasible. Perhaps the alternative is to strengthen the Commission and reduce the member states' power. After all, that was Monnet's original idea.

COURT OF FIRST INSTANCE The increasing workload of the **Court of Justice**, especially concerning disputes between management and staff in the **Community's** institutions, obliged the member states, in the 1986 **Single European Act**, to establish a Court of First Instance. Like the Court of Justice, the Court of First Instance sits in Luxembourg. It has twelve judges, appointed under the same conditions as judges on the Court of Justice. As well as management-staff disputes, the Court of First Instance has jurisdiction over cases relating to the **Coal and Steel Community** Treaty and enforcement of rules on competition policy. Appeals against its judgments are brought to the Court of Justice.

COURT OF JUSTICE The Court of Justice is one of the least known but most important **Community** institutions. Located in Luxembourg, the court currently comprises thirteen judges: one per member state plus an additional judge to provide an odd number on the bench. A judge's term is six years (renewable), with turn-over staggered in three-year cycles.

The court is responsible for the interpretation and application of Community law. The treaties and their amendments, on which Community law is based, contain many general provisions, for instance, for a **Common Agricultural Policy** (CAP) and for free movement of goods, capital, services, and labor. So-called secondary legislation translates these general principles into specific rules. Each year the court hears an average of 400 cases in the following categories: infringement (brought by the **Commission** either on its own initiative or at the prompting of a member state); application for annulment (brought by other EC institutions, member states, or private parties to review the legality of a Council or Commission act); failure to act (brought by other EC institutions, member states, and private parties against an EC institution that fails to take action stipulated by the treaties); and interpretation (brought by national courts seeking a preliminary ruling on the applicability of Community law in cases before them). Questions of interpretation constitute the largest number of cases before the Court of Justice.

Over the years, the court's judgments have been almost as important as actions by the Commission or Council in shaping the Community's development. For instance, the **Cassis de Dijon** case allowed the Commission to develop the principle of mutual recognition, thus avoiding the otherwise impossible process of harmonizing in detail the member states' diverse product standards. Mutual recognition, in turn, provided one of the most important pillars for the **single market program**.

The increasing workload of the Court of Justice, especially concerning disputes between management and staff in the Community's institutions, obliged the member states, in the (1986) **Single European Act**, to establish a "**Court of First Instance.**" As well as management-staff disputes, the Court of First Instance has jurisdiction over cases relating to the **Coal and Steel Community** Treaty and enforcement of rules on competition policy. Appeals against its judgments are brought to the Court of Justice.

-D-

DAVIGNON REPORT   As part of a proposal to "deepen" the **Community** at the same time as its first enlargement, French President **Georges Pompidou** advocated a system of foreign policy cooperation through regular meetings of foreign ministers and, possibly, the establishment of a secretariat in Paris. This smacked to the other Community leaders of a revival of the **Fouchet Plan**, although they by no means rejected the idea of foreign policy coordination among the **Six** with a view to reaching common positions. Especially in the context of Germany's *Ostpolitik*, the member states quickly grasped the utility of at least an exchange of information on each other's foreign policies. Accordingly, the leaders appointed **Etienne Davignon**, a senior Belgian Foreign

Ministry official, to prepare a report by mid-1970. Davignon's report, submitted to the foreign ministers in May 1970 and adopted the following October, struck the lowest common denominator. Instead of a permanent secretariat in Paris, as Pompidou had proposed, Davignon avoided altogether the issue of a secretariat, and therefore a location, and suggested that **European Political Cooperation** (EPC) consist of biannual meetings of foreign ministers and more frequent meetings of their political directors. The country in the presidency of the Community would also preside over EPC and provide the necessary infrastructural support.

DAVIGNON, VISCOUNT ETIENNE (1932-) "Stevy" Davignon, the Belgian public servant and, in later life, corporate businessman, played a vital role in the **Community's** development on two distinct occasions. First, as political director of the Belgian Foreign Ministry in the early 1970s Davignon chaired the committee of member state representatives that devised and launched **European Political Cooperation** (EPC). Second, as commissioner for industry in the **Roy Jenkins** and **Gaston Thorn** Commissions, Davignon worked with the CEOs of leading European manufacturers to promote collaboration in research and development and boost Europe's waning position in the global marketplace. Thus Davignon was primarily responsible for a host of Community programs in the early 1980s to improve European competitiveness, programs which helped to lay the foundation for the **single market program**.

DE GASPERI, ALCIDE (1881-1954) Like **Robert Schuman** in France and **Konrad Adenauer** in Germany, Alcide de Gasperi was a leading proponent of European integration in the immediate postwar period. Also like Schuman and Adenauer, de Gasperi was a Christian Democrat whose prewar and wartime experience had imbued in him a commitment to European reconciliation and cooperation. Despite frequent changes of government, de Gasperi's stewardship as prime minister between 1945 and 1953 allowed Italy to regain its international respectability and become a leading player in the movement for European integration. De Gasperi's specific contribution was to promote Italy's participation in the negotiations that resulted in the establishment of the **Coal and Steel Community**.

DE GAULLE, CHARLES (1890-1970)   Charles de Gaulle, president of France between 1958 and 1969, is renowned for his championing of the nation-state, hatred of supranationalism, and hostility toward the **European Community**. Indeed, de Gaulle provoked a number of crises in the Community in the 1960s, yet his contribution to European integration and his attitude toward the Community were far from negative. Despite its threat to French sovereignty, the Community offered de Gaulle an unprecedented opportunity to promote two overriding objectives. The first was French economic advancement; the second was an institutional framework in which to embed Franco-German rapprochement. Thus the Community flourished in its early years not because de Gaulle reluctantly acquiesced in it--either for legal reasons, or because his government depended on the support of the pro-EC Independents in the National Assembly, or because he was preoccupied with the war in Algeria--but because the General strongly supported a certain amount of sectoral economic integration.

Apart from industrial rejuvenation, de Gaulle saw in the European Community a unique opportunity to modernize the large and cumbersome French agricultural sector. The solution lay in the proposed **Common Agricultural Policy** (CAP), which would provide a Community-wide outlet for French produce, guarantee high prices in the EC regardless of low prices on the world market, and subsidize the export of surplus produce outside the Community itself. Thus the CAP, subsequently denigrated as a drain on Community resources and an impediment to international trade accord, owes its existence to de Gaulle. In the 1960s the CAP proved a vital instrument of Community solidarity and helped restructure declining Western European agriculture. More important, without the CAP there would not have been a Community of any kind.   Just as the French Assembly had successfully insisted on agricultural provisions in the **Treaty of Rome**, so, too, had de Gaulle demanded implementation of those provisions as a condition of implementing the treaty as a whole. The industrial customs union and common external tariff came into being because of, and not despite, the Common Agricultural Policy.

De Gaulle's generally positive position on European economic integration complemented his policy toward Germany. Whereas de Gaulle had left the French political stage in 1946 advocating a punitive policy toward a weak, divided Germany, he returned in 1958 to a radically altered European scene. With Germany reindustrialized and rearmed, de Gaulle abandoned his earlier position and espoused instead the then-orthodox French policy of reconciliation and rapprochement. De Gaulle cemented this policy in an exceptionally close relationship with Chancellor **Konrad Adenauer.** Both leaders believed that their countries' future, and the future of Europe, depended above all on close Franco-German accord. The **Elysée Treaty,** signed by de Gaulle and Adenauer in January 1963, symbolized the close friendship between them and their countries and became the institutional basis for Franco-German leadership of the European Community.

Apart from developing a close relationship with Adenauer, de Gaulle is best known in the context of the European Community for keeping Britain out and for curtailing the powers of the **European Parliament** and **Commission.** Once again, both seem negative achievements. But allowing Britain into the Community in the early 1960s would in all likelihood have thwarted the CAP, undermined economic integration, and turned the customs union into a broad free trade area. Shortly before signing the Elysée Treaty in January 1963, de Gaulle had vetoed Britain's application to join the Community. As well as economic considerations, at issue was de Gaulle's conception of the Community and his espousal of a "European Europe." The Treaty of Rome could only succeed, he thought, in the context of a broader political framework of intergovernmental cooperation. Such cooperation was an essential prerequisite for the emergence of an economically strong, politically assertive, and militarily independent Europe. As Britain's world view differed fundamentally from France's, de Gaulle could not take seriously Britain's candidacy for Community membership. He vetoed Britain's second membership application in 1967 for essentially the same reasons.

De Gaulle's stand against the Commission in 1965 epitomized his hostility to supranationalism. The epic clash between de

Gaulle and Commission President **Walter Hallstein,** personifying the conflict between nationalism and supranationalism, erupted in the infamous **"Empty Chair Crisis"** of 1965-66. An ambitious Commission proposal to fund the CAP from the Community's "own resources," and in the process to extend the parliament's budgetary power, caused de Gaulle to withdraw French representation in the **Council of Ministers** in July 1965 (hence the "Empty Chair"). But the crisis took a new twist when de Gaulle announced at a press conference in September 1965 that France would not accept a provision of the Rome Treaty, due to be implemented on January 1, 1966, introducing qualified-majority voting in the Council of Ministers on a limited range of issues. De Gaulle's attack on qualified-majority voting and insistence on a national veto over Community legislation greatly exacerbated the situation. The other member states shared France's concern about being outvoted in the Council but argued that important national interests were unlikely ever to be ignored. The results of the December 1965 French presidential election brought de Gaulle back to the negotiating table. The Community crisis dominated the election, with de Gaulle's opponents campaigning in favor of a France retaking its seat in **Brussels.** Deprived of an absolute majority in the first round of balloting, de Gaulle and **Francois Mitterrand** contested the second round alone. As expected, de Gaulle won but by the surprisingly narrow margin of 11%. The result demonstrated the domestic limits on de Gaulle's EC policy. The General got the message; a week later he announced that the French foreign minister would attend a meeting of his Community counterparts in Luxembourg.

The crisis finally ended with the so-called **Luxembourg Compromise,** which amounted to an agreement to disagree over majority voting. While maintaining the principle of majority voting, the compromise acknowledged that "when very important issues are at stake, discussions must be continued until unanimous agreement is reached." The Luxembourg Compromise heightened member states' awareness of each other's special interests and increased their reluctance to call a vote in the Council of Ministers even when no vital interest was at stake. As a result, decision making in the European Community virtually ground to a halt until the early 1980s, when a huge legislative logjam finally convinced the member states to move toward majority voting.

De Gaulle devoted his remaining years in office mostly to French foreign policy beyond the Community, notably to an effort to undermine the **North Atlantic Treaty Organization** (NATO) and establish good relations with the Soviet Union and its Eastern European satellites. These policies proved spectacularly unsuccessful. At the same time, de Gaulle neglected domestic affairs and was caught totally unaware by the student and workers' demonstrations of May 1968, which almost toppled not only his government but also the Fifth Republic. Although de Gaulle survived politically, the events of May 1968 demolished his personal popularity and fatally compromised his credibility as president. Moreover, the crisis further weakened France economically and caused serious financial instability. De Gaulle continued as president for less than a year. Defeat in two referenda in April 1969, one about the structure of local government and the other about reform of the Senate, prompted his departure. Those relatively inconsequential issues, on the outcome of which he had staked his presidency, brought the "decade of de Gaulle" abruptly to an end.

De Gaulle bequeathed a mixed legacy to the Community. On the one hand he was instrumental in getting the Community going in the early 1960s, but on the other he severely impaired the Community's development toward supranationalism. He also kept the Community small, restricting it to "Little Europe" of the **Six** centered on the Franco-German core. But Europe and the EC had changed much during his eleven years as president. Most important, Germany had grown economically and was becoming more and more assertive politically. By 1969, France was no longer economically and politically the most powerful member state. That fact was not lost on **Georges Pompidou**, de Gaulle's successor, who sought to compensate for the changing balance of power in the Community by allowing Britain to join. Thus, within three years of de Gaulle's departure, his Gaullist successor would endorse the Community's first enlargement.

DE MICHELIS, GIANNI (1940-   ) Gianni de Michelis, the flamboyant foreign minister of Italy (1989-1992), gave the

Community decisive direction during his country's presidency of
the Council of Ministers in the last six months of 1990. In
November 1989 the Berlin Wall collapsed and German
unification suddenly loomed. De Michelis understood the
importance of those developments for the Community and strove
to deepen European integration by preparing and ultimately
launching the two intergovernmental conferences on **Economic
and Monetary Union** and **European Political Union** that
culminated in the **Maastricht Treaty**. Rumors abounded in
Brussels in early 1992 about de Michelis' ambition to become
president of the **European Commission** after Jacques Delors'
departure and, in the interim, to become commissioner for
external relations. But allegations in mid-1992 of de Michelis'
involvement in widespread corruption in Italy seriously damaged
his credibility and political career.

DELORS, JACQUES (1925-   ) Jacques Delors is the longest-
serving and most powerful president in the history of the
European Commission. Delors became president in 1985, just in
time to launch the **Community**'s spectacularly successful **single
market program**. Delors was also instrumental in accomplishing
the 1986 **Single European Act**, the 1988 budget agreement
(**Delors I**), the 1989 plan for **Economic and Monetary Union**
(EMU), and the 1991 intergovernmental conferences on EMU
and **Political Union**. In 1992, the final year of his second
Commission, Delors' agenda included ratifying the **Maastricht
Treaty**, devising and securing member state support for a second
budget package (**Delors II**) to help implement the Maastricht
agreement, ratifying the **European Economic Area** treaty, and
grappling with the complex question of the Community's future
enlargement.

Few could have predicted in 1985 that, a few years later,
Delors would personify the Community's extraordinary
revitalization. Undoubtedly Delors displayed great ability as an
economist, academic, politician, and MEP before joining the
Commission, and in the mid-1980s the Community seemed on the
verge of revival. But the extent to which the single market
program took off, the suddenness of the Soviet Union's collapse,
and the magnitude of the Community's contribution to the

emerging, post-**Cold War** "New Europe" caught everyone--not least Jacques Delors--by surprise.

A sharp instinct for shifts in the international political system, a keen awareness of the ebb and flow of international economic power, and a willingness to exploit sudden opportunities account in large part for Delors' success. The fall of the Berlin Wall is a case in point. Delors immediately realized that German unification would happen sooner rather than later and would benefit the Community enormously. Accordingly, Delors gave Chancellor **Helmut Kohl** all possible moral and political support and propelled planning in the Commission for East Germany's absorption into the EC. Similarly, Delors quickly grasped the ramifications of the Soviet Union's collapse and the implications of disintegration in Eastern Europe for integration in Western Europe. He became one of the most zealous champions in the West of economic assistance for Gorbachev and, subsequently, for the former Soviet republics.

Workaholism, close attention to detail, and a clear idea of where the Community should go--Delors speaks and writes of History and Destiny as proper nouns--also account for his accomplishments. Moreover, Delors is widely respected, although not deeply loved, at the highest levels in the Community. Even before his early espousal of German unification, Delors could count on Kohl's unswerving support. Delors also numbered the prime ministers of most of the other member states as close friends or colleagues. The two exceptions were **Margaret Thatcher** and, surprisingly, **Francois Mitterrand**, a fellow socialist under whom Delors served as finance minister in the early eighties.

Delors' difficulties with Thatcher were partly personal and partly ideological. Although Thatcher supported Delors' efforts to introduce a single market, she bitterly resented his sponsorship of the so-called social dimension and especially disliked his federalist vision of Europe's future. Ideological and political differences soured relations between the two strong-willed leaders. Thatcher swore that socialism would never return to Britain "through the back Delors." For Thatcher, Delors personified all that was wrong with the Community: excessive bureaucracy, technocracy, and remoteness from reality. Personal rancor added an unusually sharp edge to the prime minister's famous anti-integration speech, delivered in Bruges in September 1988.

Delors' relationship with Mitterrand is by no means as antagonistic and far more complex. As finance minister, Delors had reversed the French government's disastrous "dash for growth" in the early 1980s, turned the economy around, and saved Mitterrand's first presidency. Perhaps Delors' domestic achievements aroused Mitterrand's envy; in any event, relations between the president of France and the new president of the Commission were markedly tense. The strain became even more apparent when the socialist government's political fortunes plummeted in 1992, culminating in Mitterrand's dismissal of Prime Minister Edith Cresson. Only Delors, one of the few senior socialist politicians still popular in France, seemed capable of redeeming the government. Yet Mitterrand was loath to recall Delors from **Brussels** and eventually decided not to at Kohl's urging. Much to Mitterrand's discomfiture, Delors is reportedly positioning himself for a French presidential bid in 1995. That raises the intriguing prospect of an avowed Euro-federalist at the helm in France in the late 1990s.

In Brussels, Eurocrats revere Delors for having instilled a renewed sense of purpose and importance in the once moribund Commission. Yet Delors' fellow commissioners and the heads of the Commission's twenty-three Directorates-General often resent their president's impatience and imperiousness. For in shaking up the Community Delors also shook up the Commission. In particular, Delors made little effort to hide his intolerance of those commissioners and senior officials who lacked acumen or commitment, regardless of their political standing at home. Unable to reorganize the Commission completely, Delors instead engineered a shift of power from the upper echelons of the Directorates-General to the commissioners' private offices (*cabinets*), of which his own is undoubtedly strongest.

Ambition for the French presidency and an innate protectionism may have intensified Delors' backing, during his second Commission, for "Eurochampions"--large European manufacturers capable of competing globally against their American and Japanese counterparts. Thus in 1991 and 1992

Delors leaned more toward **Martin Bangemann** than **Leon Brittan** in the internal Commission struggle between advocacy of industrial and competition policy. Domestic political calculation doubtless also reinforced Delors' romanticism about the role of agriculture in the Community. Although concerned about the exorbitant cost of the **Common Agricultural Policy** (CAP), Delors resisted internal Commission efforts, led by Commissioner **Frans Andriessen** and external pressure, applied primarily by the U.S., to cut drastically EC export subsidies. Delors' qualified support for CAP reform, therefore, not only exacerbated tension inside the Commission but also contributed to a marked decline in U.S.-EC relations in the early 1990s.

Growing U.S.-EC friction, sharpened by other Community policies apart from agriculture, threatened to mar Delors' outstanding record as Commission president. Moreover, despite Delors' prescience, developments inside and outside the Community in the early 1990s challenged his vision of Brussels' future. In Eastern Europe the pace of political and economic change endangered Community "deepening" by forcing a premature "widening." This led Delors, at the June 1992 Lisbon European Council, to propose additional institutional reform as a prelude to the inevitable enlargement of the Community to the north and east.

Within the Community itself, the 1991 intergovernmental conference on political union and the Danish rejection of the Maastricht Treaty in June 1992 revealed increasing member state impatience with the Commission's grasping for greater power. Delors responded by emphasizing the idea of **subsidiarity**: the Community should involve itself only in those activities that cannot be handled better at the national or regional level. In order to allay member state concerns, especially during the Maastricht Treaty ratification crisis in 1992, Delors gave substance to subsidiarity by scaling back a number of Commission proposals that seemed to intrude unduly into member state affairs, particularly on environmental issues.

Delors' espousal of subsidiarity reveals the pragmatism and resourcefulness that characterize his Commission presidency. Nevertheless expediency and compromise in no way diminish Delors' idealism or undermine his principles. On the contrary, devout Roman Catholicism, a quest for social justice, and a burning belief in Europe's destiny set Jacques Delors apart as a contemporary statesman. These unique qualities, combined with the unprecedented opportunities presented to the Community in the late 1980s, will forever distinguish his Commission presidency.

DELORS I   In February 1987, **Commission** President **Jacques Delors** unveiled a budgetary package to implement the undertaking to achieve a single market by the end of 1992 given in the 1986 **Single European Act**. Officially called "Making the Single Market a Success," the package later became popularly known as "Delors I" to distinguish it from the similar "Delors II" post-Maastricht budgetary proposals. The package had four constituent parts: a remodeled **Common Agricultural Policy** (CAP) to take account of changes in production and trade, reform of the structural funds to transform them into instruments of economic development, adjustment of the level and breakdown of "own resources," and more effective budgetary discipline.

The most controversial elements of the package concerned a doubling of structural funds to promote **cohesion** between different regions in the **Community** and an increase in the Community's "own resource" ceiling from 1.16% of GNP in 1987 to 1.4% in 1992. The Commission and the poorer, southern member states were preoccupied with the "cohesion question" because of the inherent danger of greater imbalances in a single market. However, the rich, northern countries balked at paying substantially more money to the south, and the December 1987 Copenhagen **Summit**, which should have resolved the issue, ended in bickering and failure.

Chancellor **Helmut Kohl**, then in the six-month EC presidency, convened a special summit in **Brussels** in February 1988 to try again to reach a settlement. Addressing the **European Parliament** in January 1988, Delors called the impending Brussels Summit "the moment of truth for the strategy proposed by the Commission in 1985 to revitalize the European venture." Kohl and Spanish Prime Minister **Felipe González**, representing the rich north and the poor south, respectively, hammered out an agreement that, according to some commentators, amounted to a second **Marshall Plan** for Europe.

DELORS II   Delors II is the popular name for the budgetary package proposed by **Jacques Delors**, president of the **European Commission**, to pay for implementation of the ambitious **Maastricht Treaty**.   The package, which would increase **Community** revenue by 33%, sought to cover three new Community responsibilities: a **cohesion** fund to provide assistance to the Community's poor countries (Greece, Portugal, Ireland, and Spain) in the run-up to EMU; the cost of improving EC industry's international competitiveness; and the expense of meeting the Community's greatly expanding foreign and security policy obligations.   The fate of Delors II soon became embroiled in the Maastricht Treaty ratification crisis and fell victim to Germany's inability to contribute substantially more money to the Community at a time of pressing domestic political and economic problems relating to reunification.   The June 1992 Lisbon **European Council** failed to resolve the issue.

DELORS PLAN   At a **summit** in Hanover in June 1988, the heads of state and government recalled the **Single European Act**'s reference to **Economic and Monetary Union** (EMU) and decided to appoint a committee to consider the matter further. **Commission** President **Jacques Delors** chaired the committee, which subsequently bore his name.   The other members were the central bank governors of the **Twelve**, another European commissioner, and three independent experts--all acting in a personal capacity.   The committee completed its report, officially entitled *Report of the Committee for the Study of Economic and Monetary Union* but popularly known as the Delors Plan, in April 1989.

The Delors Plan described an EMU in the **Community** and outlined three stages by which member states could achieve it. Stage one involved the establishment of free capital movement in the Community and closer monetary and macroeconomic cooperation between the member states and their central banks. Stage two called for a new European system of central banks to monitor and coordinate national monetary policies.   Stage three envisioned "irrevocably fixed" exchange rate parities, with full authority for economic and monetary policy passing to Community institutions.

The heads of state and government spent much of the June 1989 Madrid Summit discussing the Delors Plan and decided to launch stage one on July 1, 1990. Six months later, at the December 1989 Strasbourg Summit, Community leaders decided, despite British objections, to convene an intergovernmental conference (IGC) to determine the treaty revisions necessary to move to stages two and three. The IGC opened in Rome in December 1990 and concluded at the **Maastricht Summit** in December 1991. To a great extent the **Maastricht Treaty** provisions on EMU follow the contours outlined in the Delors Plan.

DENMARK Like Britain, Denmark joined the EC in January 1973. Also like Britain, the Danes were, and remain, skeptical about European integration. Once Britain applied for membership in the early 1960s, however, Denmark had little option but to follow suit. With the bulk of the country's agricultural and industrial exports going to the U.K. and Germany, it would have been economic suicide for Denmark to stay out of the enlarged **Community**. Despite familiar fears about the erosion of national sovereignty and the possible severance of traditional ties with the Nordic countries, a sizable majority of the Danish electorate voted in favor of accession in the 1972 referendum.

The role and influence of a special parliamentary committee on EC affairs has always been an unusual aspect of Denmark's EC membership. Like most member state parliaments, the Folketing jealously guards its power against any encroachment from the **European Parliament**. However, Denmark's national parliamentarians are particularly well-versed on EC issues, and the Folketing's EC committee regularly and comprehensively interrogates government ministers about their dealings in **Brussels**.

As an EC member, Denmark benefits greatly from the **Common Agricultural Policy** and from the **single market program**. Yet Danes are more ambivalent than ever about the political impact of closer integration. As well as general concerns about shared sovereignty, a strong pacifist streak makes Danes particularly sensitive to the development of a security dimension in the Community. In the early 1980s, when a number of larger member states canvassed the idea of including security and even defense issues in **European Political Cooperation** (EPC), Denmark demurred. Similarly, Denmark was one of the three smaller member states to block adoption of a defense dimension in the **Single European Act** (SEA). Although Title III of the SEA restricted EPC to the political and economic aspects of security, the Danish referendum on ratification proved contentious, not least because of the SEA's strengthening of majority voting in the **Council of Ministers**.

The security/defense question surfaced again during the 1991 intergovernmental conference on **Political Union,** with Denmark advocating a minimalist position on the scope of the proposed **Common Foreign and Security Policy** (CFSP). The role of the **Western European Union** in the CFSP became a key issue in the June 1992 Danish referendum on the **Maastricht Treaty.** At the same time, Danes grew increasingly concerned about the Community's long-term development and the seemingly inexorable centralization of power in Brussels. To everyone's surprise, a small majority of Danes voted not to ratify the Maastricht Treaty and set off a crisis that consumed the Community in late 1992.

DOOGE COMMITTEE At the **Fontainebleau Summit** in June 1984, the heads of state and government decided, almost as an afterthought, to establish an Ad Hoc Committee on Institutional Affairs to consider the **Community's** response to internal and external change. When Ireland took over the Community presidency in July 1984, Prime Minister **Garret FitzGerald** nominated his friend and former foreign minister, Jim Dooge, to chair the committee to which the other Community leaders appointed their personal representatives. The so-called Dooge Committee drew on the recent **Genscher-Colombo Proposals** and the **European Parliament's Draft Treaty on European Union** in an effort to "translate a wide range of existing views on the nature of European integration into politically acceptable reform." The Committee's report, dealing with a variety of institutional issues and a plethora of policy options from technology, to political cooperation, to the internal market generated an intense discussion on the future of European integration at the **Milan**

Summit in June 1985. As a result, and based on a majority vote of the heads of state and government, the **Ten** decided to convene an intergovernmental conference (IGC), similar to the one that recently ended in Maastricht, to propose treaty amendments. The **Single European Act** eventually emerged from that process.

DRAFT EUROPEAN ACT see **Genscher-Colombo Proposals**

DRAFT TREATY ON EUROPEAN UNION In February 1984, by an overwhelming majority of votes, the **European Parliament** passed the Draft Treaty on European Union. The treaty originated in the work of the Crocodile Club, a small group of MEPs from different political parties who shared a commitment to getting the **Community** going again in the early 1980s. **Altiero Spinelli**, the veteran Italian Euro-federalist, had convened the group in the Crocodile Restaurant in **Strasbourg**, a favorite MEP eatery. As the group grew in size, it met regularly in the European Parliament itself, before convincing the parliament to form an Institutional Affairs Committee, on which Spinelli served as rapporteur.

Spinelli and the Crocodile Club believed that, in the first direct elections held in June 1979, the European electorate had given the parliament a mandate to revise the Communities' treaties and resuscitate European integration. A consensus emerged in the Institutional Affairs Committee that a new treaty was needed to replace the existing treaties, and a new union was needed to replace the existing Communities. The union would incorporate the existing Communities' institutional structure and competencies but include numerous reforms and additional authority. However, in deference to member states' sensitivities to the centralization of power in **Brussels**, the Draft Treaty explicitly mentioned the principle of **subsidiarity**: the idea that the union would be responsible only for tasks that could be undertaken more effectively in common than by the member states acting separately.

Passage of the Draft Treaty gave a boost to the momentum then gathering in the Community for institutional reform. It coincided with developments such as the **Genscher-Colombo Proposals** and the **Stuttgart Declaration** to jolt the Community out of its political malaise in the mid-1980s. Coming only four months before the decisive **Fontainebleau Summit**, the Draft Treaty contributed to the climate of change in which the **Dooge Committee** and the 1985 intergovernmental conference took place, and the **Single European Act** was implemented.

-E-

ECONOMIC AND MONETARY UNION (EMU) EMU has been a long-standing objective of the **European Community**. The **Treaty of Rome** recognized the causal connection between a common market and EMU but did not develop the point. It was only in the early 1970s, as part of the post-**Hague Summit** initiative to deepen European integration, that the Community took its first serious steps in the direction of EMU based on the ambitious, seven-stage **Werner Plan** to achieve EMU in the Community within ten years by means of institutional reform and closer political cooperation.

In April 1972, following three years of unprecedented currency fluctuations, the Six member states hatched the "snake," a regime to keep EC currency fluctuations within a 2.5% margin inside the "tunnel" established during the Smithsonian talks of December 1971 to repair the damaged international monetary system. For the next three years the Community's currencies wiggled in and out of the snake, with the deutsche mark, buoyed by Germany's low inflation and large trade surplus, pushing through the top, and the pound, franc, and lira, weakened by their countries' high inflation and large trade deficit, falling through the bottom.

In the meantime, at their **Paris Summit** in October 1972, the heads of state and government called for EMU by 1980. Despite their optimism, the snake and the Werner Plan soon became victims of the sclerosis that beset the Community in the 1970s. High inflation rates and growing economic divergence made nonsense of the 1980 target date and consigned the Werner Plan to oblivion. The collapse of the snake in the mid-1970s ended the member states' first experiment with monetary union.

Roy Jenkins, who became **Commission** president in 1977, resolved to revive the Community by means of a monetary initiative. His original idea, greatly altered by German Chancellor **Helmut Schmidt** and French President **Valéry Giscard d'Estaing**, eventually resulted in the **European Monetary System** (EMS). Launched in March 1979, the EMS brought about a zone of relative monetary stability in Western Europe, with the deutsche mark as a reference currency. The EMS soon exceeded its authors' expectations. The ensuing fall in inflation and stabilization of prices among the participating states brought the Community back to where it had been in the 1960s, before the collapse of the Bretton Woods system. That permitted the Community to focus on the unfinished business of the internal market. Thus the EMS played a decisive role in bringing about the **single market program**, which, in turn, forced the Community to confront again the complementary questions of monetary union and a coordinated macroeconomic policy.

Commission President **Jacques Delors** needed little prompting on that score. At the request of the **European Council**, in late 1988 and early 1989 Delors chaired a committee of central bank governors of the **Twelve**, another European commissioner, and three independent experts, all acting in a personal capacity, to develop a plan for EMU. In its report, officially entitled *Report of the Committee for the Study of Economic and Monetary Union* but popularly known as the **Delors Plan**, the Committee outlined three stages by which the member states could achieve EMU. Stage one involved the establishment of free capital movement in the Community and closer monetary and macroeconomic cooperation between the member states and their central banks. Stage two called for a new European system of central banks to monitor and coordinate national monetary policies. Stage three envisioned "irrevocably fixed" exchange rate parities, with full authority for economic and monetary policy passing to EC institutions.

The heads of state and government spent much of the June 1989 Madrid **Summit** discussing the Delors Plan and agreed to launch stage one on July 1, 1990. Six months later, at the December 1989 Strasbourg Summit, Community leaders decided, despite British objections, to convene an intergovernmental conference (IGC) to determine the treaty revisions necessary to move to stages two and three. By that time the question of EMU was inextricably linked with the question of **European Political**

Union (EPU). Revolution in Eastern Europe in 1989 and German unification in 1990 had raised member states' concerns about the future of European integration and the extent of Germany's commitment to the Community. Under the circumstances, the intergovernmental conference on EMU opened at the Rome Summit in December 1990 in tandem with an intergovernmental conference on EPU. Both conferences culminated in the **Maastricht Summit** of December 1991.

To a great extent the **Maastricht Treaty** provisions on EMU follow the contours outlined in the Delors Plan. Stage two, a transitional stage of intensified economic and monetary coordination, will begin in January 1994. Monitoring of member states' policies based on broad guidelines laid down by the Council of Ministers, and treaty constraints on member states' budget deficits, will facilitate economic policy coordination. The European Monetary Institute, intended to help coordinate the member states' monetary policies, will become operational at the beginning of the second stage.

Stage three will start on January 1, 1999, at the latest. If a majority of member states (possibly excluding Britain and Denmark, if they exercise the option they won at Maastricht to opt out of EMU) meet the convergence criteria earlier, it could begin on January 1, 1997. When stage three begins, the European system of central banks, consisting of the **European Central Bank** (ECB) and the member states' central banks, will start to function; the European currency unit (ECU) will become a currency in its own right; and the rates at which member states' currencies are to be irrevocably fixed to each other and to the ECU will be determined.

There are four EMU convergence criteria:
* a high degree of price stability, judged by an inflation rate no higher than 1.5 percentage points of the best three performing member states;
* a general government deficit no greater than 3% of GDP and a government debt level no greater than 60% of GDP;
* staying in the EMS's currency exchange fluctuations margins with no devaluation against any other EMS member for at least two years;

> * interest rate levels no more than 2 percentage points higher than equivalent rates in the three lowest-inflation member states.

The entire exercise begs some interesting questions. What happens if only a small number of countries meet the convergence criteria? What happens if Germany is not one of them? More fundamentally, is a single currency economically desirable and politically necessary? These questions may become irrelevant if German public and political opinion, increasingly concerned about the loss of the beloved deutsche mark, turn against EMU and thwarts either ratification or implementation of the Maastricht Treaty.

ECONOMIC AND SOCIAL COMMITTEE (ESC) The Economic and Social Committee (ESC) consists of 189 part-time members who represent employers, trade unions, and other interested groups, such as farmers and consumers. Its members are appointed by the national governments. The ESC's purpose is to advise the **Council** and **Commission** on pending legislation. In 1991 the ESC produced 185 consultative documents, of which 172 were opinions requested by the Council or the Commission, eleven were own-initiative reports, and two were information reports. Although in some cases an ESC opinion is obligatory before proposals can become law, the Council and Commission rarely heed the ESC's advice.

ELYSEE TREATY In January 1963 President **Charles de Gaulle** and Chancellor **Konrad Adenauer** signed a treaty between their two countries at a ceremony in the Elysée Palace in Paris. In the treaty both sides pledged "to consult each other, prior to any decision, on all questions of foreign policy...with a view to reaching an analogous position." The treaty was the pinnacle of Adenauer's international achievements, symbolizing as it did reconciliation between France and Germany, to which he had dedicated his foreign policy. Yet members of Adenauer's government, not to mention the Social Democratic opposition, feared that the treaty would undermine U.S. support for Germany. Because Germany depended militarily on the U.S. during the Cold War, and General de Gaulle infuriated the U.S.

by pursuing an independent security policy, many Germans were afraid that the Franco-German treaty would alienate Washington. Accordingly, during the ratification debate in May 1963, a majority within the chancellor's own Christian Democratic Party joined the parliamentary opposition to attach a crippling codicil to the treaty. A new preamble, inserted at the insistence of a majority in the German parliament, asserted Germany's primary commitment to existing alliance obligations. Over Adenauer's objections, the Bundestag solemnly subordinated the Franco-German treaty to Germany's multilateral obligations to the **Atlantic Alliance**, the **European Economic Community** (EEC), and even the **General Agreement on Tariffs and Trade** (GATT).

Over time, the Elysée Treaty played a key role in promoting closer integration in the Community. Despite his disappointment over the Bundestag's behavior in May 1963, de Gaulle continued to attend regular bilateral meetings under the terms of the treaty. More important, subsequent French presidents and German chancellors, as well as a host of government ministers and officials, similarly stuck to a fixed schedule of bilateral meetings. With the rapid improvement of Franco-German relations in the early 1970s and the growing consensus in both countries about the utility of European integration, these frequent, institutionalized contacts became, and to a great extent remain, the motor of Community momentum.

EMPTY CHAIR CRISIS The Empty Chair Crisis, which takes its name from France's withdrawal from the **Council of Ministers** and COREPER in July 1965, brought the **Community** to a standstill until the "**Luxembourg Compromise**" of January 1966. Even after France resumed full participation, the terms of the Luxembourg Compromise impaired the Community's development for nearly twenty years, until political and economic changes in the mid-1980s obliged the member states to reform decision making in the Council.

The crisis began over the **Commission's** proposals to link a financial provision for the **Common Agricultural Policy** (CAP) with greater power for itself and the **European Parliament**. President **Charles de Gaulle** of France wanted a new financial arrangement for the CAP but not badly enough to sanction the

Commission's plan. Moreover, de Gaulle objected to the introduction of majority voting in the Council of Ministers, mandated by the **Treaty of Rome** to come into operation in January 1966. For de Gaulle, an ardent nationalist, the prospect of being outvoted and having to accept the will of the majority was unacceptable in an international organization.

De Gaulle withdrew French representation from the Community in July 1965 after the breakdown of talks to consider the Commission's CAP proposals but announced three months later that France would not retake its seat in the Council unless the member states agreed to defer majority voting. The others refused to comply. Thus the crisis seemed set to continue indefinitely, until de Gaulle suffered a serious setback in the presidential election of December 1965. Although victorious, de Gaulle had nearly lost to **Francois Mitterrand**, who ran on a pro-EC ticket. Chastened, de Gaulle decided to return to the negotiating table.

The crisis finally came to a close at a foreign ministers meeting in Luxembourg on January 28-29, 1966. The **Six** agreed to adopt an interim financial regulation for the CAP, deferring the question of additional powers for the Commission and the **European Parliament**. Majority voting in the Council of Ministers remained the outstanding issue. After restating their positions, both sides approved a short declaration, the Luxembourg Compromise, which maintained the principle of majority voting but acknowledged that "when very important issues are at stake, discussions must be continued until unanimous agreement is reached."

Apparently the result was a draw; in fact it represented a victory for de Gaulle. The Council approved temporary funding for the CAP in May 1966. In the meantime, the Commission's ambitious proposals had been soundly defeated. Moreover, despite the Five's statement of support for majority voting, the Luxembourg Compromise impeded effective decision making in the Community for many years to come. General de Gaulle's insistence on unanimity heightened the member states' awareness of each other's special interests and increased their reluctance to call a vote in the Council even when no vital interest was at stake.

EURATOM see **European Atomic Energy Community**

EUROPEAN AGREEMENTS In December 1991, the **European Community** concluded Association Agreements (called European Agreements in this case) with Czechoslovakia, Hungary, and Poland (the Visegrad Three), the most economically developed countries in Central and Eastern Europe. The agreements culminated a process that had begun in the late 1980s, during the period of reform in Eastern Europe, and gathered momentum after the revolution there in 1989. Czechoslovakia, Hungary, and Poland wanted to apply for EC membership, but the Community urged association as an interim measure. Strong protectionist pressure in the member states, especially in France, held up the Community's efforts to conclude the proposed arrangements. The Community finally signed the much-heralded European Agreements in December 1991 as a means of promoting reform and putting off for as long as possible the inevitable accession applications. Brussels hoped to conclude similar agreements with Bulgaria and Romania by the end of 1992. In the meantime, the Baltic states, Albania, the former Soviet republics, Croatia, Bosnia, and Slovenia all seek to cultivate closer contacts with the Community. None is apt to apply to join for some time, although most undoubtedly aspire to membership.

EUROPEAN ATOMIC ENERGY COMMUNITY (Euratom) Known colloquially as Euratom, the European Atomic Energy Community came into existence simultaneously with the **European Economic Community** in 1958. Moreover, the treaties establishing both Communities were signed together in Rome in March 1957.

   Jean Monnet first proposed an organization, along the lines of the successful **Coal and Steel Community** (ECSC), to promote the peaceful use of atomic energy and, at the same time, further the cause of European integration. Even while the ECSC Treaty was being negotiated, Monnet knew that coal was rapidly losing its position as the basis of industrial power and, by extension, military might. Atomic energy had already revolutionized strategic doctrine and seemed poised to replace coal and oil as the main energy source of the future. Thus Monnet proposed a

European Atomic Energy Community in order both to achieve the immediate objectives of the ECSC itself and to promote the distant goal of European federation.

The French government was well disposed toward Euratom, which offered an opportunity to share the exorbitant costs of atomic energy research and development while enjoying all the benefits. U.S. President Dwight D. Eisenhower's recent Atoms for Peace initiative had increased Euratom's attraction. Not only was the U.S. willing to share nuclear technology for peaceful purposes, but also the State Department recognized the importance of Monnet's initiative for the European integration movement. Notwithstanding U.S. support, other ECSC member states disliked the Euratom idea, not least because they distrusted French motives.

In November 1954 Monnet announced his decision to resign from the **High Authority** of the ECSC, in part to promote Euratom. He did so by establishing an elite interest group of political party and trade union leaders: the **Action Committee for a United States of Europe**. Although the Action Committee became a highly visible and successful lobby for further European integration, it failed to advance the Euratom idea over a contemporaneous proposal to establish a common market among the six ECSC member states.

Instead, at the intergovernmental conference, formed after the **Messina Conference** meeting in June 1955, to draft plans for further European integration, the member states focused on the common market proposal. Yet the **Spaak Report**, presented to the six foreign ministers in May 1956, proposed that the two objectives of sectoral (atomic energy) integration and wider economic integration (a common market) be realized in separate organizations, with separate treaties. This marked the first stage of a protracted process of intergovernmental negotiations, culminating in the signing of the **Treaties of Rome** in March 1957, establishing the European Atomic Energy Community and the European Economic Community.

From the outset Euratom was a poor relation to the EEC. When its institutions merged with those of the EEC and the ECSC in 1967, Euratom virtually lost its own identity. Moreover, the other member states' suspicion of France's nuclear policy, an abundance of cheap imported oil in the 1960s, and environmental and safety concerns about atomic energy meant that Euratom was moribund. Despite profound international change in the past twenty-five years, Euratom's situation remains largely unaltered.

EUROPEAN BANK FOR RECONSTRUCTION AND DEVELOPMENT (EBRD) The European Bank for Reconstruction and Development (EBRD) is the only international financial institution that has a specific brief to focus on Central and Eastern European countries that have embraced multiparty democracy, in order to help their transition to market economics. The EBRD originated in a French proposal to promote reform in Central and Eastern Europe (including the Soviet Union) by establishing a Bank for Europe. The French argued the need for a new bank, rather than an existing institution reoriented toward the East, to assist the transforming economies of the reforming Soviet bloc. In December 1989 the **Strasbourg European Council** endorsed the proposal for a new investment and development bank and called for intergovernmental negotiations to begin immediately.

Although initially France wanted to confine membership to the **Community**, the European Council agreed that other Western countries, notably the U.S., should be invited to participate. Negotiations opened in Paris in January 1990 and ended only five months later with an Agreement to Establish the European Bank for Reconstruction and Development. The agreement stipulated that the bank's emphasis would be on helping eligible countries with private-sector development and transition to free market economics, privatization, reform of the financial sector, stimulation of direct investment, and environmental rehabilitation. Membership in the bank was open to European countries, to non-European countries that are members of the International Monetary Fund, and to the **European Community** and the **European Investment Bank**. Thus the European Community, as well as its member states, became charter members.

The agreement entered into force, and the EBRD began operations in April 1991. Participants in the constitutive conference chose London as the EBRD's location, although in deference to France, Jacques Attali, a close adviser of President

Francois Mitterrand, was appointed its first president. Attali is a colorful and controversial character known for his anti-Americanism. As the U.S. is the largest single shareholder (although collectively the Community and its member states have far more shares), Attali's appointment institutionalized friction between the U.S. and the EC over assistance to Central and Eastern Europe.

EUROPEAN CENTRAL BANK (ECB) The European Central Bank is due to come into operation at the beginning of stage three of the plan outlined in the **Maastricht Treaty** to achieve **Economic and Monetary Union** (EMU). Depending on the member states' ability to meet EMU's convergence criteria, stage three will begin on either January 1, 1997, or January 1, 1999. The ECB will be an independent body with exclusive responsibility for the formulation and implementation of the **Community**'s single monetary policy. An Executive Board of six individuals, appointed by the **European Council** for a nonrenewable term of eight years, will run the ECB's day-to-day operations. Together with the governors of the national central banks, the Executive Board will constitute the Governing Council, the chief policy-making body of the ECB. At the Lisbon **Summit** in June 1992, eleven of the member states agreed, as part of a complex package on the location of Community institutions, that the ECB and its forerunner, the European Monetary Institute, should be housed in Bonn, the former capital of Germany. The U.K. objected, hoping to locate the ECB's operational arm in London. Although a final decision will not be made until the end of 1992, it seems likely that the ECB, in its entirety, will end up in Bonn.

EUROPEAN COAL AND STEEL COMMUNITY (ECSC) The ECSC was the first of the three **European Communities**; its inauguration in 1952 marked the birth of what is now generically known as the **European Community**.

The ECSC originated in the **Schuman Plan** of May 1950 to pool French and German production of coal and steel. Once **Robert Schuman** sold the French, German, and American governments on his plan, **Jean Monnet**, who had authored the idea, thought that the negotiations between France, Germany, Italy, Belgium, The Netherlands, and Luxembourg to establish a Coal and Steel Community would conclude quickly. They only began in earnest in August 1950 and eventually ended in April 1951. Ratification by the member states' parliaments took nearly another year, and the Coal and Steel Community finally began operating in August 1952.

The main issues to be decided concerned the proposed Community's competence, institutions, and decision-making procedures. Jean Monnet led the French side at the talks, while his friend **Walter Hallstein** headed the German delegation. What emerged was a supranational **High Authority**, the institutional depository of shared national sovereignty over the coal and steel sectors. The High Authority would be responsible for formulating a common market in coal and steel and for such related issues as pricing, wages, investment, and competition. Because of the High Authority's small size, national bureaucracies would have to cooperate closely with it in order to implement Community legislation. A separate Community institution, the **Court of Justice**, would adjudicate disputes and ensure member states' compliance with the terms of the treaty.

In a move that was to have important repercussions for the future of European integration, the other negotiators forced Monnet to accept a **Council of Ministers** in the Community's institutional framework. Initially intended to be advisory and intermediary as the embodiment of the member states' interests, the Council of Ministers would increasingly act as a brake on supranationalism within the Community. Finally, an Assembly, consisting of delegates of the national parliaments, would give the Community the appearance of direct democratic accountability.

The ECSC Treaty outlined the structure and set the rules of the new supranational organization. Together with lofty references to "world peace" and a "contribution...to civilization," the ECSC Treaty's preamble explicitly stated the Community's functionalist, as opposed to federalist, mission. Thus the Community would help to build European unity "through practical achievements which will first of all create real solidarity, and through the establishment of common bases for economic development."

The ECSC disappointed ardent European integrationists, both in its conceptual framework and in its actual operation. It was an unglamorous organization that inadequately symbolized the high hopes of supranationalism in Europe. Yet the ECSC served a vital purpose in the postwar world, in terms of promoting Franco-German reconciliation and fostering closer European integration. Moreover, the ECSC survived the failure of the **European Defense Community** and the related **European Political Community** in the mid-1950s and provided a vital basis for the subsequent resurgence of European integration at the **Messina Conference** and the intergovernmental conferences that led to the establishment of the **European Economic Community** and the **European Atomic Energy Community** (Euratom) in 1958.

The success of the far broader EEC completely overshadowed the ECSC and Euratom. From the outset of the EEC and Euratom the three Communities had a common Assembly, but each had separate executive institutions. In 1965 the **Six** signed a treaty merging the executive institutions of the three Communities, thereby establishing a single Commission and a single Council. When the **Merger Treaty** came into force on July 1, 1967, the ECSC lost its identity and importance.

EUROPEAN COMMISSION see **Commission**

EUROPEAN COMMUNITIES   There are three European Communities: the **European Coal and Steel Community**, the **European Atomic Energy Community** (Euratom), and the **European Economic Community**. Under the terms of the **Maastricht Treaty**, the European Economic Community is officially called the **European Community**.

EUROPEAN COMMUNITY This is the popular name by which all three European Communities--the **European Coal and Steel Community**, the **European Economic Community**, the **European Atomic Energy Community** (Euratom)--are known. It is also the colloquial name specifically for the EEC, the most important of the Communities. Indeed, under the terms of the **Maastricht Treaty**, the European Economic Community will officially be called the **European Community**.

EUROPEAN COUNCIL The European Council is the official name for **summit** meetings of the **Community's** heads of state and government. European Councils, often known by the name of the city where they take place, have become synonymous with breakthroughs in the Community's development. The **Maastricht Summit** of December 1991, at which the member states concluded the intergovernmental conferences on **Economic and Monetary Union** and **European Political Union,** is a classic example. Others include the **Bremen Summit** (June 1978), where the **European Monetary System** was born, and the **Fontainebleau Summit** (June 1984), where the Community's budgetary problems were resolved.

French President **Valéry Giscard d'Estaing** initiated the European Council when he proposed regular (thrice annually) summits as a means of resolving Community problems, providing general direction, and discussing international issues at the highest level. Giscard proposed informal meetings solely of the French president and the other member states' prime ministers. He did not even want the **Commission** president to attend. However, **Roy Jenkins,** who became Commission president in 1977, insisted on participating, and the prime ministers also asked to take their foreign ministers along. Soon an official note-taker was added. Thus Giscard's supposedly intimate, fireside gatherings turned into large, two-day get-togethers of nearly thirty people.

The **Single European Act** of 1986 officially recognized the European Council's existence and called for two rather than three annual meetings, at the end of each country's six-month EC presidency. In the late 1980s, with the success of the **single market program** and the emergence of the New Europe, the European Council proved an invaluable forum for promoting closer European integration. Special "emergency" summits were often held to discuss such items as German unification (Dublin, April 1990) and the **Maastricht Treaty** (Birmingham, October 1992).

France and Germany, together the motor of Community momentum, have traditionally dominated European Councils. In the 1970s Giscard and Chancellor **Helmut Schmidt,** his friend and collaborator, monopolized summit meetings. In the 1980s and early 1990s, President **Francois Mitterrand** and Chancellor **Helmut Kohl** tended to do so. Since 1985, however, a third player has emerged onto the center stage of Euro-summitry: Commission President **Jacques Delors**. Delors' assertiveness restored the Commission's confidence and provided a useful "Community"--as distinct from national--perspective at the core of European Council decision making.

EUROPEAN COURT OF JUSTICE see **Court of Justice**

EUROPEAN DEFENSE COMMUNITY (EDC)   Faced with American and British demands for German rearmament following the outbreak of the Korean War, French Prime Minister René Pleven announced in October 1950 a plan for German remilitarization under the aegis of a European Defense Community (EDC). **Jean Monnet** was the architect of the so-called Pleven Plan and of the earlier proposal for a **Coal and Steel Community** (ECSC). Apart from the conceptual similarity between both plans, Monnet authored the EDC proposal in part to save his cherished ECSC, then still being negotiated with Germany. Faced with possible German recalcitrance over the ECSC talks unless France acquiesced in German rearmament, Monnet pressed Pleven to pursue the parallel idea of a supranational organization for European security.

Negotiations for a European Defense Community, in which German units would be integrated into a European army, began in February 1951. Although Monnet was not directly involved in the EDC talks, he used his influence behind the scenes to win powerful American support for the Pleven Plan. True to form, Britain resisted American entreaties to enter the talks. Apart from disliking the idea of supranationality and apart also from their accession to the **Brussels Treaty** of 1948, the British still harbored a deep distrust of their Western European allies' military capability, based on the lessons of the French and Belgian collapse of 1940. Despite British remoteness, the **Six** persevered in their negotiations. After complex and bitter bargaining they signed the EDC Treaty on May 27, 1952, in Paris.

Having survived the penultimate negotiating stage, the EDC foundered on the rock of ratification. Gaullist hostility to sharing sovereignty over sacrosanct national defense policy, coupled with implacable Communist opposition to German rearmament, resulted, in August 1954, in defeat of the EDC Treaty in the French National Assembly. It was paradoxical that the EDC failed in France, where the original initiative had been taken in 1950 and the treaty signed in 1952. In the interim, however, Stalin's death and the end of the Korean War had lessened **Cold War** tensions and made the issue of German remilitarization far less urgent. Moreover, Paris had become increasingly preoccupied with dissipating colonial conflicts.

In retrospect, advocates of European integration see the EDC's failure as a great opportunity lost. In reality, the circumstances of the early postwar years were not propitious for a common security or defense policy. As the outcome of the 1991 inter-governmental conference on **European Political Union** indicated, the **Community's** member states remain reluctant to grasp the nettle of common defense.

EUROPEAN ECONOMIC AREA (EEA)   The European Economic Area encompasses the member states of the **European Community** and the **European Free Trade Association** (EFTA) in a single market covering northern and Western Europe. The European Economic Area (originally called the European Economic Space) grew out of the Community's concern that a flood of membership applications from the EFTA member states, precipitated by the success of the **single market program** and the end of the **Cold War** in Europe, would weaken the Community before completion of the single market and implementation of the **Maastricht Treaty.**

Following a decision at the joint Ministerial Meeting in December 1989 "to commence formal negotiations as soon as possible," exploratory talks among EC and EFTA officials began early in the new year. Based on the success of these talks, negotiations opened in June 1990 covering the free movement of goods, services, capital, and persons; flanking and horizontal policies; and legal and institutional questions. The most serious problems in the first six months of the talks were the large number of requests from EFTA countries for permanent derogations from Community legislation and the Community's unwillingness to begin substantive negotiations on institutional arrangements for the EEA. The Community's reluctance was due largely to the EFTA countries' demand for a leading role in Community decision making.

Officials on both sides overcame these difficulties in 1991 and brought the negotiations to a conclusion in October of that year. The three most contentious last-minute issues were fishing rights, Alpine trucking rights, and a **cohesion** fund for the Community's poorer members to compensate for better EFTA access to EC markets. To everyone's surprise, the EC's **Court of Justice** rejected the EEA Treaty in December 1991 on the grounds that the proposed EC-EFTA tribunal to adjudicate EEA-related disputes was incompatible with the **Treaty of Rome**. After months of legal wrangling, the Court of Justice finally approved the EEA Treaty in April 1992. At a formal ceremony on May 2, 1992, representatives of the EC and EFTA member states signed the treaty, which needs to be ratified by their legislatures and by the European Parliament. The EEA creates the world's largest trading area, encompassing nineteen countries, 380 million people, and over 40% of world trade. The Treaty is due to come into force in January 1993, simultaneously with the single market.

EUROPEAN ECONOMIC COMMUNITY (EEC)   Known colloquially--and officially since the **Maastricht Treaty**--as the **European Community**, the European Economic Communit is the most important of the three **European Communities**. Like the **European Atomic Energy Community**, the EEC was brought into being by the **Treaty of Rome** in March 1957 and began operating the following January. From the outset, the EEC shared an Assembly (later called the **European Parliament**) and a **Court of Justice**. But all three Communities had separate executives and Councils of Ministers. However, the **Merger Treaty** establishing a single **Commission** and a single **Council** came into force in July 1967.

The EEC originated in a 1952 suggestion by J. W. Beyen, foreign minister of The Netherlands, to extend the competence of the proposed **European Political Community**. The Beyen Plan, a scheme for a customs union and common market embracing the **Six** countries of the ECSC, survived the defeat of the **European Defense Community** and, consequently, the demise of the European Political Community. Beyen believed that sectoral integration alone was insufficient to promote economic development and, ultimately, political union. Instead, the Six should abolish quotas and tariffs on intra-Community trade, establish a joint external tariff, unify trade policy toward the rest of the world, devise common policies for a range of socioeconomic sectors, and organize a single internal market.

Beyen's idea was revived at the **Messina Conference**, a meeting of Community foreign ministers held in this Sicilian port city in June 1955 to discuss the future of European integration. **Paul-Henri Spaak**, the Belgian foreign minister, had prepared a memorandum, on behalf of the **Benelux** countries, suggesting further integration along the lines of **Jean Monnet's** idea for an Atomic Energy Community and Beyen's advocacy of a **common market**. The foreign ministers' decision at least to give the question of European integration further thought, by asking Spaak to form a committee and write a report on future options, constituted the first "relaunch of Europe."

During the next twelve months Spaak steered the work of a number of committees and subcommittees that drafted specific parts of a precise proposal to advance the European idea. His report, presented to his fellow foreign ministers at a meeting in Venice in May 1956, urged that the two objectives of sectoral (atomic energy) integration and wider economic integration (a common market) be realized in separate organizations, with separate treaties. The Venice foreign ministers' meeting marked the first stage of a protracted process of intergovernmental negotiations, culminating in the signing of the **Treaties of Rome** in March 1957, establishing the European Atomic Community and the European Economic Community.

The negotiations that led to the establishment of the EEC were by no means smooth. Following the failure of the EDC in 1954, supranationalism had acquired a bad name, and politicians had to proceed cautiously. Nor were all potential member states eager to embrace competition and open markets. France, in particular, was loath to abandon protectionism. **Robert Marjolin**, a senior French negotiator, fought what he called "the Battle of Paris" trying to promote French interests, on the one hand, and overcome the resistance of French politicians and civil servants, on the other.

Marjolin and others argued the case for a customs union and common market on its own merits but bolstered their position with the legitimate assertion that France could not have the desirable Atomic Energy Community without the less desirable Economic Community. Moreover, they convinced their fellow negotiators of the need to meet two fundamental French demands--the inclusion of agriculture and special provisions for France's overseas possessions in the proposed common market. The other countries agreed in part because of the benefits that would accrue to all from a common agricultural policy and because Belgium and The Netherlands would benefit as well from extending Community privileges to the member states' overseas possessions. But the main reason for the other states' acquiescence was the importance to them of including France in the Community. A Community without Britain was perfectly possible; a Community without France was impracticable. As Franco-German reconciliation lay at the core of the Community, and the Community was the key to Germany's postwar rehabilitation, Chancellor **Konrad Adenauer** was willing to pay almost any price to placate Paris.

The preamble of the EEC Treaty was far less flamboyant than its ECSC counterpart, referring only to the signatories' determination "to lay the foundations of an ever closer union among the peoples of Europe." The treaty itself outlined the essential principles of the common market: the free movement of goods, persons, services, and capital; a customs union and common external tariffs; and various Community policies. The new Communities' institutional frameworks emulated that of the ECSC but with a stronger Council of Ministers and a correspondingly weaker Commission. Because Luxembourg, home of the ECSC, did not want a further influx of foreigners, by default **Brussels**, site of the intergovernmental conferences that led to the Treaties of Rome, hosted the new Community institutions. However, the Assembly (Parliament), common to all three Communities, continued to hold its plenary sessions in **Strasbourg**.

The first EEC Commission, under the presidency of **Walter Hallstein**, set about implementing the Treaty of Rome. Its responsibilities included external economic relations, economic and financial affairs, the internal market, competition, social affairs, agriculture, transport, and relations with overseas countries and territories. In some of these areas the treaty lay down a specific timetable to implement certain measures; in others, the treaty provided no more than general guidelines and statements of principle. The most immediate and tangible task was to establish the customs union. Thanks to French financial and economic reforms, the first intra-EC tariff reductions took place on schedule, on January 1, 1959, and the customs union came into existence ahead of schedule on July 1, 1968.

Whereas tariff barriers could easily be identified and eliminated between member states, policies in areas such as competition, social affairs, transport, energy, and regional disparities were far harder to formulate. A combination of sometimes vague treaty provisions, member state apathy or outright opposition, and philosophical and ideological differences between and among the Commission and Council of Ministers--factors that are as cogent in the EC today as they were in the early years--impeded Community progress. The result was a spotty record of policy formulation and implementation.

The **Common Agricultural Policy** (CAP) was the most challenging and controversial of the EEC's early initiatives. In order to be politically acceptable and economically practicable, the CAP had to replace individual member states' systems of customs duties, quotas, and minimum prices with a Community-wide system of guaranteed prices and export subsidies. **Sicco Mansholt**, vice-president of the Commission with responsibility for agriculture, was the CAP's chief architect. Detailed discussions on the CAP's fundamental principles and procedures took place in the early 1960s, as the Commission and the member states thrashed out the precise means by which it would operate.

A dispute between French President **Charles de Gaulle** and the Commission over a financial provision for the CAP precipitated one of the worst crises in the Community's history. Realizing how eager de Gaulle was to secure the financial regulation, the Commission proposed funding the CAP by a system of Community "own resources," thereby increasing the powers of the Commission and the Parliament. De Gaulle strongly opposed a further augmentation of the Community's supranational authority and especially objected to a move, mandated under the Treaty of Rome, to replace unanimity with majority voting in Community decision making. Following a breakdown of negotiations with the Commission and the other member states, in July 1965 de Gaulle stopped French participation in the Council of Ministers and COREPER. The so-called **Empty Chair Crisis** ended in January 1966 with the "**Luxembourg Compromise**," which amounted to an agreement to disagree over majority voting. Under the terms of the Luxembourg Compromise France resumed its participation in the Community, but the consequences of the crisis, particularly in terms of the Commission's self-confidence and the Council's decision-making procedure, persisted into the early 1980s.

In the 1960s the Community also addressed the question of enlargement when Britain, Denmark, Ireland, and Norway applied to join. Accession negotiations began in 1961, but ended abruptly in January 1963 when de Gaulle announced at a press conference in Paris that Britain was not yet ready for membership. De Gaulle objected to Britain's strategic dependence on the U.S., which he thought would prevent the Community's proper political development. He vetoed Britain's second application in 1967, essentially for the same reason. Only when de Gaulle resigned as president of France in 1969 did enlargement become feasible. **Georges Pompidou**, de Gaulle's successor, called for a special **summit** of Community leaders to resolve the enlargement issue. Pompidou advocated enlargement in the context of "completion" and "deepening." "Completion" meant moving to a system of "own resources" to finance the CAP; "deepening" meant extending the Community's competence into new areas.

The **Hague Summit** in December 1969 broke the deadlock over enlargement and set the Community on course for the decade ahead. As a result of decisions taken at The Hague, the following year Community leaders endorsed two reports on "deepening." The first proposed **European Political Cooperation**, a procedure for foreign policy coordination among the member states. The second outlined a plan for **Economic and Monetary Union**. At the **Paris Summit** in October 1972, held on the eve of the Community's first enlargement (Britain, Denmark, and Ireland joined in January 1973), the member states declared their intention "before the end of the present decade to transform the whole complex of their relations into a **European Union.**" This was an extraordinary statement even by the standard of European Community rhetoric and illustrates the member states' high hopes for European integration at the beginning of the 1970s. As the decade progressed, however, and the Community became bogged down in high inflation rates, soaring unemployment, and low economic growth, European Union grew more and more remote.

Thus the 1970s was a disastrous decade for the Community. "Euro-pessimism" replaced the "Euro-optimism" of 1971 and 1972. The Middle East war in October 1973 and the ensuing oil embargo and price rises threw the member states' economies into chaos. Instead of pursuing a joint approach to their common problems, the member states took individual action. Coupled with the demise of Community solidarity, bureaucratic inertia in Brussels and decision-making paralysis in the Council of Ministers (a legacy of the Luxembourg Compromise) virtually brought the Community to its knees. An effort by French President **Valéry Giscard d'Estaing** to revive the Community, by institutionalizing summits of heads of state and government in a new **European Council,** served only to emphasize the extent of the Community's malaise.

Yet the Community survived the disastrous 1970s and revived spectacularly in the 1980s. The seeds of the Community's revival were sown in the late 1970s, during the **Roy Jenkins** presidency (1977-81), and reaped in the following years. At that time the member states finally endorsed a long-standing scheme for direct elections to the European Parliament, the first of which took place in June 1979. The new, directly elected Parliament proved much more assertive than its predecessor and, under the leadership of **Altiero Spinelli,** drafted a revised constitution for the European Community. The **Draft Treaty on European Union,** passed by the EP in February 1984, contributed to the momentum then developing in the Community to strengthen European integration.

Also during the Jenkins presidency the Community concluded Greece's accession and began negotiations on Spanish and Portuguese membership. The accession of Greece and imminent accession of Spain and Portugal forced member states to tackle the Community's decision-making problems, which otherwise would become much worse in a Community of **Ten** and eventually **Twelve**. The member states' willingness to reform the Community's decision-making procedure coincided with the Draft Treaty and with the **Genscher-Colombo Proposals** for institutional reform and greater involvement in foreign and security policy.

A third extremely beneficial development during the Jenkins presidency was the launching of the **European Monetary System** (EMS) in March 1979. Eighteen months earlier Jenkins had made an important speech advocating monetary union. After initial hesitation, Chancellor **Helmut Schmidt** of Germany warmly embraced Jenkins' initiative and, at the **Bremen Summit** in July 1978, unveiled a Franco-German proposal to establish a zone of relative monetary stability in a world of wildly fluctuating exchange rates. The ensuing EMS was an immediate success and helped participating member states to fight inflation and recover economic growth. It also gave the Community the confidence necessary to embark on the **single market program**. The single market program, which epitomized for many the Community's resurgence in the 1980s, thus emerged from a background of growing Community self-assurance. It was a response not only to the Community's failure to date to bring about a real common market but also to Europe's perceived declining competitiveness vis-à-vis the U.S. and Japan, especially in the high-technology sector. **Etienne Davignon**, a vice-president of the **Gaston Thorn** Commission (1981-85), developed extensive contacts with European industrialists and promoted close Commission-industry cooperation in research and development. His enterprise spawned a number of collaborative ventures in the early 1980s and helped to generate enthusiasm among industrialists and business people for the single market initiative.

Arthur Cockfield, a vice-president in the first **Jacques Delors** Commission (1985-89), with responsibility for the internal market, launched the single market program in 1985. Lord Cockfield produced a **White Paper**, or policy document, outlining the steps necessary to bring about a Community in which people, capital, goods, and services could move freely. But such an ambitious plan was unlikely to succeed without a radical reform of decision making in the Community. Nor could the Community have made much progress as long it remained embroiled in a bitter controversy over Britain's budgetary contribution, which **Margaret Thatcher** reopened as soon as she became prime minister in 1979. Resolution of the British budgetary question at the **Fontainebleau Summit** in June 1984, after nearly five years of frustration and aggravation, freed the Community's leaders to set their sights on a higher goal.

This was the climate in which the **European Council** convened in Milan in June 1985. In an unprecedented move, a majority of Community leaders outvoted the recalcitrant minority--Britain, Denmark, and Greece--and called for an intergovernmental conference (IGC) to revise the Treaty of Rome. The IGC produced the **Single European Act** (SEA) in early 1986. The SEA set a target date of December 31, 1992, for completion of the single market program; stipulated that most of the single market decisions would be subject to majority voting in the Council; and brought EPC, the environment, research and development, and regional policy explicitly within the treaty framework. Full ratification of the SEA was delayed until mid-1987. More hard negotiating followed, especially on compensation for poorer countries in the single market, before the program took off in 1988 and 1989.

Jacques Delors personified the Community's extraordinary revitalization at that time. Energetic, ambitious and farsighted, Delors gave the Commission a new sense of purpose. His close friendship with Chancellor **Helmut Kohl** of Germany and political affinity with President **Francois Mitterrand** of France gave Delors exceptional influence in the European Council. However, Delors soon ran afoul of Thatcher, especially for his espousal of a **Social Charter** to allow workers in the Community to enjoy the benefits of the single market. Thatcher directed much of her hatred of socialism, supranationalism, and European federalism at Delors and the Brussels bureaucracy.

Thatcher also opposed Delors' effort to cement the single market by relaunching Economic and Monetary Union (EMU). In April 1989 Delors produced a plan (the **Delors Plan**) to achieve EMU in three stages: by promoting economic convergence, establishing a European central bank, and ultimately creating a single currency. Despite his misgivings about currency union, Kohl supported the Delors Plan, and Mitterrand was enthusiastic. The Spanish government, then in the six-month rotating EC presidency, strongly supported Delors' initiative. At the Madrid Summit, in June 1989, the Twelve agreed that the Delors Plan provided a blueprint for EMU and decided to launch the first stage by July 1, 1991.

In and of itself the single market program was insufficient to maintain a powerful momentum toward EMU. Yet the contemporaneous revolution in Eastern Europe and the imminent reunification of Germany gave a huge boost to EMU and added **European Political Union** (EPU) to the agenda. Delors rapidly realized that what he called the "acceleration of history" in Central and Eastern Europe afforded the Community a unique opportunity to reaffirm its political objectives and to expedite EMU. The other member states' consent to German unification was the bargain upon which the Community's future hinged. The deal was struck at the Strasbourg Summit in December 1989. An exuberant Chancellor Kohl sought to allay his partners' anxieties about German unification and especially to overcome deep French suspicion. At the end of the historic meeting, the other member states acknowledged Germany's right to self-determination, but only in the context of European integration and unification. In concrete terms, that meant an end to German foot-dragging over EMU and a commitment to proceed on EPU.

This set the stage for two years of frenetic discussions among the member states and the Commission about the nature, scope, and competence of the "new" European Community in the "new" Europe. In the course of 1990 the member states decided to convene two parallel intergovernmental conferences, one on EMU and the other on EPU. Both conferences opened in Rome in December 1990 and culminated at the **Maastricht Summit** twelve months later.

Of the two IGCs, the one on EMU made most progress. After all, the Delors Plan already existed as a blueprint. The Twelve, including a more compliant United Kingdom following Thatcher's departure, began to tackle the plan's most pressing particulars, notably convergence criteria, composition of the **European Central Bank** (ECB), and the ECB's relationship to other EC institutions and the member state governments. At Maastricht the heads of government and state effectively adopted the Delors Plan but set the definitive date of 1999 for a single currency in the Community.

By contrast, the parallel intergovernmental conference on EPU lacked focus and direction. Negotiations covered a wide range of issues, including institutional reform, the Social Charter, and foreign and security policy. The Dutch, who took over the Community presidency in July 1991, proposed that the Community embrace EMU, foreign and security policy, cooperation on home affairs, and the Social Charter. The other member states, however, preferred to keep foreign and security policy and home affairs on an intergovernmental basis, outside the formal treaty framework. As a result, the Maastricht Treaty established a European Union that resembled a temple resting on three separate pillars: the Communities, a **Common Foreign and Security Policy**, and cooperation on justice and home affairs. Moreover, British Prime Minister **John Major**'s opposition to the Social Charter obliged the other member states at the last minute to remove it entirely from the proposed union.

Thus the Maastricht Treaty identified the European Community (henceforward the official name for the European Economic Community) as part of the Communities pillar of the union. The treaty also reformed decision making in the Community, notably by strengthening the power of the European Parliament. Finally, the treaty extended the Community's competence to include such matters as education, culture, and consumer protection.

The Maastricht Treaty was to have been ratified in 1992 in order to be implemented in 1993. However, Denmark's rejection of the treaty in a referendum in June 1992 sparked a ratification crisis throughout the Community, especially in the United Kingdom. At the very least, the Danish vote caused a serious legal problem: even if the other eleven member states ratified the treaty, Denmark's rejection obviously undermined its validity. At worst, the failure of the Maastricht Treaty would scuttle the European Union and set back the Community's rapid progress in the late 1980s and early 1990s. But the soundness of the Community itself is not in doubt. During the past thirty-five years the Community has had a profound impact on the political and economic development of its member states; doubtless it will continue to do so for many years to come.

EUROPEAN FREE TRADE ASSOCIATION (EFTA)   In the early 1960s it was often said that Europe was "at Sixes and Sevens." "Sixes" referred to the **European Economic Community**, which had six member states, and "Sevens" referred to the European Free Trade Association, with its seven member states. The term not only made a clever numerical distinction between the two recently established organizations but also indicated a degree of competition and conflict between them.

During the **Messina Conference** in the mid-1950s the U.K. had proposed establishing a Free Trade Association instead of the putative European Economic Community. The British preferred a limited, intergovernmental free trade area rather than a comprehensive, supranational **European Community** and feared that the EEC would be protectionist and damaging to non-member state interests. Some Scandinavian countries, as well as neutral Austria and Switzerland, favored Britain's approach. But the **Six** persevered with their negotiations and launched the EEC in 1958.

Britain nevertheless pressed ahead with the idea of a free trade area that would incorporate and possibly supplant the new Community.   Having decided not to pursue Community membership, the British sought instead to enjoy the benefits of free trade in Europe while eschewing a common external tariff, a common agricultural policy, and any form of economic integration.   President **Charles de Gaulle** of France especially disliked the proposal's implications for agriculture, a sector specifically excluded from the proposed free trade area. Although talks about a possible free trade area to include the Six and the other Western European countries had continued since the second half of 1956, de Gaulle brought them to an abrupt end in November 1958, soon after coming to power. Undaunted, in 1960 Britain formed the European Free Trade Association with Austria, Denmark, Norway, Portugal, Sweden, and Switzerland.

Using a small secretariat in Geneva and occasional ministerial meetings, EFTA restricted its activities solely to promoting free trade among its member states. By contrast, the Community established a customs union, a common external tariff, and a **Common Agricultural Policy** (CAP). In the early 1960s and 1970s the Community negotiated trade agreements with each of the EFTA countries, and the relationship between both organizations became cooperative and harmonious. After all, the member states of both organizations continued to trade actively with each other.

Paradoxically, it was Britain, the country that had pushed the EFTA idea, that almost immediately broke ranks with the other EFTA member states and applied to join the Community in 1961. Prime Minister **Harold Macmillan** advocated Britain's accession to the **Treaty of Rome** for negative rather than positive reasons. By the end of the 1950s Macmillan grasped that EFTA and the British Commonwealth were inadequate vehicles through which to promote British influence and prosperity in the world. He saw EC membership as the only response to Britain's declining economic position. Denmark, economically dependent on Britain, followed suit and also applied to join the Community. Both countries eventually did so in 1973.

The remaining EFTA member states (later increased in number by the accession of Iceland, Finland, and Liechtenstein) were content to remain outside the Community, although the Luxembourg Declaration of 1984 stressed both sides' interest in developing a closer relationship. The launch and spectacular success of the **single market program** in the late 1980s gave added impetus to the Luxembourg Declaration. EFTA member states feared that they would be blocked out of the Community's expanded, frontier-free market. At the same time, reform and revolution in Eastern Europe abruptly ended the **Cold War**, removing the strategic obstacle that the neutral EFTA states believed existed to EEC accession. Attracted by the single market and unencumbered by the Cold War conception of neutrality, Austria applied for membership in 1989, with Sweden, Finland, and Switzerland following suit over the next three years.

The Community was simultaneously flattered and alarmed by the prospect of so many new applicants, especially as the single market had not been completed and the **Maastricht Treaty** was still under negotiation. In an effort to ward off EFTA applicants for EC membership, at least for a few years, and at the same time extend the benefits of the single market to the wealthy EFTA countries, the Community proposed a joint EC-EFTA European Economic Space, later called the **European Economic Area** (EEA).

Negotiations for an EEA Treaty began in June 1990 and ended in October 1991. The three most contentious issues, unresolved until the last moment, were fishing rights, Alpine trucking rights, and a **cohesion** fund for the Community's poorer members to compensate for better EFTA access to EC markets. To everyone's surprise, the EC's **Court of Justice** rejected the EEA Treaty in December 1991 on the grounds that the proposed EC-EFTA tribunal to adjudicate EEA-related disputes was incompatible with the Treaty of Rome. After hasty renegotiations in early 1992 the Court removed its objections. That left the EC and EFTA member states free to ratify the EEA Treaty so that it could come into force in January 1993, simultaneously with the single market.

EUROPEAN INVESTMENT BANK (EIB) The European Investment Bank (EIB) began operating in 1958 to support **Community** policies and objectives, notably regional economic development and overseas assistance. Initially the Bank gave most of its loans to projects in the impoverished south of Italy. Italy remains the bank's largest borrower, receiving over 30% of its loans in 1990. France, Spain, and the U.K. come next, with approximately 14% each. The bank supports a wide variety of projects, mostly in transportation, telecommunications, environmental protection, and industry for both public and private companies. Since the revolution in Eastern Europe the bank has lent an increasing amount of money to Germany--to help cover the costs of reunification--and to the newly independent countries of Central Europe. Based in Luxembourg, the EIB raises most of its money on the international market.

EUROPEAN MONETARY SYSTEM The launch in March 1979 of the European Monetary System (EMS), an initiative to establish a zone of relative monetary stability in a world of wildly fluctuating exchange rates, marked an important milestone in the

Community's history. The EMS was a striking success psychologically as much as financially, helping the Community to acquire the characteristics of a fixed exchange rate regime, with the German mark playing the part of a reference currency. The consequent fall in inflation and stabilization of prices among the participating states brought the Community back to where it had been in the 1960s, before the collapse of the Bretton Woods system. That, in turn, permitted the Community to direct its attention to the unfinished business of the single market. According to the 1984 **Dooge Report**, the EMS "enabled the unity of the **Common Market** to be preserved, reasonable exchange rates to be maintained, and the foundations of the Community's monetary identity to be laid."

The story of how the EMS began has the ingredients of a political thriller: **Commission** President **Roy Jenkins'** courage and prescience in proposing a monetary initiative after the failure of the **Werner Plan** and the currency **snake**; German Chancellor **Helmut Schmidt's** sudden espousal of a scheme for exchange rate stability and his determination to see it through despite strong domestic opposition; French President **Valéry Giscard d'Estaing's** less enthusiastic but nonetheless strong support and apparent U-turn at the last moment; the efficacy of the Franco-German alliance, particularly at the June 1978 **Bremen Summit**, in convincing the Community to adopt the EMS; Britain's refusal to take part in the exchange rate mechanism (ERM) of the EMS; and the value of the **European Council** for rapid decision making at the highest level.

The Franco-German proposal presented at the Bremen Summit called for an exchange rate mechanism using a parity grid and a divergence indicator based on the European currency unit (ECU). Although still open to amendment, the Bremen proposal became the basis of the future EMS, which the member states hoped to implement as early as January 1979. In the meantime, officials worked diligently in a number of specialized committees to thrash out details of the scheme. At a political level, one of the most contentious last-minute questions concerned compensation for poorer participating countries. Both Ireland and Italy demanded an increase in the Regional Fund and subsidized loans for infrastructural development. The problem of resource redistribution became politically charged when France and Britain insisted that their shares of a larger Regional Fund be equal to their shares of the existing fund, and Germany balked at paying the bill. Nor would Giscard approve the amount of subsidized loans that Ireland and Italy requested. This bickering did not augur well for the Brussels Summit of December 4-5, 1978, the decisive European Council before the expected implementation of the EMS. Only a last-minute compromise by Schmidt at the Brussels Summit in December 1978 broke the "concurrent measures" deadlock and ensured that the remaining member states would participate in the scheme.

But the EMS did not come into operation in January 1979 because of a new problem involving its impact on the CAP. The issue had to do with Giscard's demand for the abolition of monetary compensatory amounts (MCAs), a mechanism introduced in the early 1970s to cushion the CAP from exchange rate fluctuations. This proved politically unacceptable to Germany, where MCAs helped to prop up agricultural prices. A meeting of agriculture ministers on December 19, only two weeks before the proposed launch of the EMS, failed to find a solution. Giscard's last-minute intransigence over MCAs baffled his Community counterparts, although it made sound political sense in France, especially in the prelude to the first direct elections to the European Parliament. In the end, however, Giscard's abandonment of the MCA issue was as swift as his embracing of it. Following an agreement at a meeting of Agriculture Ministers in early March 1979 ultimately to abolish MCAs, without specifying a timetable, Giscard announced his unconditional support for the EMS. On March 13, 1979, the system finally came into operation.

The apparent success of the EMS contributed not only to the launch of the **single market program** but also to a revival of interest in **Economic and Monetary Union** (EMU) at the end of the 1980s, culminating in the **Delors Plan**. In November 1990 a reluctant Britain finally joined the ERM, and by early 1992 Greece was the only Community member state not participating fully in the system. Apart from the British pound, the Spanish peseta, and the Portuguese escudo, participating currencies fluctuated within a 2.25% band above or below bilateral exchange rates with the other ERM currencies. The three exceptional currencies fluctuated within a wider 6% band. According to the **Maastricht Treaty**, successful participation in the EMS is a precondition for charter membership in EMU.

Yet by mid-1992 economic divergence rather than convergence between participating countries in the EMS, together with the Maastricht Treaty ratification crisis, caused severe strains in the system. The EMS had increasingly become a fixed-rate system rather than a system of fixed but adjustable rates. The fundamental weakness of the Italian economy, and the weakness of the British economy plus the unacceptably high parity at which the pound sterling had joined the system, caused both countries to withdraw their currencies from the EMS in September 1992. That led to British charges that the system itself was seriously flawed. However, the system's surviving participants, especially the German government, maintained steadfastly that the problem lay primarily in poor British and Italian economic performance. Whatever the ultimate goal of EMU, at least the EMS survived the political and currency crises of 1992.

The EUROPEAN MOVEMENT The European movement (with a lower-case "*m*"; the European *M*ovement was a specific group within the broader movement) is the name of the popular and political drive for cooperation and integration that swept Europe in the immediate postwar years. Repugnance against the slaughter of two European civil wars in as many generations, and the economic depression and political extremism of the intervening years, fueled widespread support for a reorganization of the international system. Words like "federation," "union," and "supranationalism" were bandied about as panaceas for Europe's ills. This gave rise in the late 1940s to the European movement, a loose collection of individuals and interest groups, ranged across the political spectrum from the noncommunist left to the discredited far right, that had in common a shared advocacy of European unity.

The intellectual ancestry of the European movement stretched into antiquity, but its immediate roots lay in the interwar years. In 1923 an Austro-Hungarian aristocrat, Count **Richard Coudenhove-Kalergi**, buoyed by the success the previous year of his book, *Pan-Europa*, launched an organization of the same name. Inspired as much by the devastation of the Great War as by the emergence during it of a powerful United States and a nascent, but menacing, Soviet Union, Pan-Europa quickly acquired an ardent following, not least among influential politicians. The zenith of the pan-European movement was a stirring speech by Aristide Briand, then French foreign minister, before the League of Nations in 1929. But the lofty ideals of European unity were soon swept aside by the floodtide of fascism in the 1930s. It took the bitter experience of defeat and occupation in 1939 and 1940 for pan-European ideas to revive and flourish in European minds.

The wartime resistance movement, itself a loose collection of individuals and groups opposed to Axis occupation, took up the cause of European unity as one plank of a proposed radical reorganization of postwar politics, economics, and society. Resistance literature, secretly circulated in occupied Europe, espoused the goal of international cooperation and integration as a basis for future peace and prosperity. In 1944, **Altiero Spinelli**, a fervent federalist and a future commissioner and member of **European Parliament** (MEP), helped to write one of the most influential wartime tracts on integration, the Draft Declaration of the European Resistance.

The legacy of the prewar Pan-Europa and of the wartime resistance movement generated a ground swell of support for European unity in the early postwar years. Politicians as diverse as **Konrad Adenauer**, a German Christian Democrat; **Paul-Henri Spaak**, a Belgian Socialist; and **Winston Churchill**, an English Conservative, espoused the cause of economic and political integration. Such diverse individuals, sharing a determination to promote European cooperation and reconciliation, came together in May 1948 at the **Hague Congress**, a glittering gathering of more than 600 influential Europeans from sixteen countries. The **Council of Europe**, which emerged from their lengthy deliberations, represented the high point of the European movement. Thereafter political interest in European integration concentrated more on sectoral economic integration, culminating in the establishment of the three **European Communities** in the 1950s.

EUROPEAN PARLIAMENT (EP)   The European Parliament (EP) is arguably the **Community's** best known institution. It has 518 members (81 each from Germany, France, Britain, and Italy; 60 from Spain; 25 from The Netherlands; 24 each from Belgium, Greece, and Portugal; 16 from Denmark; 15 from Ireland; and 6 from Luxembourg), elected directly every five years. Voting systems and constituency sizes vary from country to country, and balloting is spread out over a week in some member states, but elections to the Parliament constitute a unique, Community-wide exercise in direct democracy.

A need to involve the member states' citizens closely in European integration impelled **Jean Monnet** and his colleagues to include an Assembly in the **Coal and Steel Community's** institutional framework. Later, when the **European Economic Community** and the **European Atomic Energy Community** came into being, the ECSC Assembly broadened its scope to become the Assembly of all three Communities. In 1962, the Assembly changed its name to the European Parliament. To symbolize European reconciliation, the Assembly met from the outset in **Strasbourg**, a city contested for centuries by France and Germany. To the detriment of its credibility and efficiency, the Parliament continues to hold monthly plenary sessions in Strasbourg. MEPs and their staff spend the rest of the month close to the **Council** and **Commission** in **Brussels**, two hundred miles to the north, where they hold committee and political group meetings. To compound its peripatetic nature, the European Parliament's secretariat is located in Luxembourg.

To a great extent, the EP is still more symbolic than real. Although its power has increased considerably--from having a purely consultative role at the beginning to getting budgetary authority in the early 1970s; to securing "cooperation" with the Council in specific legislative areas under the terms of the 1986 **Single European Act**; to extending cooperation to additional areas and attaining more far-reaching "co-decision" for a limited legislative agenda under the terms of the **Maastricht Treaty**--the European Parliament remains relatively ineffectual. It is cumbersome, unwieldy, badly organized, and plagued by linguistic problems (there are nine official Community languages; many MEPs know only their own language, and many of those fluent in another Community language sometimes refuse to speak it for political reasons).

By their nature all institutions crave more power. The European Parliament bases its claim to greater responsibility on the twin propositions that a putative legislature should be allowed to legislate and that the only directly elected Community institution should, by right, have more authority. The Council of Ministers disputes both claims by arguing, first, that the institutional structure of the Community is unique. The EP was never intended to become the Community's legislature, along the lines of an assembly in a liberal-democratic state. Legislative responsibility needs to be shared between the Council of Ministers, representing the member state governments, and the European Parliament, representing Community-wide social and political interests.

Second, the Council points out that the Parliament may be the only *directly* elected Community institution, but it is not the only *elected* Community institution. After all, the Council consists of ministers who are members of elected governments. Thus the Council is accountable to the electorate. If the Council takes decisions that prove unpopular in a particular member state, the government of that member state will have to explain why to its citizens, especially during the next election. Yet this is a weak argument because the Council increasingly takes decisions by qualified majority rather than by unanimity, thus allowing ministers to avoid their constituents' wrath by claiming to have been outvoted. On more solid ground, the Council contends that Parliament has a weak legislative record to date. Attendance in plenary sessions when the Parliament votes on important issues is generally poor, as is the level of many MEPs' interest in or awareness of critical Community issues.

Nor does the Parliament's organization bolster its case for greater power. The distribution of seats between member states is patently unfair: Germany, with a population of 80 million, has 81 seats; Ireland, with a population of 3.5 million, has 15 seats. Responsibility for the distribution of seats, a highly sensitive political issue, rests with the member states. But the member states stick with this inequitable ratio (although under the terms of the Maastricht Treaty Germany will receive more seats as a result of unification) largely because MEPs still think and act like national representatives, not Community representatives. Community-wide political parties have failed to emerge, in part because, despite sitting in Strasbourg in transnational groupings, MEPs continue to behave in a predictable national fashion.

The way in which Parliament selects a president is another example of dubious democracy. The Socialist Group (180 seats) is the largest political grouping in Strasbourg. It would not be surprising, therefore, for the president of the Parliament, elected by its members, to be a Socialist. Yet by arrangement between the Socialist Group and the European Peoples Party (the next-largest grouping, with 121 seats), the presidency has alternated during the Parliament's current five-year term between each group. The groups claim that this arrangement improves relations between them and increases Parliamentary efficiency. Yet it hardly strengthens the case for an additional transfer of power to Parliament on the basis of a supposed "democratic deficit."

Apart from granting legislative co-decision to the European Parliament, the Maastricht Treaty gives Parliament a limited role in selecting future Commission presidents. Beginning in 1994, the heads of state and government, in consultation with the president of the Parliament, will choose Commission presidents. The entire Parliament will then be able to accept or reject the other commissioners (collectively, not individually), nominated by the member states. The EP already has the power to vote the whole Commission out of office, a power it has never exercised. By giving the Parliament a say in the Commission president's selection and in the composition of his Commission, the member states took a step to give the Commission some democratic accountability.

The argument about Parliament's power has always been circular. Would greater parliamentary authority increase public interest and involvement in direct elections, or vice versa? As it is, the turnout every five years for Euro-elections is low, and few people follow what happens in the Parliament's plenary sessions or committee meetings. More than likely, only when the Parliament moves permanently to Brussels, acquires a uniform voting system for direct elections, improves its rules of procedures, and exploits legislative cooperation and co-decision to the full will it earn more public interest and respect and secure greater political power.

EUROPEAN POLITICAL COMMUNITY   Like the proposed **European Defense Community** (EDC) from which it emerged, the European Political Community never came into being. Article 38 of the EDC Treaty had called for the establishment of a supranational political authority to direct the Defense Community. Deferring to domestic parliamentary opinion, in September 1952 the foreign ministers of the **Six** acted on a resolution passed by the **Council of Europe's** Consultative Assembly to entrust a parliamentary body with the task of implementing Article 38 by drafting the statute of a supranational European Political Community. Reflecting, perhaps, the Six governments' indifference toward the proposed Political Community and doubts that it would ever come to anything, the foreign ministers asked a special committee of the newly established **European Coal and Steel Community** (ECSC) Common Assembly to draft a treaty.

The so-called constitutional committee drew up plans for a Political Community that would not only encompass the EDC and ECSC but also embrace foreign, economic, and monetary policy coordination. The result would have been a community more advanced along the road of European integration than the most optimistic EC member states in the recent intergovernmental conferences had thought likely to emerge from the December 1991 **Maastricht Summit**. Even in the extraordinary climate of the early 1950s, with the worsening **Cold War** and the attendant acceptance of German rearmament acting as a spur to greater European integration, the Six balked at the consultative committee's extravagant recommendations. In any event, the issue became moot when the French Parliament failed to ratify the EDC Treaty in 1954, and the proposed Defense Community died on the drawing board.

EUROPEAN POLITICAL COOPERATION (EPC)   European Political Cooperation began in the early 1970s as an effort both to deepen European integration and to enhance the member states' collective international identity. At the **Hague Summit** of December 1969, French President **Georges Pompidou** advocated a system of foreign policy cooperation through regular meetings of foreign ministers and, possibly, the establishment of a secretariat in Paris. This smacked to the other **Community** leaders of a revival of the **Fouchet Plan**, although they by no means rejected the idea of foreign policy coordination among the **Six** with a view to reaching common positions. Especially in the context of Germany's *Ostpolitik*, the member states quickly grasped the utility of at least an exchange of information on each other's foreign policies. Accordingly, the heads of state and government appointed **Etienne Davignon**, a senior Belgian Foreign Ministry official, to prepare a report by mid-1970.

The **Davignon Report**, submitted to the Council of Ministers in May 1970 and eventually adopted the following October, struck the lowest common denominator. Instead of a permanent secretariat in Paris, as Pompidou had proposed, Davignon avoided altogether the issue of a secretariat, and therefore a location, and suggested that European Political Cooperation consist of biannual meetings of foreign ministers and more frequent meetings of their political directors. The country in the presidency of the Community would also preside over EPC and provide the necessary infrastructural support. A second report (the Copenhagen Report of July 1973) completed the foundations of EPC. Moreover, beginning in 1974, with the inauguration of the **European Council**, the heads of state and government discussed international affairs in the framework of EPC at their regular **summit** meetings.

At a lower level, working groups of Foreign Ministry officials dealt on a regular basis with such regional and thematic issues as the Middle East, South Africa, arms control proposals, and Ostpolitik. EPC proved invaluable in coordinating the member states' positions in the **Conference on Security and Cooperation in Europe**, both in the original negotiations leading up to the 1975 Helsinki Accords and in the numerous follow-up conferences. In marked contrast to other efforts to "deepen" European integration in the 1970s, EPC was a striking success.

In the early 1980s, during a period of renewed **Cold War** tension between the superpowers, a number of member states attempted to restructure EPC. The member states' poor response to the Soviet invasion of Afghanistan in December 1979 had highlighted the need for reform. Lord Carrington, the British foreign secretary, took the lead during his country's EC presidency and proposed a number of improvements. The ensuing London Report of October 1981 tightened up EPC procedurally and for the first time mentioned the controversial word "security." Pacifist Denmark, quasi-neutral Ireland, and obstructionist Greece all objected to EPC's encroaching into the military or defense domain. Accordingly, the June 1983 **Stuttgart Declaration**, which further reinforced EPC, merely called for coordination of the member states' positions on "the political and economic aspects of security."

The **Single European Act** (SEA) of 1986 was the next EPC milestone. Title III of the SEA provided a constitutional basis for EPC, bringing it for the first time under the aegis of the **Treaty of Rome**. Developments in the early 1990s, in the aftermath of revolution in Eastern Europe and the end of the Cold War, tested EPC to the full. Despite the rhetoric of foreign policy cooperation, member states did not "speak with one voice" on such crucial issues as the Gulf War and the disintegration of Yugoslavia. Fortunately for the Community, these events coincided with the intergovernmental conference on **European Political Union** and focused attention on the need to supplant EPC with a **Common Foreign and Security Policy** (CFSP). Under the terms of the **Maastricht Treaty**, the CFSP will form a pillar of the **European Union**. Like EPC, the CFSP will be inter-governmental, although it will have far greater scope and may ultimately form the basis of a Community defense policy.

During the Maastricht ratification process, the prospects for EPC and the CFSP did not seem bright. The war in Bosnia strained foreign policy cooperation among the member states and highlighted the Community's international impotence. Nor did French President **Francois Mitterrand**'s gesture of flying to Bosnia in June 1992 strengthen Community solidarity. Mitterrand left for Bosnia from the Lisbon Summit, where the heads of state and government had just decided to coordinate their foreign policies more closely. Despite that commitment, Mitterrand did not inform his fellow Community leaders of his impending initiative.

EUROPEAN POLITICAL UNION (EPU) European Political Union encompasses the noneconomic aspects of European integration: the **Community's** institutional structure, decision-making process, competence, **European Political Cooperation** (EPC) and a **Common Foreign and Security Policy** (CFSP), and cooperation on judicial and home affairs. EPU is a subset of, and a step toward, full **European Union.** Most recently interest in EPU revived not only because of the success of the **single market program** but also because of the revolution in Eastern Europe and German unification. **Commission President Jacques Delors** realized that what he called the "acceleration of history" in Central and Eastern Europe threatened to derail the single market program and undermine European integration. He seized the opportunity to rethink the Community's political agenda and expedite **Economic and Monetary Union** (EMU).

Delors received a huge boost from German Chancellor **Helmut Kohl** and French President **Francois Mitterrand.** In a famous letter in April 1990, both leaders endorsed European Union and called for "fundamental reforms--economic and monetary union as well as political union--(to) come into force on January 1, 1993." That proved the starting point for two years of frenetic discussions in the Community, including the intergovernmental conference of 1991, about the nature, scope, and competence of EPU. The outcome of the negotiations at the **Maastricht Summit** in December 1991 was a **Treaty on European Union** that included an increase in majority voting in the Community, greater competence for **Brussels,** more power for the **European Parliament,** a CFSP, and cooperation on judicial and home affairs.

EUROPEAN UNION (EU) European Union has always been the objective of European integration. A common analogy describes European Union as the destination toward which the **European Community** train is heading. But European Union is an ill-defined terminus. The preamble of the **Treaty of Rome** calls for "an ever closer Union" among the peoples of Europe, and the preamble of the **Single European Act** cites European Union as the ultimate goal of European integration. Neither document spells out exactly what the competence or structure of the European Union will be, although its membership is explicitly confined to countries that are European and have liberal-democratic, free-market systems.

In the **Maastricht Treaty**, the member states of the Community
defined European Union for the first time and, indeed,
established it. The treaty declared that the union is founded
upon the **European Communities** supplemented by a **Common
Foreign and Security Policy** (CFSP) and cooperation on judicial
and home affairs. The treaty sets out the union's objectives: to
promote economic and social progress; to assert its identity on
the international scene; to strengthen and protect the rights of its
citizens; to develop close cooperation on justice and home affairs;
and to maintain in full the body of existing Community law.

At the same time one of the treaty's "Common Provisions"
states that the treaty "marks a new phase in the process of
creating an ever-closer union among the peoples of Europe."
Thus the European Union established at Maastricht appears not
to be final or definitive. In that sense, despite the Maastricht
Treaty, European Union remains an imprecise destination.

-F-

FITZGERALD, GARRET (1926-) Garret FitzGerald, the Irish
    politician and statesman, strove to bring his country to the
    forefront of European integration first as foreign minister (1973-
    77) and then as prime minister (1981-82 and 1982-87). As
    foreign minister, FitzGerald presided over the **Council of
    Ministers** during the first six months of 1975; as prime minister,
    he presided over the **European Council** during the last six months
    of 1984. FitzGerald strongly supported the **single market
    program** and helped to revive the **Community** in the mid-1980s.
    He sometimes had difficulty at that time reconciling his
    obligations as Ireland's prime minister with his aspirations as a
    European integrationist. The two most troubling tasks were to
    assert Ireland's neutrality (with which he disagreed) during
    discussions in the Community about acquiring a security and
    defense identity and to defend Irish dairy farmers (with whom he
    surely also disagreed) from badly needed reform of the **Common
    Agricultural Policy** (CAP). On one celebrated occasion,
    FitzGerald stormed out of a European Council meeting in
    deference to the Irish agricultural lobby.

FONTAINEBLEAU SUMMIT   The June 1984 Fontainebleau
Summit, held in the old royal palace outside Paris, was one of the
most important in the **Community's** history. For the previous five
years the Community had been bogged down in a debilitating and
aggravating dispute over Britain's budgetary contribution. At
issue was Prime Minister **Margaret Thatcher's** claim that Britain
paid too much into the Community and received too little in return. Few doubted that Thatcher had a valid point. The high
volume of food and industrial imports into the U.K. meant that
Britain contributed a lot in customs duties and agricultural levies
to **Brussels**, but Britain's small and highly efficient farm sector
meant that London benefited little from the **Common Agricultural Policy**, which accounted for over 70% of EC expenditure.

Yet the size of Britain's rebate request and Thatcher's
aggressive style infuriated her Community counterparts. A series
of summits in 1983 and early 1984 had ended in deadlock.
French President **Francois Mitterrand**, who presided over the
Fontainebleau Summit, did his utmost in the preceding weeks to
broker a settlement.   At the summit itself Thatcher proved
surprisingly conciliatory. For their parts the other member states
desperately wanted not only a resolution of the British budgetary
question but also a comprehensive settlement of other budgetary
problems. After much hard bargaining Thatcher won a rebate in
the amount of 66% of Britain's annual net contribution.   The
other two elements of the overall budgetary agreement were a
curtailment of CAP expenditure and an increase in the
Community's "own resources," effective no later than January
1986, from 1.0% to 1.4% of the value-added tax (VAT) collected
in each member state.

The Fontainebleau Summit finally ended the British budgetary
dispute and allowed the heads of state and government to
concentrate instead on the Community's future direction. Almost
as an afterthought at the summit, the leaders decided to establish
an Ad Hoc Committee on Institutional Affairs to consider the
Community's response to internal and external change. Known
by the name of its chairman, the **Dooge Committee** drew on the
recent **Genscher-Colombo Proposals** and **Draft Treaty on European Union** and tackled a variety of institutional issues and a
plethora of policy options, from technology, to political cooper-

ation, to the internal market. The Dooge Committee started the process that led ultimately to the **Single European Act.**

FOUCHET PLAN The failed Fouchet Plan was the means by which French President **Charles de Gaulle** sought to bring about a "Union of States" in Europe. De Gaulle's idea was to involve the **Six Community** countries in a new intergovernmental organization to coordinate foreign and defense policy. A series of bilateral meetings between France and its Community partners in the summer and fall of 1960 paved the way for a **summit** of the Six in Paris, in February 1961. This resulted in a decision to continue intergovernmental discussions under the chairmanship of Christian Fouchet, French ambassador to Denmark.

At a summit in Bonn in July 1961 the leaders of the Six asked Fouchet to draft "proposals on the means of giving the union of their peoples a statutory character." Before the end of the year Fouchet submitted a design for a confederation of European states. With the goal of a common foreign and defense policy, as well as cooperation on cultural, educational, and scientific matters, the Fouchet Plan outlined an institutional framework that included a Ministerial Council, a Commission of senior Foreign Ministry officials, and a Consultative Assembly of delegated national parliamentarians.

Apart from German Chancellor **Konrad Adenauer,** however, leaders of the other member states were less than enthusiastic about the Fouchet Plan. In particular Josef Luns, the Dutch foreign minister and a future Secretary-General of the **North Atlantic Treaty Organization** (NATO), questioned de Gaulle's motivation and purpose. Resentment of an apparent Franco-German fait accompli fueled Luns' concerns about the future of the Community, the likely reaction of the United States, and the role of the United Kingdom. Luns' intransigence augured ill for the future of the Fouchet Plan. A series of acrimonious meetings in early 1962 caused the Fouchet Committee to collapse. Later that summer de Gaulle abandoned his grandiose scheme for a Union of States, and the Fouchet Plan came to nothing.

FRANCE From the outset, France has been the most influential **Community** member state. The Community was a French invention: **Robert Schuman** proposed it and **Jean Monnet** designed it. The Community's bureaucratic structure is quintessentially French, and the **Common Agricultural Policy** was included at French insistence. As the economically most powerful and politically most assertive member state in the 1950s and 1960s, France set the pace of European integration. Even in the 1970s, when the United Kingdom joined and Germany became an industrial giant, France remained the most prominent member state because Britain never sought a leadership role and Germany never emerged from the political shadow of World War II. Nor has the situation changed drastically, even in the aftermath of German unification.

France has traditionally supported European integration as a means of achieving economic modernization and international security. But domestic opinion differs sharply on the degree of integration either necessary or desirable. President **Charles de Gaulle** personified the minimalist position. In July 1965 de Gaulle caused the **"Empty Chair Crisis"** and nearly destroyed the Community. At issue was de Gaulle's insistence on maintaining unanimity, rather than introducing majority voting, in the **Council of Ministers**, the Community's decision-making body. De Gaulle fiercely defended his country's right not to be out-voted on a question of vital national interest.

De Gaulle returned to the negotiating table and approved the January 1966 **"Luxembourg Compromise"** in large part because of growing domestic opposition. De Gaulle had suffered a serious setback in the December 1965 presidential election. Although victorious, de Gaulle had been forced into a second ballot against none other than **Francois Mitterrand**, the present president of France, who personifies the maximalist French position on European integration.

In 1981, shortly after becoming president, Mitterrand made the case for more majority voting in the Council. He acknowledged the irony that unanimity, which had stymied the Community's development during the previous fifteen years, was the legacy of a former French president. Mitterrand also abandoned his initial program for economic development in France because it involved a "national," rather than a "Community," approach and jeopardized France's position in the **European Monetary System**

(EMS).   Subsequently, Mitterrand and his former finance minister, **Jacques Delors**, became the primary instigators of the Community's spectacular revival in the mid-1980s.   The turn-around in the Community's fortunes came during the French presidency of the Council of Ministers, in the first half of 1984. Thereafter Mitterrand helped to launch the **single market program**, engineer the **Single European Act**, anchor the Community's position in the "New Europe" that emerged after the collapse of the Soviet empire in 1989, and set the agenda for **Economic and Monetary Union** and **European Political Union** in the intergovernmental conferences that culminated in the **Maastricht Treaty**.

If de Gaulle and Mitterrand represent opposite ends of the spectrum, former President **Valéry Giscard d'Estaing** straddles the middle ground of French attitudes toward the Community. Giscard claimed to support European integration, but he loathed the **Commission**. He believed that the Community should be run intergovernmentally, not supranationally.   However, he far exceeded de Gaulle in his willingness to involve France deeper in economic integration. Without Giscard's support, the EMS would never have been launched.

Despite differences among de Gaulle, Giscard, and Mitterrand, the French, compared to other European advocates of closer integration, tend toward caution.   Traditionally France has preferred intergovernmentalism to supranationalism, hence French opposition to greater power for the **European Parliament**. Hence also France's refusal to bring **European Political Cooperation** and its successor, the **Common Foreign and Security Policy,** under the aegis of supranational decision making. President Mitterrand's gesture at the end of the June 1992 Lisbon **Summit**, when he flew to the besieged Bosnian city of Sarajevo without informing the European Council, was typically French. Indeed, it was worthy of de Gaulle.

Calling a referendum on the Maastricht Treaty in the aftermath of the Danish "no" vote on June 2, 1992, was another typically Gaullist gesture.   Mitterrand was confident of a resounding French "yes" that would not only rally support throughout the Community for the beleaguered Maastricht Treaty but also split the domestic French opposition parties. As September 20--the date of the French referendum--approached, the alarming prospect of defeat grew larger by the day. French repugnance of the treaty and of Mitterrand was widespread. In the end, a narrow majority (51%) voted in favor, thus keeping the treaty alive and saving Mitterrand's political skin. If France had rejected the treaty, the damage to European integration would have been incalculable.

-G-

GENERAL AGREEMENT ON TARIFFS AND TRADE (GATT)

The GATT is one of the international institutions launched in the late 1940s to try to regulate economics and trade in the post-World War II world. After six years of warfare, countries sought to avoid the excessive nationalism and protectionism of the 1930s that had given rise to the latest, most destructive conflict in European history. The purpose of the GATT was to promote employment and general prosperity by the substantial reduction of tariffs and other trade barriers and the elimination of discrimination.

Concluded in October 1947, the GATT codified trade relations among the signatory states. Since that time, the scope and membership of the GATT have increased enormously. Over 100 countries are now members, and most economic sectors are covered. Negotiations for tariff reductions and other trade reforms take place in a series of rounds that bear the names of either key individuals (e.g., Kennedy Round) or key locations (e.g., Tokyo Round). The GATT has a small secretariat in Geneva headed by a director-general. GATT also has a Council of Representatives and a number of committees.

The practice of reaching decision by consensus greatly impedes the GATT's progress. This is especially evident in the current round, named after the country where it began (Uruguay). The **European Commission** negotiates in the GATT on behalf of the **Community's** member states. In the Uruguay Round, the U.S. and other agricultural exporting countries severely criticized the Community for maintaining high agricultural export subsidies as part of the **Common Agricultural Policy** (CAP). The Community was in the process of reforming the CAP in any case, although the proposed reforms have not gone far enough to satisfy the Community's critics.   Without further reform of agricultural export subsidies, the Community's negotiating partners may not make the other concessions necessary to bring the Uruguay Round to a successful conclusion.

The Uruguay Round of the GATT is a serious bone of contention in U.S.-EC relations.   The breakdown of the December 1990 GATT negotiations in Brussels, convened to resolve the outstanding Uruguay Round problems, marred the **U.S.-EC Declaration** concluded only the previous month to promote harmonious economic and political relations between both sides. Extensive international criticism of the Community in the GATT has exacerbated strains within the Commission, most dramatically between Agriculture Commissioner **Ray MacSharry** and Commission President **Jacques Delors**, who in late 1992 came out squarely against concessions to the U.S.   Nor have the Community's heads of state and government changed the Commission's mandate in favor of a compromise. Such is the power of the farming lobby in the Community and the domestic political importance of being seen to resist American diplomatic pressure.

GENSCHER-COLOMBO PROPOSALS Officially called the **Draft European Act**, the Genscher-Colombo Proposals take their popular name from **Hans-Dietrich Genscher** and Emilio Colombo, the German and Italian foreign ministers who launched the initiative in November 1981. The purpose of the proposals was to shake the **Community** out of its political and institutional malaise in the early 1980s by advocating reform of the decision-making process, an end to the increasingly artificial distinction between **European Political Cooperation** (EPC) and EC external economic policy, and the extension of EPC into the security and defense domain.

British Prime Minister **Margaret Thatcher** disliked the call for greater security cooperation, lest it upset Washington.   For different reasons a number of smaller Community member states also disliked Genscher-Colombo's emphasis on closer security cooperation. Despite its **North Atlantic Treaty Organization**

(NATO) membership, Denmark resisted efforts to increase the Community's competence in the security domain. Despite its NATO membership, too, under the newly elected Socialist government Greece opposed deeper European integration in general and closer security cooperation in particular. Finally, sensitivity to domestic public opinion, which liked nonmembership in NATO and generally supported an otherwise ill-defined "neutrality," caused the Irish government to object to any initiative on security and defense in the Community.

Under the circumstances, Genscher-Colombo failed to achieve its foreign policy objectives. In November 1981 the **European Council** asked the **Ten** foreign ministers to consider and report back on the proposals. The foreign ministers failed to agree on a way forward and could not concur on the relatively mild foreign and security policy proposals contained in the draft act. Consequently, their report to the heads of state and government, meeting in Stuttgart on June 19, 1983, was weak. It gave rise only to the **"Solemn Declaration on European Union,"** a vague, insubstantial assertion of the Community's international identity.

GENSCHER, HANS-DIETRICH (1927-   )   For twenty-three consecutive years Hans-Dietrich Genscher served in the German government, including eighteen consecutive years as foreign minister (1974-1992).   As chairman of the small but disproportionately influential Free Democratic Party, Genscher wielded considerable domestic political power.   For instance, his switch of coalition partners from the Social Democrats to the Christian Democrats in 1982 ousted **Helmut Schmidt** as chancellor and brought **Helmut Kohl** instead to office. Similarly, his unexpected resignation as foreign minister in 1992 further weakened Kohl's already deteriorating political position.

Genscher had a reputation for being equally Machiavellian in international affairs.   Certainly Britain's Prime Minister **Margaret Thatcher** disliked him for that reason, as did successive American statesmen.   But American dislike of Genscher went deeper that mere personal mistrust.   Americans especially distrusted what they termed Genscherism: the foreign minister's efforts to balance the Federal Republic's opening to the East with its commitments to the **European Community** and the **Atlantic Alliance** in the

West. To a great extent, Genscherism was an extension of Chancellor **Willy Brandt's** *Ostpolitik* (Eastern policy) of the early 1970s, which America had also abhorred. In Genscher's case, personal considerations added poignancy to his Eastern policy: Genscher had been born in what became, after 1949, the German Democratic Republic.

In practice, Genscherism meant strong support for the **Conference on Security and Cooperation in Europe** (CSCE), the pan-European diplomatic arrangement that flourished during the period of detente in the mid-1970s, and provided a valuable forum in which the U.S. and U.S.S.R. could at least communicate with each other during the height of the "Second Cold War" in the early 1980s. Inevitably, Genscherism reached its zenith at the time of German reunification in 1991. Like Kohl, Genscher seized the opportunity presented by the revolutions in Eastern Europe in 1989 to advance and quickly achieve the coveted goal of national unity. Genscher had been the first Western leader to back Gorbachev and was the last to drop him. He also remained a strong supporter of massive Western aid to the U.S.S.R. and to the successor Soviet states.

Despite American fears, for all his enthusiasm for a positive Eastern policy Genscher never wavered from his commitment to the European Community. Genscher always saw integration as an essential means to achieve the related goals of German and Western European prosperity and security and (ultimately) German and European reunification. In the early 1980s Genscher was instrumental in helping to revive the **Community** with his so-called **Genscher-Colombo Proposals**. For Genscher the dramatic events of 1989 and 1990 vindicated the often maligned policy that bore his name. Moreover, the inter-governmental conferences of 1991, in which he played a leading role, culminated in a treaty that anchored united Germany firmly in the Community.

By the time he voluntarily left office in 1992, however, Genscher's reputation was tarnished. Kohl's firm grip on unification policy and U.S.-EC relations, and the foreign minister's unseemly rush to recognize Croatia's independence during Yugoslavia's fragmentation, suggested that Genscher was finally beginning to lose his once magical touch.

GERMANY   Just as France is the most influential **Community**
member state, Germany is the most important.   Without
Germany there would not be a **European Community**.   The
movement for European integration grew out of the experience
of World War II, with the objective of promoting reconciliation
and preventing future conflict.   As the apotheosis of European
integration, the Community seeks to tie Germany economically
and politically to its neighbors, making future German aggression
impossible.   The original proposal by **Robert Schuman** and **Jean
Monnet** was to end competition and encourage cooperation in the
coal and steel sectors of France and Germany.   Since then, the
Community has increased its competence and extended its
membership enormously, but the basic premise remains valid.
This became strikingly apparent in the prelude to German
unification in 1990, when other member states responded by
accelerating the pace of European integration, notably by
convening an intergovernmental conference on **Political Union** to
coincide with the intergovernmental conference on **Economic and
Monetary Union.**

From the outset, Germany has willingly participated in
European integration both because of the Community's intrinsic
economic merit and because of the country's need to reassure its
erstwhile adversaries. Additionally, Chancellor **Konrad Adenauer**
realized that postwar Germany would never regain full
sovereignty but could hope only to share sovereignty with its
neighbors. Hence his enthusiasm for the **Schuman Declaration**
and, especially, for the proposed **European Defense Community**
(EDC). Adenauer was eager to remilitarize and saw the EDC as
an ideal opportunity to do so. The collapse of the EDC, due to
continuing distrust of Germany, threatened to torpedo European
integration. Only when British Prime Minister Anthony Eden
mollified Germany and appeased France by bringing Germany
into NATO through the **Western European Union** was the contentious question of rearmament resolved and the future of
integration secured. At the subsequent **Messina Conference**, Germany wholeheartedly endorsed the proposed **European Economic
Community** and the **European Atomic Energy Community.**

Adenauer pursued an extremely close relationship with France,
largely through his friendship with President **Charles de Gaulle.**

Many Germans fretted about Adenauer's dependence on de Gaulle and especially about the January 1963 **Elysée Treaty** signed by both leaders, because of its possible negative impact on relations with the U.S. But nobody in Germany disputed the importance of a close accord with France. On the contrary, the new Franco-German entente became the motor of European integration and a prerequisite for progress in the Community. The friendship between Chancellor **Helmut Schmidt** and President **Valéry Giscard d'Estaing** cemented that entente in the 1970s, as did the friendship between Chancellor **Helmut Kohl** and President **Francois Mitterrand** in the 1980s and early 1990s.

Although Germany is the Community's most important member state, Germans have not excelled in **Brussels**. Apart from **Walter Hallstein**, the **Commission's** first president, and other notable exceptions, Germans have not been as prominent in the Community's institutions as the size of their country would suggest. This is due partly to personal considerations (for instance, Schmidt detested the Commission and would not send his best people there) and partly to historical factors (Germans are sensitive to concerns that they seek to dominate internationally and accordingly have not been as assertive as others in international organizations). In the **European Council** and the **Council of Ministers**, by contrast, German ministers have not been shy to advance their country's interests. Between 1974 and 1992 **Hans-Dietrich Genscher**, Germany's foreign minister, was a key figure in the Council's deliberations.

German industry has benefited enormously from Community membership, and the small but politically important farm sector has benefitted from the **Common Agricultural Policy**. But Germany also contributes a lot to the Community's coffers, prompting a famous remark by Chancellor **Willy Brandt** that his country was becoming the "paymaster of Europe." Resentment in Germany against the entitlement mentality of other member states, particularly the poor southern countries, has grown throughout the 1970s and 1980s. The **"Delors I"** budgetary package, with its proposed doubling of "structural funds" for the poor south to compensate for any distortions in the emerging single market, nearly foundered in 1988 over Germany's refusal to foot the bill. Similarly, the **"Delors II"** package, intended to help the same countries in the run-up to EMU, was in serious difficulty in 1992 over Germany's far-greater reluctance to pay, not least because of the cost to Germany of reunification.

As a federal, decentralized state, Germany has consistently advocated federalism in the Community. Throughout the years, Germany has been a persistent champion of supranationalism and greater power for the **European Parliament**. Germany attempted to advance these claims during the 1991 intergovernmental conference on Political Union, partly as a trade-off for concessions in the parallel intergovernmental conference on EMU. In the end, Germany agreed to a single currency by 1997 or 1999 at the latest, but the other member states did not go far in the direction of meeting Germany's political demands. This fueled latent resentment in Germany against the Community, as did the prospect of giving up the tried and trusted deutsche mark for an untested new Euro-currency. These factors complicated the **Maastricht Treaty** ratification debate in Germany and increased the political pressure on Chancellor Kohl in 1992.

German unification has given rise to predictable alarm that Germany will either dominate the Community or lose interest in European integration. Neither scenario seems feasible. Given the distribution of seats in the European Parliament, the distribution of votes in the Council of Ministers, and the structure of the European Commission, no single country can "dominate" the Community. Nor is it in Germany's economic interests to forsake European integration. Notwithstanding concern in Germany over specific aspects of the Maastricht Treaty, developments since unification in October 1990 suggest that the country is more committed than ever to the European Community.

GISCARD D'ESTAING, VALERY (1926-) As president of France between 1974 and 1981, Giscard d'Estaing helped to steer the **Community** through a period of economic stagnation and political malaise that sapped the movement for European integration. Giscard became president of the Fifth Republic at approximately the same time that **Helmut Schmidt** became chancellor of Germany; for the next seven years both leaders were friends and collaborators in the **European Community**, virtually running the show between them. At a time of demoralization and weakness in the **Commission**, the Franco-German alliance was the sole motor of Community momentum. Going well beyond the framework of the **Elysée Treaty**, Giscard and Schmidt got together often for dinner, spoke at least weekly on the telephone, and caucused regularly on the fringes of multilateral meetings. To facilitate communication, Giscard and Schmidt spoke two common languages: economics and English.

Giscard's greatest contribution to the Community was the **European Council**, which he inaugurated at a **summit** meeting of heads of state and government in Paris in 1974. The idea was typically Giscardian: regular meetings of Community leaders, without an army of advisers, to give the Community overall direction and resolve outstanding problems. Giscard also organized the annual summit meetings of the major industrialized countries (now called the G7 Summit) along the same exclusive lines. With his knowledge of economics (he had been finance minister in France for nearly ten years) and grasp of international affairs, Giscard was in his element in small, elite groups of politicians and statesmen.

The European Council proved its worth at the end of the 1970s in relation to the Franco-German initiative for a **European Monetary System** (EMS). Regular meetings of the Community's leaders provided Schmidt and Giscard with an opportunity to promote their monetary proposal and a forum in which to approve the EMS at the highest possible decision-making level in the Community. The EMS also was a classic example of the Franco-German alliance at work. Without French backing, Schmidt's initial idea for an EMS would not have succeeded; with French backing, success was assured.

Although Giscard is closely associated with the EMS initiative, his last-minute concerns about the impact of the EMS on the **Common Agricultural Policy** (CAP) almost prevented the EMS from coming into operation. Giscard's intransigence on the issue baffled his Community counterparts but earned him political points at home in France. Following an agreement at a meeting of agriculture ministers in early March 1979 ultimately to abolish monetary compensatory amounts in the CAP, Giscard announced his unconditional support for the EMS. On March 13, 1979, the EMS finally started to function.

As president of France, Giscard grew aloof, remote, and patronizing. The presidential election of 1981 brought him crashing back to earth. **Francois Mitterrand's** victory removed Giscard from the Elysée Palace. Thereafter Giscard returned to the French Parliament but resigned in 1989 to stand for election to the **European Parliament** (EP), where he has since led the Liberal group. During that time he has become an advocate of additional power for the Parliament and of greater supranationality in the Community, causes he opposed as president of France.

GONZALEZ, FELIPE (1942-) Felipe González, Spain's young and charismatic prime minister (1982-), is an unequivocal supporter of the **European Community** and a self-avowed "Euro-fanatic." Under González, Spain saw its fortunes change from an economy plagued by General Franco's legacies of inefficiency and underdevelopment to one of Europe's strongest economies, experiencing the highest growth rate in Europe in the late 1980s. After he took Spain into the Community in 1986, González distinguished himself as an ardent European, wholeheartedly accepting the **single market program** and consistently supporting moves toward deeper integration.

When González's Socialist government came to power in 1982, Spain was still recovering from the effects of forty years of Francoism: backward industry, soaring unemployment, and rampant inflation. In addition, accession negotiations between Spain and the EC, which began in 1979, were at a standstill. Over the next few years González introduced a series of measures designed to restructure Spanish industry and otherwise modernize Spain's sagging economy. While intra-Community obstacles continued to plague Spain's already protracted negotiations, in the first two years of his stewardship González was instrumental in ensuring that Spain would join the Community without further delay; the close relationship he cultivated with his French counterpart and ideological soul mate, **Francois Mitterrand**, was perhaps his most notable achievement in this regard. Meanwhile, to demonstrate his commitment to Western Europe, González refuted his initial opposition to **North Atlantic Treaty Organization** (NATO) membership (Spain had joined the

Atlantic Alliance in 1982 under the centrist government of Adolfo Suarez) and mobilized public opinion in favor of continued NATO membership in the 1986 referendum.

EC membership, along with a favorable global economic environment, provided the boost that Spain's economy needed. After a brief period of adjustment, the Spanish economy soared, thanks largely to a surge in foreign investment encouraged by lowered trade barriers. Politically, EC membership represented a return to international respectability. By the late 1980s, as Spain's leading spokesman for modernization and closer ties to the rest of Europe, González came to personify Spain's youthful democracy, prosperity, and hope for the future.

Yet as Spain's financial contribution to the EC budget increased with its prosperity and high spending, the benefits of Community membership became less tangible. The government realized that Spain, like Britain in the 1970s, would become a net contributor to the EC in the years ahead. Thus, while González supported moves in the late 1980s and early 1990s toward deeper integration, he insisted that any **European Union** treaty must also make provisions for a "**cohesion** fund" to help narrow the disparities between the Community's core and periphery. In a feat of diplomatic deftness and political will, González got his way: the **Maastricht Treaty** calls for the establishment of a cohesion fund by the end of 1993.

Another provision of the Maastricht Treaty, however, proved more problematic. As part of the agreement to implement **Economic and Monetary Union** (EMU) by the end of the decade, the **European Council** decided on the so-called convergence criteria--economic requirements that any country wishing to enjoy the full benefits of EMU would have to meet. To achieve these goals Spain faces years of austerity. Not all sectors of Spanish society share González's Euro-fever, not least trade unions intent on maintaining Spain's liberal unemployment benefits. Nor is the Spanish Socialist Party in complete accord with its leader's tilt to the right. By 1992, despite the conspicuous lack of any formidable opposition, González's political position had weakened. At the same time González was touted in Community circles as a possible successor to **Commission** President **Jacques Delors**, a prospect he reportedly found congenial.

GREECE Greece is the **European Community's** problem child. Greece applied for membership in the mid-1970s, following the collapse of the military regime and the restoration of democracy there. The **Commission** concluded that Greece was economically unfit to join, but the **Council of Ministers** decided that Greek membership was politically imperative. How could the **Community** remain faithful to its democratic ideals, the Council argued, if it excluded the cradle of democracy? How could Greece remain democratic unless the Community provided a support structure by allowing it to join?

Privately, many European politicians and Community officials now regret the decision to allow Greece in. The Commission was right: economically Greece remains far behind the rest of the Community and has made little effort to improve. Moreover, politically Greece has proven a thorn in the Community's side. Throughout the 1980s, the Greek Socialist government of Andreas Papandreou pursued a virulently anti-Western policy that quickly alienated the other member states. Papandreou blocked the Community's political development, especially in **European Political Cooperation** (EPC). Even when he tried to be helpful--for instance, when he attempted to broker a settlement of the British budgetary dispute at the December 1983 Athens **Summit**--Papandreou succeeded only in irritating his Community counterparts further. The Athens Summit was the only **European Council** to end without a communiqué agreed by the heads of state or government.

In the late 1980s a Conservative government returned to power in Greece. The new administration tried to regain control of the economy but to no avail. Politically, the new government sought to build bridges in **Brussels** by becoming a model Community member. However, problems persist in EPC. The difficulty no longer lies with procedure but with policy. For instance, Greece's preoccupation with Cyprus prevents the Community from developing better relations with Turkey, and Greece's insistence that Macedonia change its name precludes the Community from recognizing the independence of the former Yugoslav territory.

No sooner had the countries of Central and Eastern Europe regained their independence in 1989 than they cited the case of Greece a decade earlier as an argument in favor of Community membership. Little did they realize that, as far as the other member states were concerned, the Greek experience was a compelling reason not to have another enlargement. By the same token, Greek officials surely realize how fortunate they are that their country regained democracy fifteen years before other countries in the region. Otherwise, Greece would surely be in the long line of countries now queuing up for Community membership.

-H-

The HAGUE CONGRESS A glittering gathering of over 600 influential Europeans from sixteen countries, the Hague Congress took place in May 1948 to plan a strategy for European unity. The congress was characterized by a conflict between European "unionists" and "federalists." The former, personified by **Winston Churchill**, advocated intergovernmental cooperation while the latter, personified by **Altiero Spinelli**, espoused supranationalism. Both positions were based on different political, economic, and cultural experiences, largely between the continental and the geographically peripheral countries. The unionists and the federalists agreed only on the desirability of European unity and on the need to institutionalize that ideal by establishing an international organization with a parliamentary body. Thus the amorphous **Council of Europe** emerged from their deliberations.

The HAGUE SUMMIT The Hague Summit of December 1969 relaunched the **European Community** after **Charles de Gaulle's** departure from the French presidency earlier that year. With de Gaulle gone and enlargement once again at center stage, most member states anticipated a decisive breakthrough at the summit. Aware of Western apprehension about Germany's new *Ostpolitik* and domestic pressure for a French initiative in the EC, President **Pompidou**, de Gaulle's sucessor, called for the special **summit**-- the first meeting of **Community** leaders since the tenth anniversary celebration of the **Treaty of Rome** in 1967--to promote what he called "completion, deepening, enlargement." "Completion" meant finalizing the financing of the **Common**

Agricultural Policy (CAP), a cherished French objective put in abeyance since the 1965 **"Empty Chair Crisis."** "Deepening" meant going beyond the Community's existing agenda by embracing foreign policy cooperation, macroeconomic coordination, and even currency harmonization. "Enlargement" meant finally admitting Britain and the other applicant countries to the Community. As a result of the process set in train at The Hague, the member states soon agreed on a system of "own resources" to fund the CAP, approved the idea of foreign policy cooperation, took the first steps toward **Economic and Monetary Union,** and decided in principle to extend the Community's membership from **Six** to **Nine.**

HALLSTEIN, WALTER (1901-1982) Walter Hallstein was the first president of the **Commission** of the **European Economic Community.** Apart from an academic interest in European integration, his initial involvement in the **European movement** came in the early 1950s, when Chancellor **Konrad Adenauer** asked him to represent Germany in the negotiations to bring the **Schuman Plan** to fruition. Accordingly, Hallstein worked closely with **Jean Monnet** to bring about the **Coal and Steel Community.**

In the mid-1950s Hallstein served as state secretary in the German Foreign Office before taking up his appointment as president of the EEC Commission in 1958. From the beginning of his presidency Hallstein had used every opportunity to espouse **European Union** along federal lines, and he sought to turn the Commission into an embryonic government of a supranational **Community.** This ambition, as well as Hallstein's "presidential" behavior, infuriated French President **Charles de Gaulle,** who bitterly opposed any extension of the Commission's power. Although a protégé of Konrad Adenauer's, Hallstein evidently lacked the old chancellor's extreme deference to the French president.

The looming confrontation between de Gaulle and Hallstein came to a head in early 1965, when Hallstein introduced proposals to link completing the **Common Agricultural Policy's** financial arrangement (due to take place on July 1 that year) with greater budgetary power for the **European Parliament** and executive authority for the Commission. **Robert Marjolin,** a vice-president of the Commission, warned Hallstein not to persist with his CAP and decision-making proposals. Although de Gaulle wanted a new financial regulation for the CAP, he wanted even more to thwart Hallstein's ambition. In a conflict between both men, Marjolin knew, de Gaulle would easily come out best.

But Hallstein pressed ahead and took the additional inflammatory step of announcing the proposals first not to the **Council of Ministers in Brussels,** but to the **European Parliament in Strasbourg.** Storm clouds immediately gathered. De Gaulle made clear to his Community counterparts that France would reject the Commission's proposals. The crucial Council of Ministers meeting opened on June 28 and ended two days later in deadlock. De Gaulle promptly recalled his permanent representative to Paris and announced that French officials would no longer participate in the Council of Ministers or its numerous committees, thus precipitating the so-called **Empty Chair Crisis.**

The crisis ended seven months later at a foreign ministers meeting in **Luxembourg** on January 28-29, 1966. The **Six** agreed to adopt an interim financial regulation for the CAP, deferring the question of institutional reform. Majority voting in the Council of Ministers, which de Gaulle opposed and linked to a resolution of the crisis, remained the outstanding issue. After restating their positions, both sides approved a short declaration, the "**Luxembourg Compromise,**" which amounted to an agreement to disagree over majority voting. While maintaining the principle of majority voting, the compromise acknowledged that "when very important issues are at stake, discussions must be continued until unanimous agreement is reached."

Ostensibly, the outcome was a draw or even a victory for the Community. The French presidential election result of December 1965 had apparently clipped de Gaulle's wings, the Five had not reneged on majority voting, and the Community soon resumed full operation. In reality, however, the crisis ended in victory for de Gaulle. The Council approved temporary funding for agriculture, and the CAP continued to function effectively. In the meantime, the Commission's ambitious proposals to revise budgetary procedures had sunk out of sight. From de Gaulle's point of view, the situation in early 1966 was highly satisfactory. Not only was the CAP secure, but also Hallstein's supranational

ambitions were severely set back. As a result, the crisis had
profoundly undermined both Hallstein's credibility and the
Commission's confidence. Thereafter the Commission refrained
from asserting itself in the Community for well over a decade.

De Gaulle exacted his revenge on Hallstein when the member
states discussed the composition of the new, merged Commission
of the Communities, due to come into office in July 1967. Kurt
Kiesinger, the German chancellor, wanted to nominate Hallstein
as Commission president, but de Gaulle strenuously opposed.
The issue quickly degenerated into an undignified squabble, with
a possible compromise involving Hallstein's appointment for one
year only. In May 1967 Hallstein settled the matter by
announcing his impending resignation, and he stepped down on
July 6, 1967.

HEATH, EDWARD (1916-) As prime minister of Britain Edward
Heath brought his country into the **European Community** in
1973, and he remains Britain's most pro-European politician. He
first became involved with the **Community** in 1960, when **Harold
Macmillan**, Britain's then prime minister, appointed him to the
Cabinet as lord privy seal in charge of European affairs. With
that imposing title Heath conducted Britain's first entry
negotiations in Brussels, in 1962 and 1963. French President
Charles de Gaulle abruptly ended those difficult negotiations at
a press conference on January 14, 1963, by vetoing Britain's
membership application. Heath was bitterly disappointed but
persevered in his determination to bring Britain into the
Community.

His next opportunity to do so came in 1970 when he became
prime minister after his Conservative Party's election victory.
Harold Wilson, his predecessor as prime minister, had submitted
Britain's second application for Community membership in 1967,
but de Gaulle had again exercised a veto. De Gaulle's
resignation in 1969 and replacement by **Georges Pompidou**
augured well for a reactivation of Britain's application. Heath's
election one year later gave added impetus to Britain's effort to
join.

Yet few of Heath's fellow Conservative Party members shared
the prime minister's ardor for European integration. Most saw

Community membership largely in negative terms--as Britain's only feasible option. On the other side of the political divide the issue split the opposition Labour Party. Harold Wilson, the Labour Party leader, now equivocated. As the entry negotiations unfolded, Wilson moved from ambivalence toward open opposition of British accession, bringing the bulk of Labour with him.

Following the political breakthrough at the **Hague Summit**, Britain's entry negotiations began on June 30, 1970, in Luxembourg and ended almost a year later in **Brussels**. Familiar issues from Britain's previous applications resurfaced in the new discussions. However, the talks were far less contentious and protracted than in the early 1960s. For one thing, Heath was so eager for membership that he quickly settled any differences. For another, Commonwealth and **European Free Trade Association** concern about British membership in the Community had abated in the intervening decade. The impact on the Commonwealth of Britain's accession to the Community now focused exclusively on specific problems like imports of Caribbean sugar and New Zealand dairy products. Nevertheless the negotiations occasionally stalled, particularly on the controversial questions of Britain's budgetary contribution during the transition phase and the related issue of the dubious benefit to Britain of the **Common Agricultural Policy**.

A meeting between Heath and Pompidou in Paris, on May 20-21, 1971, helped to resolve the outstanding problems and set the tone for Britain's first year in the Community. So harmonious was the Heath-Pompidou relationship, in marked contrast to the **Willy Brandt**-Pompidou relationship, that Britain seemed set to replace Germany as France's favored partner in the Community. Yet, the leadership of all three countries changed at approximately the same time in early 1974, and the old pattern of Franco-German leadership soon reasserted itself. **Valéry Giscard d'Estaing** succeeded Pompidou, **Helmut Schmidt** replaced Brandt, and Heath lost the February 1974 general election to Harold Wilson.

Soon afterward, Heath lost the Conservative Party's leadership to **Margaret Thatcher**. The political and personal differences between them could not have been more striking, not least on

European issues. Heath remained avidly committed to the Community, whereas Thatcher strongly opposed deeper integration. Heath suffered through Thatcher's eleven years in office and repeatedly attacked her negativism and obstructionism toward the Community. His numerous House of Commons speeches denouncing Thatcher's Community policy were especially prescient and enlightening.

HIGH AUTHORITY The High Authority of the **European Coal and Steel Community** (ECSC) was the supranational institution responsible for formulating a common market in coal and steel and for such related issues as pricing, wages, investment, and competition. **Jean Monnet**, author of the **Schuman Plan** that gave rise to the ECSC, became the High Authority's first president in 1952. In 1965 the **Six** signed a treaty merging the executive institutions of the three **Communities**, thereby establishing a single Commission and a single Council. When the **Merger Treaty** came into force on July 1, 1967, the High Authority ceased to exist.

-I-

IRELAND For the first four decades of its existence as an independent state Ireland pursued a policy of economic self-sufficiency. Moreover, Ireland's neutrality during World War II led to a period of diplomatic isolation in the postwar period. Ireland declined to join the **North Atlantic Treaty Organization** (NATO) in 1949 and was admitted to the UN only in 1955.

Yet it would have been absurd economically for Ireland to stay outside the EC once Britain went in. Elements of economic and political opportunism complemented this sense of determinism. The former had to do with the expected windfall for Irish farmers of participation in the **Common Agricultural Policy** (CAP), as well as a host of other benefits, mostly in the form of grants and loans, that would accrue to Ireland in the **Community**. The element of political opportunism, by contrast, consisted of the anticipated impact of Community membership on Anglo-Irish relations. EC membership afforded Ireland the chance to break out of a suffocatingly close relationship with Britain and place Anglo-Irish relations in a broader, more equitable, multilateral context. It was little wonder that an overwhelming majority endorsed EC membership in the May 1972 referendum.

As expected, EC membership proved a bonanza, especially for Irish farmers. Ireland's relatively small industrial work force fared less well, and high unemployment--currently running at approximately 20%--has characterized the country's membership in the Community. The compatibility of Ireland's neutrality, narrowly defined as nonmembership of an existing military alliance, with participation in **European Political Cooperation** (EPC) has always been a sensitive domestic political issue. A challenge on that score by an Irish citizen against the constitutionality of the **Single European Act** (SEA) delayed ratification of the SEA in Ireland, and therefore throughout the Community, in 1987. Apart from the contentious neutrality question, the compatibility of Ireland's constitutional ban on abortion with the provisions of the **Maastricht Treaty** became a major domestic issue and dominated the June 1992 referendum debate, which nonetheless resulted in a resounding endorsement of the treaty.

Given the importance of the primary sector in the Irish economy, one of the country's preoccupations in the Community has been to limit the extent of CAP reform. In 1983 the Irish prime minister, **Garret FitzGerald**, stormed out of an EC **summit** to protest proposed curbs on milk production. The Irish government was especially concerned about the 1991 agricultural reforms introduced by Commissioner **Ray MacSharry**, who is, ironically, an Irishman.

Membership in the Community has had little or no impact on the conflict in Northern Ireland.

ITALY Along with France and Germany, Italy was one of the "Big Three" founding member states of the **European Community**. **Alcide de Gasperi**, Italy's postwar prime minister, steered his country along the path of European integration. Like French Foreign Minister **Robert Schuman** and German Chancellor **Konrad Adenauer**, de Gasperi was a Christian Democrat and an active participant in the **European movement**. Italy accepted with alacrity Schuman's offer to take part in the negotiations to launch the **Coal and Steel Community**. Subsequently, Italy played a prominent part in the intergovernmental conference following the **Messina Conference** that resulted in the **Treaties of Rome**.

Membership in the European Community had an immediate impact on the Italian economy. The northern, industrial part of the country prospered, but the southern, rural part remained impoverished. The government hoped that the **Community's** nascent regional policy and new **European Investment Bank** would help to lift southern Italy's abysmal economic level. Despite a massive infusion of money from **Brussels** and Luxembourg over the next thirty years, the disparity between both parts of the country only widened.

As a relatively new country with a strong sense of regional rather than national identity, Italy is one of the Community member states least concerned about supranationalism. For many Italians, Brussels is no more remote, politically and psychologically, than Rome. Thus, throughout the Community's history Italy has consistently advocated a stronger **Commission** and a more powerful **European Parliament**. Italy also advocates greater Community competence, especially over military and defense issues. During the intergovernmental conference that preceded the **Maastricht Summit**, Italy pushed for a more ambitious **Common Foreign and Security Policy** than eventually emerged in the **Treaty on European Union**. Gianni de Michelis, Italy's flamboyant foreign minister during the conference, seized on the outbreak of the Gulf War and the Yugoslav conflict to press for a close link between the Community and the **Western European Union**.

Because of frequent changes of government in Rome and chronic corruption Italy is often dismissed as an insignificant, underdeveloped country. Yet the ministerial merry-go-round belies Italy's relative political stability. Moreover, socioeconomic indicators put Italy squarely at the top flight of industrialized countries in the world. The Italian prime minister attends the annual "G7" summit meetings of the world's economically strongest countries. Italy would not have been able to attain that position without full participation in the European Community's economic policies and programs.

-J-

JENKINS, ROY (1920-   )   Roy Jenkins was a prominent British Labour politician before becoming president of the **European Commission** in 1977.   Jenkins had been leader of the pro-**Community** faction in the deeply divided Labour Party during Britain's 1970-71 entry negotiations, when the Conservatives were in power.   Labour leader **Harold Wilson's** support for a national referendum on the issue provoked Jenkins to resign from the Party's Front Bench.   During the referendum that followed Britain's renegotiation of membership terms, in June 1975, Jenkins chaired the "Britain in Europe" campaign.

In 1976, as **Francois-Xavier Ortoli's** term came to an end, the other member states agreed that Britain, a large recent arrival, should nominate the next Commission president.   As much to get him out of Britain as in recognition of his impeccable pro-Community credentials, the Labour government chose Jenkins for the job.   Having spent his entire career in British politics, and with little experience of foreign affairs, Jenkins was a **Brussels** outsider.   Largely because he succeeded the uninspiring Ortoli, Jenkins' arrival in Brussels aroused inflated expectations.   Yet, by his own account, his first year there was a disaster.   It soon looked as if Jenkins' Commission presidency would be as undistinguished as any of his predecessors' since **Walter Hallstein**.

Yet three events ultimately set Jenkins' presidency apart, although two of them had been set in train before he arrived in Brussels.   One was Greece's accession to the EC, which took place on January 1, 1981.   The other was the first-ever direct elections to the **European Parliament**, which were held in June 1979.   Unlike these two events, the third development that characterized Jenkins' presidency, and helped to get the Community going again, owed a great deal directly to him.   This was the **European Monetary System** (EMS), an initiative to establish a zone of relative monetary stability in a world of wildly fluctuating exchange rates.   The EMS was an immediate success and helped participating member states to fight inflation and recover economic growth.   It also gave the Commuity the confidence necessary to embark on the **single market program**. Jenkins used the occasion of the inaugural **Jean Monnet** Lecture

at the Community-sponsored European University Institute in
Florence, in October 1977, to fly a trial balloon. Rather than
present a precise proposal, Jenkins sought to reopen the debate
about monetary union in the context of the Community's political
and economic infirmity in the late 1970s and argued that
monetary union would have the macroeconomic advantages of
lowering inflation, increasing investment, and reducing
unemployment. Nor, if properly implemented, would monetary
union exacerbate regional economic disparities or intensify
institutional centralization in Brussels.

But Jenkins' idea would not have gone anywhere without
powerful political support in the Community. That support came
largely from **Helmut Schmidt**, who grasped the importance of
Jenkins' initiative in early 1978. Schmidt's sudden espousal of a
scheme for exchange rate stability and his determination to see
it through despite strong domestic opposition made the EMS
possible. Regular meetings of the **European Council** gave
Schmidt an opportunity to promote the monetary proposal and
a forum in which to approve the EMS at the EC's highest
possible decision-making level. The July 1978 **Bremen Summit**
marked a decisive stage in the gestation of the EMS. Schmidt's
forceful chairmanship contributed to a general acceptance of the
scheme, although Britain's unwillingness to participate in the
future EMS became obvious as the summit progressed.

The EMS that eventually came into operation in March 1979
was substantially different from what Jenkins had originally envisioned. Nevertheless it was to Jenkins' credit that a monetary
initiative of any kind had been taken in the late 1970s. Without
it, the single market program and the relaunch of plans for
Economic and Monetary Union in the mid-1980s would have
been based on less solid foundations. That is Roy Jenkins'
impressive legacy to the Community.

-K-

KOHL, HELMUT (1930-) Kohl will forever be known as the
chancellor of German reunification. In November 1989, after the
collapse of the Berlin Wall, Kohl lost no time in pressing the

Soviet Union and his Western allies for an immediate end to Germany's postwar partition. In response, **Mitterrand** wavered; **Thatcher** resisted; Bush gave his blessing; **Delors** enthused; and Gorbachev acquiesced. The reestablishment of German unity in October 1990 was the unexpected culmination of Kohl's political career. His only miscalculation was the domestic economic cost, and his only mistake a refusal to tell the German people that any financial stringency would follow. Kohl paid the political price in 1992, as his coalition government suffered electoral setbacks and high-level defections in the cold dawn of post-unification euphoria.

Reunification could not have come about so soon after the collapse of communism in Eastern Europe had Kohl not stressed Germany's continuing commitment to Western European integration. This was not a ploy on the chancellor's part. Kohl was a lifelong supporter of supranationalism and had consistently advocated a stronger **Commission** and more powerful **European Parliament.** When German reunification first appeared possible in early 1990, Kohl and Mitterrand presented a proposal to their fellow heads of government for closer political integration. During the intergovernmental conferences the following year, Kohl advocated **European Political Union** (EPU), not only in its own right but also as the concession that other member states would have to make in order to secure Germany's consent to **European Monetary Union** (EMU). The bargain struck at **Maastricht** disappointed Kohl by not going far enough to strengthen supranationalism in the **Community.** Nor did ratification of the **Maastricht Treaty** prove as straightforward as Kohl had assumed, although more because of Germans' deep attachment to the deutsche mark than resentment over the lackluster nature of political union.

Kohl's handling of the extremely sensitive reunification issue, his unchallenged control over the Christian Democratic Party, and his forceful chancellorship since 1982 belie the popular image of him as incompetent and obtuse. Despite his considerable international achievements, Kohl never enjoyed domestic adulation or affection. In the **European Council,** by contrast, he is held in great respect, not least because he represents the economically--and increasingly politically--most important member state. Well before the intergovernmental conferences on EMU and EPU got off the ground, Kohl had contributed greatly to the EC's development. For instance, Kohl's presidency of the European Council in 1988 helped to break the deadlock over the "**Delors I**" budget package. Without Delors I the **single market program** would never have been a success. By contrast, for domestic political and economic reasons--Germany was less well off two years after than two years before reunification--Kohl protested the "**Delors II**" budget package to implement the Maastricht agreement. But Kohl's position on Delors II by no means indicated a waning interest in European unification. In or out of office, in good times or bad, Kohl always was and always will be a staunch supporter of the European Community.

-L-

LUXEMBOURG Luxembourg is both a founding member state of the **Community** and the location of a number of Community institutions. As a small member state Luxembourg has always advocated closer European integration, a development bound to increase its influence internationally. Before the EC came into existence Luxembourg had become economically integrated with Belgium and The Netherlands in the **Benelux** group of countries, which enthusiastically endorsed the Community's establishment. Since that time Luxembourg has championed such pro-Community proposals as majority voting in the **Council of Ministers**, a stronger **Commission** and **European Parliament**, the **Single European Act**, and the **Maastricht Treaty**.

Luxembourg's enthusiasm for the Community owes something to the benefits it derives from hosting Community institutions. In the early 1950s, during the launch of the **European Coal and Steel Community** (ECSC), **Jean Monnet** proposed a special "European District" to house the new Community's institutions, along the lines of the District of Columbia in the U.S. Monnet's proposal fell flat, and the member states instead settled on Luxembourg as the ECSC's home. Later in the 1950s, when the **European Economic Community** (EEC) and the **European Atomic Energy Community** (Euratom) were established, Monnet revived his proposal, equally unsuccessfully. By that time Luxembourg had become inundated with ECSC and associated personnel, and its government declined to host the new institutions. Subsequently, however, Luxembourg grew to like the infusion of money and people that came with Community institutions. Thus the Grand Duchy now hosts the **Court of Justice**, the **European Investment Bank**, and the Secretariat of the European Parliament. In 1992 Luxembourg made an unsuccessful effort to attract the new **European Central Bank**.

LUXEMBOURG COMPROMISE The Luxembourg Compromise of January 1966 ended the "**Empty Chair Crisis**," which had erupted in July 1965 when France walked out of the **Council of Ministers**. The dispute between France and the other Five (plus the **Commission**) centered on French objections to enhanced supranational power for the Commission and the **European Parliament** and the introduction of majority voting in the Council of Ministers, mandated by the **Treaty of Rome** to come into operation in January 1966. For French President **Charles de Gaulle**, an ardent nationalist, the prospect of being outvoted in the Council and having to accept the will of the majority was unacceptable in an international organization.

De Gaulle only returned to the negotiation table after suffering a scare in the presidential election of December 1965. Although victorious, de Gaulle had nearly lost to **Francois Mitterrand**, who ran on a pro-EC ticket. Once both sides started talking again, the crisis was finally resolved at the foreign ministers meeting of January 28-29, 1966, in Luxembourg After restating their positions, France and the other Five approved a short declaration, the "Luxembourg Compromise," which maintained the principle of majority voting but acknowledged that "when very important issues are at stake, discussions must be continued until unanimous agreement is reached."

The Luxembourg Compromise represented a victory for de Gaulle and a serious setback for the **Community**. Specifically, it impeded effective decision making in the Council of Ministers for the next twenty years. De Gaulle's insistence on unanimity heightened the member states' awareness of each other's special interests and increased their reluctance to call a vote in the

Council even when no vital interest was at stake. Only in the mid-1980s, impelled by the need to implement the **single market program**, did the member states decisively tackle, in the **Single European Act,** what Commission President **Jacques Delors** called "the ball and chain of unanimity."

-M-

MAASTRICHT SUMMIT At the **European Council** meeting of December 9-10, 1991, in the southern Dutch town of Maastricht, the heads of state and government concluded the inter-governmental conferences on **Economic and Monetary Union** and **European Political Union** and drafted the **Treaty on European Union,** known also as the **Maastricht Treaty.**

MAASTRICHT TREATY The popular name for the **Treaty on European Union** drafted at the **European Council** meeting of December 9-10, 1991, in the southern Dutch town of Maastricht, and signed there on February 7, 1992.

MACMILLAN, HAROLD (1894-1986) Harold Macmillan led Britain's first unsuccessful effort to join the **European Community.** He had become prime minister in 1957, replacing Anthony Eden after Britain's disastrous military intervention in Suez. By 1960 Macmillan was convinced of Britain's need to join the **Community.** As his biographer, Alistair Horne, has written, this "was perhaps the biggest single decision of [Macmillan's] premiership." It was certainly a fateful and far-reaching decision for Macmillan, the United Kingdom, and the Community itself.

Macmillan advocated Britain's accession to the **Treaty of Rome** for negative rather than positive reasons. By the end of the 1950s Macmillan grasped that the Commonwealth was an inadequate vehicle through which to promote British influence and prosperity in the world. By contrast, the EC flourished. Yet deep suspicion of European integration and a lingering inclination toward isolationism tempered Macmillan's enthusiasm. The prime minister had to purge his cabinet of a few anti-Marketeers, and he faced an opposition Labour Party deeply divided on the issue.

The decision to apply for Community membership complemented Macmillan's foreign policy priority: restoring and
maintaining the Anglo-American "special relationship." That
meant repairing the damage caused by the Suez crisis of 1956 and
cultivating a close friendship first with Eisenhower (alongside
whom Macmillan had served in North Africa during World War
II) and then with Kennedy, a much younger man.   Yet
Macmillan's success in re-establishing close relations with
Washington ultimately destroyed his chances of bringing Britain
into the Community, for French President **Charles de Gaulle**
distrusted Britain's Atlanticism and doubted the country's
commitment to its continental neighbors.

Entry negotiations began in 1961 but quickly bogged down in
a morass of technical detail. The main sticking points were the
Common Agricultural Policy (CAP), the Commonwealth, and the
European Free Trade Association (EFTA). But matters came to
a head over Anglo-American relations, when Macmillan and
Kennedy signed the Nassau Agreement in December 1962, under
the terms of which Britain would use American Polaris missiles
as the delivery system for British nuclear warheads. Moreover,
Britain's nuclear force would be integrated into the **North
Atlantic Treaty Organization** (NATO), except when the
government "may decide that supreme national interests are at
stake." This represented for de Gaulle, then struggling to develop
the French nuclear force, a damning surrender of British
sovereignty to the United States. There could have been no
more graphic demonstration of Britain's irreconcilability with de
Gaulle's conception of a "European Europe."

De Gaulle responded dramatically at a press conference on
January 14, 1963. In a long, wide-ranging response to a planted
question, de Gaulle cataloged the history of Britain's relationship
with the Community and concluded by effectively vetoing Britain's
membership application.   The ensuing suspension of entry
negotiations was a serious setback for Macmillan and contrasted
starkly with his apparent success in concluding the Nassau
Agreement one month before. Undoubtedly it undermined
Macmillan's domestic political position. He resigned as prime
minister in October 1963, due to a purportedly terminal illness,
but went on to enjoy twenty-three years of robust retirement.

MACSHARRY, RAY (1938-) Ray MacSharry was commissioner for agriculture in the second **Commission of Jacques Delors** (1989-92). Because of Ireland's small size and the **Common Agricultural Policy's** importance in the **Community**, this was an unusual portfolio for Ireland's commissioner to have. Yet precisely because of the economic importance of agriculture in Ireland, MacSharry's portfolio boosted his political standing both at home and in **Brussels** and raised Ireland's profile in the Commission.

Paradoxically, MacSharry became agriculture commissioner at exactly the time when the Community increased its efforts to cut overproduction of agricultural products by reforming the CAP. The 1991 reform plan, which bears MacSharry's name, tried to reconcile the dilemma of maintaining high farm incomes and keeping people on the land with reducing obscene agricultural surpluses and lowering trade-distorting export subsidies. MacSharry's plan earned him the ire of Community farmers, including his Irish constituents, who fiercely opposed any reform, and American trade negotiators, who complained that the proposed export subsidy cuts did not go far enough to make possible a successful conclusion of the Uruguay Round of the **General Agreement on Tariffs and Trade** (GATT).

MAJOR, JOHN (1943-) John Major came seemingly out of nowhere to replace **Margaret Thatcher** as Conservative Party leader and prime minister in November 1990. Major's relative obscurity was an advantage in the succession struggle. It allowed him to be seen as all things to all men: a Thatcherite to the Tory right wing and a "wet" to the Tory moderates. All agreed that Major's civility and charm would at least improve the image of Britain's government after more than a decade of Thatcher's abrasive rule.

Major's attitude toward the **Community** was a decisive issue over which Thatcher's supporters and opponents in the Conservative Party disagreed. Would he maintain her implacable hostility to deeper European integration, including **European Monetary Union** (EMU) and **European Political Union** (EPU), or would he bring Britain into the mainstream of Community developments? Major's immediate courting of Chancellor

Helmut Kohl suggested the latter. However, the 1991 intergovernmental conferences and the concluding **Maastricht Treaty** presented a decisive test case. Major performed a masterful balancing act by committing Britain to EMU, subject to a vote in the House of Commons before EMU enters its final phase, and opting out of the treaty's Social Chapter (or, rather, having the other Eleven take the Social Chapter out of the Community).

Yet the result of Major's maneuvering was to reinforce the impression in other member states that Britain is still not enamored of European integration and remains, to use the title of a recent book on the subject, "an awkward partner." Major's initial response to the Maastricht Treaty ratification crisis in the summer of 1992, and to the currency crisis in September 1992, suggested that his apparent commitment to the Community was indeed shallow. But in October 1992 Major confronted the strong Euro-skeptic wing of the Conservative Party and gave the Maastricht Treaty his full political backing.

Possibly because of his wavering position on the Community, Major has not been able to restore the hallowed Anglo-American "special relationship" to its former glory in the Reagan and Thatcher days. As long as Britain is only a bit player in the European Community, the U.S. has little incentive to revive the special relationship in order to try to influence developments in **Brussels.**

MALFATTI, FRANCO (1927-) Franco Malfatti replaced **Jean Rey** as president of the **Commission** in 1970. Malfatti's tenure was undistinguished: although the **European Community** was then in the throes of "completion, deepening, enlargement" (French President **Georges Pompidou**'s prescription), the Commission remained seriously weakened following the "**Empty Chair Crisis.**" Nor did Malfatti, a former Italian politician and government junior minister, have the stature or enthusiasm to restore the Commission's confidence. Malfatti dealt the Commission's prestige a further blow by retiring before the end of his two-year term as president in order to reenter Italian politics. He went on to have a distinguished career in Rome, becoming a senior minister in the government.

MANSHOLT, SICCO (1908-   )   Sicco Mansholt served as a European commissioner from January 1958 until January 1973. For the last few months of that time he replaced **Franco Malfatti**, who retired to reenter Italian politics, as **Commission** president. Mansholt's exceptionally long tenure as a commissioner spanned the formation of the **European Economic Community** in 1958, the establishment of the Customs Union in the early 1960s, the "**Empty Chair Crisis**" of 1965-66, and the Community's revival after French President **Charles de Gaulle's** resignation in 1969.

Mansholt's greatest contribution to the Community was to implement the **Common Agricultural Policy** (CAP) and, subsequently, to sound a warning about the CAP's excesses. Coming from a Dutch farming background and having been agriculture minister in The Netherlands before moving to **Brussels**, Mansholt had a profound grasp of Europe's agricultural needs. As vice-president of the Commission with responsibility for agriculture, Mansholt convened a conference of Commission officials, member state delegates, and representatives of farmers' groups in Stressa, in July 1958, to draw up blueprints for the CAP. Detailed discussions on the CAP's fundamental principles and procedures continued during the next eighteen months, before the Commission submitted a proposal to the **Council of Ministers** in June 1960. The Council's approval six months later paved the way for the series of complex and rancorous negotiations that preoccupied the Community in the early 1960s, as the Commission and the member states thrashed out the precise means by which the CAP would operate. In December 1964 the Council adopted the "Mansholt Plan," establishing a fixed price for wheat and feed grains throughout the Community for the farm year beginning July 1, 1967, the date set for frontier-free trade in most agricultural products.

By that time Mansholt was concerned about the impact of guaranteed high prices on agricultural production in the Community. He also sought to rationalize the agricultural industry by cutting down on the number of small, inefficient farms in the Community. His proposed reforms in that regard made economic but not political sense. Although the member state governments appreciated the wisdom of his proposals, none was willing to risk the inevitable farmers' protests. Paradoxically,

Mansholt left the Commission distrusted by Community farmers for his reform proposals, although his design and implementation of the CAP was the basis of their prosperity in the 1960s and 1970s.

MARJOLIN, ROBERT (1911-1986) As **Jean Monnet's** right-hand man in the mid-1940s and as a vice-president of the **European Commission** in the 1960s, Robert Marjolin played an extremely influential part in the **European Community's** origin and early development. In the immediate postwar years Marjolin worked with Monnet on the French Modernization Plan. He then became secretary-general of the **Organization for European Economic Cooperation** before returning to French public service in 1955.

Perhaps Marjolin's greatest contribution to the Community came in the mid-1950s, during the intergovernmental conference that led to the establishment of the **European Economic Community** and **European Atomic Energy Community (Euratom)**. At that time Marjolin was an adviser to the foreign minister and a chief French negotiator. His task was not only to strike the best bargain for France in the intergovernmental negotiations but also to overcome deep-rooted French hostility to the removal, even gradual, of the protection that French industry then enjoyed. In addition to fighting in France's corner in the intergovernmental negotiations in Brussels, Marjolin also found himself waging a rear guard action at home: what he called in his memoirs the "Battle of Paris." Marjolin's ultimate victory made French participation in the proposed common market possible and therefore secured the Community's future.

As a senior member of **Walter Hallstein's** Commission during the first ten years of the EC's existence, Marjolin distinguished himself by his pragmatism and realism, in contrast to some of his colleagues' fervent Euro-federalism. The contrast was most striking in the run-up to the **"Empty Chair Crisis"** in 1965, when Marjolin urged Hallstein and other commissioners not to push French President **Charles de Gaulle** too far by proposing greater supranational powers for the Commission and the **European Parliament.** Marjolin's advice went unheeded, and, as he predicted, de Gaulle crushed the Commission in the ensuing crisis.

Marjolin retired from the Commission in 1967 and turned his extensive experience and considerable ability as an economist to the service of European industry. A decade later he returned briefly to the center stage of European integration. That was to act as one of the "Three Wise Men," who, at the suggestion of French President **Valéry Giscard d'Estaing**, prepared a report on Community reform. Published in 1980, the report made a number of realistic proposals to improve decision making in the Community but disappointed Giscard by not going far enough in endorsing a more powerful **European Council**. Accordingly, the Wise Men's report was politely shelved. Six years later Commission President **Jacques Delors** commented that this report is still topical. All the problems that have to be settled in order to improve the functioning of the Community are clearly set out in it and the solutions offered are still valid." Delors' efforts to implement some of those solutions during his dynamic Commission presidency were a suitable tribute to Marjolin.

MARSHALL PLAN Probably the best known American international initiative ever, the Marshall Plan was the means by which the U.S. sent massive economic assistance to post-World War II Europe. The Marshall Plan--or the European Recovery Program, as it was formally called--had many origins and objectives, all of them interconnected. One goal was humanitarian, another was strategic: U.S. economic assistance would stabilize Western Europe politically and undermine indigenous support for Communist parties. At the same time, this assistance would bolster Western Europe's ability to defend itself in the event of a direct Soviet attack. As part of America's strategic approach to Western Europe at the outset of the **Cold War**, the Marshall Plan also sought to encourage European integration. This it would do by insisting that the recipient countries formulate a joint approach to aid solicitation and distribution.

General George Marshall, the U.S. secretary of state, announced the plan in a commencement address at Harvard University on June 5, 1947. Almost immediately the American administration set about convincing a skeptical Congress that it was in the country's interests to allocate large-scale assistance to Western Europe. In Western Europe itself the French and

British governments took the lead in organizing a multilateral response to the American offer. To meet the American prerequisite for Marshall Plan assistance, the recipient countries established the **Organization for European Economic Cooperation** (OEEC), an umbrella body to solicit U.S. funds. But the OEEC was too large and diverse to act as an institutional instrument of integration. Its eighteen members varied greatly in size, population, and economic well-being. Perhaps more important, widely differing political cultures and wartime experiences made the prospect for agreement on integration extremely remote. Thus the OEEC failed to live up to American expectations.

But the Marshall Plan nonetheless played a pivotal role in promoting European integration by indirectly inspiring the **Schuman Declaration.** Because the Marshall Plan involved the reconstruction of Western Germany as an integral part of the reconstruction of Western Europe, it therefore set the stage for a series of diplomatic decisions that would gradually rehabilitate the former enemy, much to the consternation of Germany's neighbor to the west. The threat to France's own economic recovery, let alone intrinsic security, was immense. Here was the crisis on which Monnet seized in order to convince first Schuman, and then the dubious French government, that it was imperative for France to accept the inevitability of German economic recovery and to make a virtue of necessity by proposing the pooling of French and German production of coal and steel. Thus the Marshall Plan was an important antecedent of the **European Coal and Steel Community**.

MERGER TREATY The Merger Treaty establishing a single **Council** and a single **Commission** for the three **European Communities** came into force on July 1, 1967, more than two years after it was signed by the **Six** on April 8, 1965. The treaty was intended as a first step in the merger of the Communities themselves, although this has not yet happened.

The new Commission of the Communities began functioning on July 6, 1967; simultaneously the terms of office of the members of the **European Coal and Steel Community** (ECSC) **High Authority** and of the **European Economic Community** (EEC) and the **European Atomic Energy Community** (Euratom)

Commissions came to an end. Because of General **Charles de Gaulle's** opposition, **Walter Hallstein,** outgoing president of the EEC Commission, was not nominated to become president of the new, single Commission of the Communities. Instead, **Jean Rey** became the first president.

MESSINA CONFERENCE In June 1955, in Messina, Sicily, the foreign ministers of the six member states of the **European Coal and Steel Community** (ECSC) met to discuss both the future of the ECSC, in view of **Jean Monnet's** decision to resign as president of its **High Authority,** and the future of European integration. **Paul-Henri Spaak,** the Belgian foreign minister, had prepared a memorandum on behalf of the **Benelux** countries suggesting further integration along the lines of Monnet's idea for an **Atomic Energy Community** and a separate proposal for a common market. The foreign ministers' decision at least to give the question of European integration further thought, by asking Spaak to form a committee and write a report on future options, constituted the first "relaunch of Europe." The success of the Spaak Committee's deliberations subsequently established the Messina meeting as the point at which the EEC and Euratom originated.

MILAN SUMMIT The June 1985 Milan Summit proved a watershed in the **Community's** history. Two main items were on the agenda: the **Commission's White Paper** of measures necessary to achieve a single market by 1992 and the **Dooge Report.** The heads of state and government quickly approved the White Paper, but they argued fiercely over the Dooge Report's recommendations for reform of the Community's institutions and decision-making procedure and for an extension of Community competence. Without at least a curb on unanimity in the **Council of Ministers,** the heads of state and government realized that the **single market program** would never be implemented. But British Prime Minister **Margaret Thatcher,** Danish Prime Minister Poul Schlüter, and Greek Prime Minister Andreas Papandreou resisted the other leaders' efforts to amend the **Treaty of Rome** and instead advocated informal arrangements to improve decision making in the Council.

Finally Italian Prime Minister Bettino Craxi forced the issue by calling, under Article 236 (EEC), for an intergovernmental conference to negotiate a treaty of foreign policy and security cooperation and a revision of the Treaty of Rome to improve decision-making procedures and extend the Community's competence. When Thatcher, Schlüter, and Papandreou continued to object, Craxi took the unprecedented step at a European Council of calling for a vote. The three recalcitrants lost. Accordingly, the Community launched the intergovernmental conference that culminated six months later in the **Single European Act**. At the time the Milan Summit seemed a disaster, with Britain, Denmark, and Greece isolated. Later, the summit came to represent a decisive first step on the road to a revitalized and transformed Community.

MITTERRAND, FRANCOIS (1916-   )   Francois Mitterrand became the fourth president of the French Fifth Republic in 1981. Unlike his predecessors, Mitterrand was always enthusiastic about the **European Community**. Despite the rhetoric, an impassioned section of Mitterrand's famous May 1984 speech to the **European Parliament** fairly reflects his involvement in the movement for European integration: "When, in May 1948, exactly three years after the end of the war, the idea of Europe took shape at the **Hague Congress**, I was there and I believed in it. When, in 1950, **Robert Schuman** launched the proposal for a **European Coal and Steel Community**, I agreed with it and I believed in it. When, in 1956, work started on the vast building site of the **Common Market** with the very active participation of the French government of that time, I was there and I believed in it. And today, when we have to pull the Europe of the **Ten** out of its quarrels and resolutely steer it on the path of the future, I can say again that I am there and I believe in it."

That speech came in the closing phase of France's EC presidency, a presidency distinguished by the highly successful **Fontainebleau Summit** of June 1984. At Fontainebleau, thanks in part to Mitterrand's diplomacy and perseverance, the member states finally resolved the bitter dispute over Britain's budgetary contribution, which had ensnared the Community since 1979. Mitterrand had set out in January 1984 to resolve the issue by the end of his presidency. Despite a setback at the Brussels **Summit** in March 1984, when last-minute objections by Germany and Ireland snatched a solution from Prime Minister **Margaret Thatcher's** hands, Mitterrand began again to build a consensus for a budgetary settlement in time for the Fontainebleau Summit. His success in doing so was a personal triumph that made it possible for the member states to turn their attention instead to much more important and edifying issues, such as the **single market program** and the **Single European Act**.

For all his genuine enthusiasm for European integration, Mitterrand championed the Community cause as president of France only after overcoming a serious economic setback in the early 1980s. When he became president in 1981, Mitterrand introduced new economic policies, based on socialist principles, in an effort to fuel growth and promote employment. The result had little impact on productivity or unemployment but caused a surge in inflation that impaired France's international competitiveness and imperiled the recently launched **European Monetary System**. A sudden U-turn in 1983, under the direction of **Jacques Delors**, Mitterrand's finance minister, restored the country's economic equilibrium and made it possible for France to play a leading role in reviving the Community economically and politically.

Mitterrand's close friendship with **Helmut Kohl**--a personal manifestation of the Franco-German alliance that lies at the heart of the Community's history--helped enormously to get the EC going again in the mid-1980s. Mitterrand's miscalculation at the time of the Berlin Wall's collapse in 1989, when he seemed to oppose imminent German unification, threatened to rupture his rapport with Kohl, sunder Franco-German friendship, and derail the Community's development. Once he realized the inevitability of German unity, however, Mitterrand quickly switched from undisguised concern to wholehearted support. Moreover, he and Kohl jointly proposed embedding united Germany in a more deeply integrated European Community. Accordingly, the impetus for the 1991 intergovernmental conferences on **European Monetary Union** (EMU) and **European Political Union** (EPU), culminating in the **Maastricht Treaty**, came largely from Paris and Bonn.

Paradoxically, a political miscalculation by Mitterrand exacerbated the Maastricht Treaty ratification crisis in the summer of 1992. Immediately after the Danish rejection of the treaty, in an effort both to rally support for it throughout the Community and to split the domestic opposition parties, Mitterrand called for a French referendum to be held on September 20. Mitterrand's gesture backfired, as opposition to Maastricht snowballed in France and threatened not only to win the referendum but also to rob Mitterrand of political credibility. In the end, a narrow majority (51%) voted in favor, just enough to keep the treaty and Mitterrand's political career alive.

Regardless of the Maastricht ratification debacle, to a great extent the shape of the European Community in the 1990s bears Mitterrand's imprint. Yet Mitterrand's influence on the Community's development has not always been positive. Mitterrand's negative contribution could be summed up in two words: greater protectionism. The impact of that outlook is most clearly apparent in three policy areas: support for "national" and "European Champions" in manufacturing; unwillingness to cut subsidies in agriculture, with potentially calamitous consequences for the Uruguay Round of the **General Agreement on Tariffs and Trade** (GATT); and resistance to opening Community markets to Central and Eastern European exporters, with possibly disastrous repercussions for the stability of the "New Europe."

MONNET, JEAN (1888-1979) Jean Monnet is best known as the father of European integration and architect of the **European Community**. His direct involvement in the movement for European integration spanned the first three decades of the post-World War II period and included such major initiatives as the **Schuman Plan**, the Pleven Plan, and the proposal for a **European Atomic Energy Community**. Monnet presided over the **European Coal and Steel Community**'s first **High Authority**; later he organized and led the **Action Committee for a United States of Europe**, a high-level interest group that urged member states to share greater sovereignty.

Throughout his long life Monnet strove to promote international reconciliation and cooperation. His abiding objectives were the erosion of national sovereignty and the

promotion of supranationality as an essential means to achieve
peace and prosperity in Europe. The outbreak and persistence
of the **Cold War** during the most productive phase of Monnet's
career as a Euro-federalist, however, ensured that his vision of a
united Europe was firmly confined to *Western* Europe. Moreover,
as an implacable Cold War warrior, Monnet saw European
integration also as a way to strengthen the West against the evils
of the East. Thus the Cold War caused Monnet to blur the
distinction between "Europe" and "Western Europe" and
reinforced his inclination to limit the geopolitical scope of the
Community to a core group of countries centered on the Rhine.

Monnet was completely atheoretical and pragmatic in his
approach to the herculean task of furthering European
integration. His memoirs clearly describe his method. "Nothing
is possible without men; nothing is lasting without institutions,"
Monnet wrote. His statement that "people only accept change
when they are faced with necessity, and only recognize necessity
when a crisis is upon them" offers a further insight into Monnet's
modus operandi. On two occasions during the world wars,
sudden crises had impelled Monnet and others to propose
ambitious international schemes, one successful, one unsuccessful.
The successful occasion was in 1917, when Germany declared
unrestricted submarine warfare and began sinking huge quantities
of Allied shipping. That crisis caused the Allied governments to
accept Monnet's proposal to pool scarce shipping resources,
which diminished the destructiveness of the new German tactic.

The unsuccessful occasion came in June 1940, when France was
on the verge of military defeat and political capitulation.
Desperate to keep France in the war, Monnet proposed to Prime
Minister **Winston Churchill**, who in turn proposed to the British
cabinet, an "Indissoluble Union" between both countries. By
offering common citizenship, forming a joint government, and
pursuing a single war strategy, Monnet hoped to strengthen the
French government's flagging position. In any event, the offer
came too late to prevent the French prime minister's resignation
and replacement by the defeatist Marshal Pétain.

Following the fall of France, Monnet remained in the U.K. and
later moved to the U.S. to direct Allied economic planning. His
experience there convinced him of the potential of peacetime

economic planning. At the end of the war, **Charles de Gaulle**, then leader of the provisional government, appointed Monnet to head the newly established "Commissariat-General of the French Modernization and Investment Plan." It was an inspired choice. Apart from his experience as an economic planner during both world wars, Monnet had spent many years working in the private and public sectors, in France and abroad. Monnet had never attended university, but as a young man he had acquired an invaluable practical education and a thorough knowledge of English as a salesman in his family's brandy business. Nor was Monnet politically motivated or ideologically inclined, a fact that made it easier for him to succeed as a high-level bureaucrat.

As its name implies, the purpose of the French Modernization Plan was to overhaul the French economy, which had shown signs of serious sickness well before the damage and dislocation of World War II. Given his conviction that Europe could not be united unless France was resurgent, the plan was an inherent strand of Monnet's strategy for European integration. Based on lengthy consultations with employers, workers, and consumers, Monnet's office team set production targets, foreign trade goals, and employment objectives. Few were ever met, but the plan instilled badly needed confidence and a sense of mission in French society, both of which helped the country achieve an enviable economic recovery, although not by later German standards.

During that time Monnet stood aloof from the **European movement** of the postwar years and from the **Council of Europe** to which it gave rise. Monnet's detachment was due largely to disdain for the populism and pontification of the European movement and its constituent parts. Monnet was an elitist and a pragmatist. His road to European unity would follow the unglamorous path of functional integration. Close cooperation between countries in specific economic sectors, Monnet believed, held the key to overcoming national sovereignty and ultimately achieving European federation. And decisions to implement functional economic cooperation would be taken not by 600 delegates at the Congress of Europe but by powerful politicians in the privacy of their government ministries.

That approach helps to explain the secrecy and speed with which Monnet organized the **Schuman Declaration**. The opportunity to do so came in early 1950, when the U.S. and British governments pressured France to permit greater production of German coal and steel. The prospect of greater German productivity not only alarmed French opinion but also threatened to undermine the Monnet Plan, which was based on a projection of limited postwar German output. Monnet decided to make a virtue of necessity. Long a believer in functional economic integration and elite political initiatives, Monnet acquiesced in growing Allied pressure for a relaxation of France's punitive policy toward Germany and approached French Foreign Minister **Robert Schuman** with the imaginative idea of a coal and steel community. Thus the lifting of Allied restrictions on German steel production provided the crisis that, Monnet was certain, would force his government to take a dramatic step on the road to Franco-German reconciliation and European integration.

Schuman reacted enthusiastically to Monnet's proposed Coal and Steel Community. Both men worked frantically to win the support of the French *cabinet*, as well as the German and American governments. Monnet's friendship with high-level American officials, cultivated assiduously during his years in Washington, proved invaluable. U.S. Secretary of State **Dean Acheson**, by chance in Paris on May 7, 1950, endorsed Monnet's idea. On Tuesday morning, May 9, German Chancellor **Konrad Adenauer** approved the plan. Within the hour, the French cabinet followed suit. A public announcement--the famous Schuman Declaration--came immediately afterward at a hastily convened press conference in the French Foreign Ministry.

Negotiations to establish the Coal and Steel Community began in June 1950 and ended in April 1951. Monnet led the French delegation and persuaded Adenauer to appoint **Walter Hallstein**, the future president of the **European Economic Community's** (EEC) first **Commission**, to lead the German team. Despite the close affinity between Monnet and Hallstein, the ECSC talks proved arduous. The crisis of German rearmament, brought about by Anglo-American pressure in September 1950 in response to the outbreak of the Korean War, nearly derailed them entirely. In an effort to save the ECSC negotiations and further the cause of European integration, in October 1950

Monnet convinced French Prime Minister René Pleven to propose the **European Defense Community** (EDC). The same six countries then negotiating the ECSC also took part in the EDC negotiations, culminating in the EDC treaty of May 1952. But two years later the French parliament voted against ratification, thus wrecking the proposed Defense Community.

Undaunted, Monnet persevered with his push for European integration. In the interim the ECSC had begun operations, with Monnet as president of its High Authority (equivalent of the later EEC Commission), a job he held for only three years. Disappointed with the Coal and Steel Community's progress, concerned about the consequences for integration of the EDC's failure, and impatient to play a more active and aggressive role in advocating European unity, Monnet in November 1954 announced his decision to resign from the High Authority. Instead of operating from within the Community to advance European integration, Monnet chose to work from without by establishing a small, elite interest group of political party and trade union leaders: the Action Committee for a United States of Europe.

Monnet envisioned the Action Committee as a powerful pressure group for his latest proposal, a European Atomic Energy Community (Euratom). Realizing that coal was rapidly losing its position as the basis of industrial power and, by extension, that military might and that atomic energy seemed to be the energy source of the future, Monnet suggested an Atomic Energy Community along the lines of the Coal and Steel Community. Here was another example of Monnet's imaginative yet functional approach to European integration.

Surprisingly, Monnet's idea never amounted to much. After lengthy negotiations between the Six, the Atomic Energy Community came into existence in 1958 but failed to develop fully. The other member states' suspicion of France's nuclear policy, an abundance of cheap imported oil in the 1960s, and environmental and safety concerns about atomic energy meant that Euratom remained moribund. Instead, a contemporaneous proposal by J.W. Beyen, the Dutch foreign minister, to establish a **Common Market** among the Six provided the impetus for further integration. Paradoxically, Monnet dismissed Beyen's idea, which led directly to the European Economic Community, as impracticable and over-ambitious. Thus the Action Committee concentrated in the mid-1950s on bringing Monnet's proposed Atomic Energy Community to fruition.

In June 1955 the foreign ministers of the Six, meeting in Messina, Sicily, discussed both Monnet's idea for an Atomic Energy Community and Beyen's proposal for a common market. The foreign ministers' decision to give at least further thought to the question of European integration, by asking their Belgian colleague, **Paul-Henri Spaak**, to form a committee and write a report on future options, constituted the first "relaunch of Europe." Spaak's report, presented to his fellow foreign ministers at a meeting in Venice in May 1956, proposed that the two objectives of sectoral (atomic energy) integration and wider economic integration (a common market) be realized in separate organizations, with separate treaties. The Venice foreign ministers' meeting marked the first stage of a protracted process of intergovernmental negotiations, culminating in the signing of the **Treaties of Rome** in March 1957 that established the European Atomic Energy Community and the European Economic Community.

Monnet's advocacy of Euratom rather than the EEC had not undermined his credibility, and he continued to work tirelessly behind the scenes to promote closer integration. His influence in France, then the most economically powerful and politically influential member state, suffered a grievous blow when de Gaulle returned to power in 1958. Despite their cooperation in the immediate postwar years, de Gaulle had grown to dislike Monnet intensely for his espousal of supranationalism. De Gaulle, the arch-nationalist and intergovernmentalist, despised Monnet's efforts to weaken the power and authority of the nation-state, especially the *French* nation-state. The inherent conflict between de Gaulle's and Monnet's visions of European union came to a head in the **"Empty Chair Crisis"** of 1965-66. Monnet's Action Committee lobbied hard to end the crisis by bringing France back to full participation in the Community. But Monnet had no influence or support in Gaullist government circles. In the end Monnet played little part in the conflict's resolution.

By that time Monnet was in his late seventies. He spent the
remainder of his life in retirement but available always to counsel
European leaders on the best course to take to advance
European integration. In the last decade of Monnet's life,
however, the Community was stuck in the mire of economic
recession and political malaise. Yet Monnet made two final
contributions, one witting and the other unwitting, to the
Community's survival in the 1970s and eventual revival in the
1980s. The first, conscious contribution was his proposal to
institutionalize regular meetings of Community heads of state and
government, which French President **Valéry Giscard d'Estaing**
took up and launched in 1974 as the **European Council**. The
second, unintentional contribution was to the **European Monetary
System**. In early 1978 German Chancellor **Helmut Schmidt**
surprised Commission President **Roy Jenkins** by enthusiastically
supporting Jenkins' call for a monetary policy initiative in the
Community. Schmidt later ascribed his position on what became
the EMS to Monnet's memoirs, which he had just read at the
time. The EMS struck Schmidt as the kind of bold, imaginative
initiative that Monnet himself would have taken. Doubtless
Schmidt was right.

-N-

The NETHERLANDS Like its **Benelux** partners, The Netherlands
was an original **Community** member state. Also like Belgium
and Luxembourg, The Netherlands is extremely enthusiastic about
European integration. Historically The Netherlands shared its
small neighbors' fate of invasion and occupation in two world
wars. Economically The Netherlands is a great manufacturing
and trading country that immediately grasped the potential of a
customs union. Politically The Netherlands supports supranationalism and espouses strong Community institutions.

Throughout the Community's history, Dutch politicians have
promoted greater integration among the member states. Most
recently, in the intergovernmental conference on **Political Union**,
the Dutch pushed hard to have the three "pillars" of **European
Union**--revisions of the original treaties, a **Common Foreign and**

Security Policy, and cooperation on home and judicial affairs--combined into a single legal and institutional "tree." This proved too ambitious for the other member states and caused criticism of The Netherlands' direct and sometimes aggressive negotiating style. In addition, some countries thought that The Netherlands had abused its position in the Community presidency to advance blatantly its own agenda. In any event, the **Treaty on European Union,** signed in the southern Dutch town of Maastricht in February 1992, did not go as far in advancing supranationalism as The Netherlands wanted.

The NINE With the accession of Denmark, Ireland, and the U.K. in 1973, the **Six** member states of the **Community** became Nine, the name by which the Community was popularly known until the accession of Greece in 1981 (when the Nine became **Ten**) and the accession of Spain and Portugal in 1984 (when the Ten became **Twelve**).

NINETEEN NINETY-TWO (1992) see **Single Market Program**

NOEL, EMILE (1922-) Between 1958 and 1987, during almost thirty years as secretary-general of the **Commission,** Emile Noël served under Commission Presidents **Walter Hallstein, Jean Rey, Franco Malfatti, Sicco Mansholt, Francois-Xavier Ortoli,** and **Roy Jenkins.** As secretary-general Noël played a key role in the **Community's** development over three decades: from the establishment of the customs union in the first decade of the Community's existence, to the **"Empty Chair Crisis"** provoked by **Charles de Gaulle** in the mid-1960s, to the economic doldrums of the 1970s, and finally to the Community's revitalization by the **single market program** and the **Single European Act** in the mid-1980s. Often it was Noël's brilliant insights and subtle suggestions that cut to the core of a particular problem or helped to resolve an otherwise intractable issue.

Noël's formal involvement in European affairs began in the **Council of Europe,** where he served as secretary of the General Affairs Committee of the Consultative Assembly between 1949 and 1952. For two years after that he directed the Secretariat of the Constitutional Committee of the ad hoc Assembly charged with drafting plans for a **European Political Committee.** In the mid-1950s Noël served as chief personal assistant to Guy Mollet, first when Mollet was president of the Consultative Assembly of the Council of Europe and later when Mollet became prime minister of France. Thus Noël was intimately involved in Mollet's maneuvering during the disastrous Anglo-French military intervention in Suez in 1956.

Noël's service to European integration did not end with his departure from the Commission in 1987. Far from taking well-earned retirement, Noël instead became president of the European University Institute in Florence. In that capacity, and based on the high esteem and deep affection in which he is held throughout Western Europe, Noël continued to play an important part in shaping the "New Community" of the 1990s.

NORTH ATLANTIC COOPERATION COUNCIL (NACC) At their historic November 1991 summit meeting in Rome, leaders of the **North Atlantic Treaty Organization** (NATO) agreed to create a North Atlantic Cooperation Council as a framework for cooperative management of Europe's security problems. The NACC includes the sixteen NATO member states, the former Warsaw Pact countries, and the former Soviet republics. In effect, the establishment of the NACC brings NATO's former adversaries into the Alliance's consultative process.

NORTH ATLANTIC TREATY ORGANIZATION (NATO) From its inception in 1949 until the end of the **Cold War** in 1990, the North Atlantic Treaty Organization (NATO) provided the necessary military security for Western Europe's political and economic development. NATO emerged out of the collapse in the immediate postwar years of the wartime "Grand Alliance" between the U.S., Britain, and the Soviet Union. As Soviet hostility toward Western Europe increased and the Cold War intensified, Britain, France, and the **Benelux** countries, which signed the **Brussels Treaty** in 1948, realized that they could not face the Soviet threat without massive American military assistance. The deteriorating security situation in 1948--the Soviet blockade of Berlin, the communist coup in Czechoslovakia, and the continuing civil war in Greece--convinced the U.S. to reverse its traditional noninvolvement in peacetime military alliances. In April 1949, the U.S., Canada, Britain, France, Italy, Belgium, The Netherlands, Luxembourg, Denmark, Iceland, Norway, and Portugal signed the Washington Treaty to establish NATO. Greece and Turkey joined in 1952, Germany in 1955, and Spain in 1982, bringing NATO's membership to sixteen countries.

France has been NATO's most difficult member state. In 1966 French President **Charles de Gaulle** pulled France out of NATO's integrated military command in order to maximize French independence and protest American hegemony in the alliance. The question of U.S.-Western European relations within the alliance has always been testy, particularly over the share of the alliance's financial burden borne by each side. NATO survived enormous political stress in the early 1980s during the "Euromissile" crisis, when public opinion in Western Europe turned against the alliance's decision to deploy cruise and Pershing II intermediate-range nuclear missiles to counter the earlier Soviet deployment of SS-20 missiles. By contrast, during the revolution in Eastern Europe in 1989 and the subsequent disintegration of the Soviet Union, a triumphant mood swept the alliance.

Yet the end of the Cold War cast NATO's future in doubt. The "London Declaration on a Transformed Atlantic Alliance," issued by NATO's heads of state and government at a meeting in London in July 1990, sought to redefine NATO for a political and security role in the post-Cold War world, especially in association with the **Conference on Security and Cooperation in Europe** (CSCE). Moreover, in 1991 NATO launched the **North Atlantic Cooperation Council** (NACC) as a means of reducing tension and promoting peace with its erstwhile enemies in the former Warsaw Pact.

NATO's relationship with the **European Community** has always been close and complementary. Ireland is the only EC member state not in NATO. By fostering economic development in Western Europe, the **Community** indirectly assisted NATO by building a solid economic base for Western Europe's defense. Similarly, by providing a security umbrella, NATO allowed the Community to thrive politically and economically. NATO and the Community both have their headquarters in Brussels and are only five miles apart. The **Western European Union** (WEU), the institutional device through which Germany joined NATO, was reactivated in the mid-1980s to tie NATO and the EC more closely and formally together. The **Maastricht Treaty** of February 1992 solidifies the EC-WEU link and points the way to the Community eventually assuming a military and defense identity, in the context of either NATO or a new, post-NATO transatlantic security arrangement.

-O-

ORGANIZATION FOR ECONOMIC COOPERATION AND DEVELOPMENT (OECD) The OECD was founded in 1960 to promote high economic growth and employment, promote economic and social welfare, and encourage and harmonize its members' efforts to aid developing countries. The OECD has twenty-four member states, including the **European Community** countries, other Western European countries, the U.S., Canada, Japan, Australia, and New Zealand.   The OECD emerged out of the **Organization for European Economic Cooperation (OEEC)**, which coordinated recipient countries' responses to the **Marshall Plan.** In the late 1950s, when Europe was "at Sixes and Sevens" with the establishment of the **European Economic Community** and the **European Free Trade Association**, the OECD seemed an ideal structure to bridge both organizations and involve the world's other democratic industrialized countries. Today the OECD is the largest source of comparative data on the industrial economies in the world and produces a wealth of publications, surveys, statistics, and policy recommendations on a wide range of economic issues.

ORGANIZATION FOR EUROPEAN ECONOMIC COOPERATION (OEEC) The OEEC was established in 1948 to channel **Marshall Plan** assistance from the United States to the countries of Western Europe. As a condition of sending such massive assistance, the U.S. insisted on a joint European response in order to encourage a prototypical organization for European integration.   To meet the American prerequisite for Marshall

Plan assistance, the recipient countries established the OEEC, an organization too large and diverse to act as an institutional instrument of integration. Its eighteen members varied greatly in size, population, and economic well-being. Perhaps more important, widely differing political cultures and wartime experiences made the prospect for agreement on integration extremely remote. Thus the OEEC failed to live up to American expectations. Instead, shortly after the EEC began functioning in 1958 it turned into the **Organization for Economic Cooperation and Development** (OECD), the Paris-based body for international economic research and analysis.

ORTOLI, FRANCOIS-XAVIER (1925-) Francois-Xavier Ortoli was president of the **European Commission** between 1973 and 1976. Before that he had served in a number of senior French government positions and was finance minister between 1968 and 1969. Despite his experience in French government and his grasp of economics, Ortoli was a poor Commission president. His tenure coincided with a downturn in the **Community's** fortunes as the "relaunch" of the early 1970s gave way to the high inflation and unemployment of the post-oil embargo period. Moreover, Ortoli was exceptionally cautious and unwilling to advance the Commission's interests or agenda. Unusually, he remained in the Commission after his term as president expired, serving as a vice-president first under **Roy Jenkins** and then under **Gaston Thorn**. He eventually left the Commission in 1984.

OSTPOLITIK When he came to power in 1969, German Chancellor **Willy Brandt** elevated *Ostpolitik* (policy toward the East) to a central tenet of German foreign policy. Ostpolitik replaced the inflexible Hallstein Doctrine of nonrecognition of any Western state that recognized East Germany diplomatically. The Christian Democrats, in opposition for the first time in the history of the Federal Republic, denounced Ostpolitik as a sell-out of German interests in the East and a threat to Germany's interests in the West by the new Social Democratic government.

Indeed, some of Germany's allies fretted about the implications of Ostpolitik for Bonn's commitments to the **Community** and to the **North Atlantic Treaty Organization** (NATO). Allied and

internal Christian Democratic concern about Ostpolitik obliged
Brandt to emphasize his support for European integration, which
in any event he genuinely espoused. Moreover, Brandt stressed
the importance of British accession as a means of reassuring
those Community member states that feared Germany's
resurgence. In the U.K. Prime Minister **Harold Wilson** used
Ostpolitik to further his goal of EC entry by arguing that British
accession would restrain German nationalist ambition. In France
President **Georges Pompidou** also cited Ostpolitik as a reason to
enlarge the Community. Thus Ostpolitik was a relevant factor in
breaking the deadlock over the Community's first enlargement.
By the same token, once the Community's leaders had decided in
principle, at the **Hague Summit** in December 1969, to relaunch
the Community, Brandt felt secure enough to make his first
overtures to the East.

Similarly, Ostpolitik played an important part in the launching
and early development of **European Political Cooperation** (EPC).
At the Hague Summit President Pompidou had suggested that
the Community's member states attempt to coordinate their
foreign policies. Especially in view of Germany's new policy
toward the East, the member states quickly grasped the utility of
at least an exchange of information on each other's foreign
policies. Accordingly, the leaders appointed **Etienne Davignon**,
a senior Belgian Foreign Ministry official, to prepare a report by
mid-1970. The **Davignon Report** laid the foundation for EPC.

Germany immediately seized on EPC as a means of building
a Community-wide base for Ostpolitik. At the first meeting of
the **Six** foreign ministers "in EPC"--as distinct from a meeting of
the **Council of Ministers**--coincidentally held in Munich in
November 1970 during Germany's presidency, the German
foreign minister stressed the importance of EPC as "a potential
contribution to détente in Europe." By that time Ostpolitik was
well on track: Germany and the Soviet Union signed a treaty in
August 1970 after months of intense and highly complex
negotiations, although ratification awaited a Four Power
agreement on the status of Berlin. Enjoying only a narrow
majority of seats in the German parliament, Brandt was especially
vulnerable to continuing Christian Democratic opposition to
Ostpolitik. EPC helped at least to quell the domestic opposition's

clamor by providing an additional forum for Brandt to explain his eastern initiative to Germany's western neighbors.

By 1973 Ostpolitik had resulted in treaties between Bonn and Moscow, Warsaw and Prague, a Four Power agreement on Berlin, and an accord between the two Germanys. The pace of Bonn's diplomatic offensive in the East slowed down in the mid-1970s but never stopped thereafter, even during the height of the "Second Cold War" in the early 1980s. On the contrary, in a less visible form Ostpolitik became a fixture of Germany's foreign policy until reunification in 1990, although for much of that time it was known as "Genscherism," after **Hans-Dietrich Genscher**, Germany's long-serving foreign minister.

-P-

PADOA-SCHIOPPA REPORT In April 1987 Tommaso Padoa-Schioppa, deputy director-general of the Bank of Italy, submitted a report to the **Commission** entitled "Efficiency, Stability and Equity: A Strategy for the Evolution of the Economic System of the **European Community**." Commission President **Jacques Delors** had asked Padoa-Schioppa and six other experts to prepare the report in order to assess the impact of the accession of Spain and Portugal, and the single market program, on the Community's economic system. Just as Delors hoped that it would, the report set four main priorities for the Community: (1) the need to complete the **single market program**, which was already behind schedule; (2) the need to develop a united monetary policy; (3) the need to promote **cohesion**; and (4) the need to devise a macroeconomic strategy.

The Padoa-Schioppa Report focused especially on the "serious risks of aggravated regional imbalances in the course of market liberalization." While conceding that the single market program could improve opportunities for economic convergence between the rich north and poor south of the **Community**, in a memorable passage the report warned that "any easy extrapolation of 'invisible hand' ideas into the real world of regional economics in the process of market opening measures would be unwarranted in the light of economic history and theory." Coming only two months after the Commission unveiled the **"Delors I"** budgetary package, the Padoa-Schioppa Report played an important part in the ensuing dispute between the member states that ended in a decision at the February 1988 Brussels **Summit** to increase substantially the size of the structural funds for the development of the Community's poorer regions.

PARIS SUMMIT French President **Georges Pompidou** convened the Paris Summit in October 1972 to set the **Community's** agenda in the post-enlargement period. The summit is famous--or infamous--for the last sentence of a "solemn declaration" that prefixed the concluding communiqué: "The member states of the Community, the driving force of European construction, affirm their intention before the end of the present decade to transform the whole complex of their relations into a **European Union.**" This was an extraordinary statement even by the standard of **European Community** rhetoric and illustrated the member states' high hopes for European integration at the beginning of the 1970s. As the 1970s passed, however, the Community became bogged down in high inflation rates, soaring unemployment, and low economic growth.   With nothing remotely resembling European Union on the horizon, the Paris declaration served only to highlight the extent of the Community's disarray by the end of the decade.

POLITICAL UNION see **European Political Union**

POMPIDOU, GEORGES (1911-1974) Georges Pompidou succeeded **Charles de Gaulle** as president of France in 1969 and struggled immediately with de Gaulle's mixed legacy to the **Community**. Having served as prime minister of France between 1962 and 1968, Pompidou was steeped in Gaullism. When de Gaulle dismissed Pompidou at the height of the student unrest in 1968, relations between both men quickly soured. Pompidou exacted sweet revenge by winning the presidential election in 1969, and set about charting his own European policy.

But in one respect at least, Pompidou remained faithful to de Gaulle: he disliked supranationalism and espoused inter-governmentalism. As for enlargement, Pompidou was in a dilemma. For Gaullist diehards, whose support Pompidou could not easily sacrifice, the veto of Britain's EC membership application had become sacrosanct. Yet for a growing body of French opinion, and for France's EC partners, revoking the veto was the only means by which France could possibly retain influence and credibility in the Community.

Regardless of his personal and political preferences, there was an obvious objective change in France's circumstances in the late 1960s that impelled Pompidou toward accepting enlargement. The events of 1968 had enfeebled France economically. Moreover, by the late 1960s Germany had grown increasingly powerful. Not only was Germany economically resurgent, but under the new chancellor, **Willy Brandt**, the Federal Republic was also politically assertive. In addition, the new German government was about to launch an ambitious initiative toward Eastern Europe and the Soviet Union. The combination of Germany's growing economic power and rising political confidence made enlargement a more appealing alternative for Pompidou. Together, Britain and France in the West might counterbalance Germany's increasing weight in the East and establish geopolitical symmetry in the Community.

Faced with incipient Western apprehension about the impact of *Ostpolitik* and domestic pressure for a French initiative in the EC, Pompidou called a special **summit** of the Community's heads of state and government for December 1969. The **Hague Summit**--The Netherlands then held the rotating EC presidency-- was the first meeting of Community leaders since the tenth anniversary celebration of the **Treaty of Rome** in 1967. With de Gaulle gone and enlargement once again at center stage, most member states anticipated a decisive breakthrough; in the end, the summit spawned the "spirit of The Hague," a feeling that the Community was once more on the move. Pompidou's slogan, "completion, deepening, enlargement," summed up the prevailing mood.

"Completion" meant finalizing the **Common Agricultural Policy**, a cherished French objective put in abeyance since the **"Empty Chair Crisis."** "Deepening" meant extending the Community's competence beyond existing policies and activities. "Enlargement," of course, meant allowing Britain to join. A meeting between British Prime Minister **Edward Heath** and Pompidou in Paris in May 1971 helped to resolve the outstanding problems. The surprisingly close rapport between both men convinced others in the Community that France had finally jettisoned its lingering opposition to enlargement. To assuage domestic opinion and split the left-wing opposition, Pompidou called a referendum on the issue in March 1972. Despite the poor turnout, a majority of the electorate endorsed the president's position.

The French referendum result removed the remaining political obstacle to enlargement. In the meantime, the accession negotiations had concluded satisfactorily. Finally, on January 1, 1973, Britain, Ireland, and Denmark joined the Community. Three months previously Pompidou had convened another summit to chart the Community's agenda in the post-enlargement period. But Pompidou did not live long enough to enjoy the fruits of enlargement or to witness the Community's economic decline in the aftermath of the oil embargo. He died in April 1974, after a long illness.

PORTUGAL   Along with Spain, Portugal is the **Community**'s newest member state. An undemocratic regime kept Portugal out of the mainstream of European economic and political development for much of the postwar period. It was only when the authoritarian, right-wing regime was ousted in the mid-1970s that the country became a serious candidate for Community membership. Politically, Portugal saw accession to the **Treaty of Rome** as a means of strengthening its tenuous hold on democracy. Economically, Portugal saw Community membership as the key to prosperity.

Indeed, Portugal has prospered in the Community, and the country's commitment to democracy seems unquestionable. Portugal benefited greatly from the doubling of "structural funds" in the 1988 "**Delors I**" budgetary package and stands to gain as much again from the "**Delors II**" package. As Community president in the first half of 1992, Portugal hoped to secure agreement on Delors II, but the northern member states balked at such a large increase in the Community budget. The other disappointment for Portugal during its presidency was the deepening crisis over ratification of the **Maastricht Treaty**. Portugal hoped to hand over to the British presidency in July 1992 an EC committed to the **Treaty on European Union** and in accord on the reallocation of resources to help the poor member states meet the challenge of **Economic and Monetary Union**. Through no fault of its own, Portugal instead gave Britain the presidency of an increasingly fractious and divided Community.

Greater political and economic contact between Lisbon and Madrid has been a welcome side effect of Portuguese and Spanish membership of the Community. Before 1986, when both countries joined, Spain and Portugal had few direct dealings with each other. Now their prime ministers meet regularly in the **European Council**, their government ministers are in frequent contact at **Council** meetings, and their officials see each other weekly at a host of Community events. Thus, Community membership has not only helped both countries to develop politically and economically but also has fostered a growing friendship between two historical rivals.

-R-

REY, JEAN (1902-1983) Jean Rey, a Belgian politician, was the first president of the combined **Commission** of the **European Communities**. During his years as Commission president (1967-70) the **Community** slowly recovered from the shock of the **"Empty Chair Crisis"** and, after **Charles de Gaulle's** resignation as president of France in 1969, gradually moved toward the first enlargement. Yet the Commission remained demoralized following **Walter Hallstein's** humiliation by de Gaulle. Rey was unable to raise the Commission's self-confidence or improve its fortunes. His presidency was the first in a series of undistinguished Commission presidencies that ended only a decade later.

-S-

SCHENGEN AGREEMENT In June 1985, Belgium, The Netherlands, Luxembourg, France, and Germany announced their intention to conclude an agreement on the free movement of people between their countries. It took five years of negotiations before they concluded, in June 1990, the Schengen Agreement to that effect, named after the town in Luxembourg where it was signed. The purpose of the agreement was to hasten the removal of barriers to the movement of people in the **Community** before completion of the **single market program**. Italy, Spain, and Portugal subsequently signed the Schengen Agreement, with which Greece is also associated. However, only France, The Netherlands, and Luxembourg had ratified the agreement by 1992. Immigration aspects and implications of the Schengen Agreement are addressed in Title VI of the **Maastricht Treaty**.

SCHMIDT, HELMUT (1918-) Helmut Schmidt, chancellor of Germany between 1974 and 1982, was surprisingly ambivalent about the **European Community**. On the one hand he strongly supported the Community as a means of promoting Western Europe's economic prosperity and international influence (especially vis-à-vis the U.S.); on the other hand he despised the **Commission** and implicitly reinforced intergovernmentalism.

During the late 1970s, Schmidt and French President **Valéry Giscard d'Estaing** ran the Community like a personal fiefdom. The Commission was weak and demoralized, and the other heads of government lacked their French and German counterparts' knowledge of economics and grasp of international affairs. The Franco-German alliance, personified by the friendship between Giscard and Schmidt, was the sole motor of Community momentum. Going well beyond the framework of the **Elysée Treaty**, Giscard and Schmidt, both former finance ministers, got together often for dinner, spoke at least weekly on the telephone, and caucused regularly on the fringes of multilateral meetings. They communicated in English.

The **European Council**, Giscard's brainchild, was the institutional vehicle through which he and Schmidt ran the Community. The European Council proved especially useful in bringing Schmidt's initiative for a **European Monetary System (EMS)** to fruition. At the **Bremen Summit** in July 1978, Schmidt's forceful chairmanship contributed to a general acceptance of the monetary proposal, although Britain's unwillingness to participate in the future EMS became obvious as the European Council progressed. The EMS is also an example of the strength of the Franco-German alliance and of the Giscard-Schmidt friendship. Without Giscard's backing, Schmidt's initial idea for an EMS would not have succeeded; with French backing, it was assured success.

Concern about what he saw as America's abdication of Western leadership led Schmidt to propose the EMS. On diplomatic and security issues, Schmidt was equally alarmed about perceived U.S. weakness. Personally and politically, Schmidt despised U.S. President Jimmy Carter, whom he blamed for many of Europe's problems in the late 1970s. This led Schmidt to try to bolster the European Community as a powerful pillar of the **North Atlantic Treaty Organization** (NATO). Even after the change of administration in Washington, when President Ronald Reagan came to office, Schmidt continued to advocate a strong European counterbalance to the U.S. in the alliance. **Hans-Dietrich Genscher**, Schmidt's foreign minister, attempted to introduce a security and defense dimension into the Community in the early 1980s, but to no avail.

Schmidt's influence on international politics and economics came to an abrupt end in 1982, when shifts in his governing coalition suddenly robbed him of enough parliamentary support to stay in power. Thereafter Schmidt joined **Willy Brandt** as one of Germany's leading elder statesmen, devoting his time to writing and lecturing mostly about international affairs.

SCHUMAN DECLARATION The Schuman Declaration was the public announcement, made by **Robert Schuman** at a press conference in the French Foreign Ministry on May 9, 1950, of a plan to pool French and German production of coal and steel. Behind the scenes, **Jean Monnet** had formulated the plan. The Schuman Declaration was the first formal step on the road to establishing the **European Coal and Steel Community**.

SCHUMAN PLAN The Schuman Plan was a proposal to pool French and German production of coal and steel, announced publicly by French Foreign Minister **Robert Schuman** at a press conference in Paris on May 9, 1950. The Schuman Plan became

the basis of the **European Coal and Steel Community**, launched
by France, Germany, Italy, Belgium, The Netherlands, and
Luxembourg in April 1952.

SCHUMAN, ROBERT (1886-1963) The name of the daring plan
to pool French and German coal and steel production, which
gave rise not only to the **Coal and Steel Community** (ECSC) but
also to the **European Community** as we know it today, bears
Robert Schuman's name. The idea was **Jean Monnet's**, but
Schuman was French foreign minister at the time. On May 9,
1950, Schuman made a public announcement--the famous
Schuman Declaration--at a crowded press conference in the
French Foreign Ministry.

Schuman's background lent particular poignancy to the coal
and steel proposal. Coming from the disputed province of
Alsace, where he had suffered personally from the incessant
conflict between France and Germany, Schuman sought above all
to promote reconciliation between both countries. As a Christian
Democrat, Schuman's political principles reinforced his personal
convictions. Constrained by the climate of retribution toward
Germany that pervaded postwar France and by a natural reserve
and inhibition, Schuman had hitherto refrained from taking any
conciliatory steps in the direction of the erstwhile enemy.
Emboldened by Monnet's suggestion, and by the swing in official
French opinion toward economic accord with Germany, Schuman
enthusiastically endorsed the fateful proposal. Buoyed by U.S.
Secretary of State **Dean Acheson's** endorsement and German
Chancellor **Konrad Adenauer's** approval, Schuman had little
difficulty garnering support for the scheme among his *cabinet*
colleagues.

Schuman's period as foreign minister, from 1948 to 1953, was
decisive for France. At a time of frequent government changes,
Schuman held on to the Foreign Ministry and provided essential
stability and direction for French foreign policy. After leaving
office, Schuman remained deeply involved in the movement for
European integration. In 1958 he became the first president of
the joint ECSC-**Euratom**-EEC Parliament. He continued to
serve as a member of the **European Parliament** until his resignation from the **Strasbourg** Assembly in 1963.

SINGLE EUROPEAN ACT (SEA)   The Single European Act (SEA) originated in the **Community's** decision to launch the **single market program** in the mid-1980s and in the member states' desire to strengthen Community decision making and extend Community competence by reforming the **Treaty of Rome**. These related objectives dominated the intergovernmental conference that began after the **Milan Summit** in June 1985-- despite British, Danish, and Greek objections--and ended at the Luxembourg **Summit** the following December.   The inter- governmental conference produced a single treaty (the Single European Act) to extend the Community's power to new fields, strengthen its institutional framework, and formalize **European Political Cooperation** (EPC) by amending the Treaty of Rome.

The SEA committed the Community to six objectives: completion of the single market program by December 31, 1992; increased economic and social **cohesion**; a common scientific and technological policy; further development of the **European Monetary System** (EMS); the emergence of a European social dimension; and coordinated action on the environment. These clear-cut tasks comprise a comprehensive plan linked in the SEA's preamble to the ultimate goal of **European Union**. The SEA also extended majority voting to cover most of the proposed single market legislation, in order to ensure that directives would not be unduly delayed in the **Council of Ministers**. Another notable institutional innovation was the introduction of a "cooperation procedure" to involve the **European Parliament** more fully in Community decision making. Finally, Title III of the SEA provided a constitutional basis for EPC.

Member states signed the SEA in early 1986, with a view to ratifying it before the end of the year so that it could come into effect in January 1987. However, a challenge by a private citizen to the constitutionality of the SEA in Ireland necessitated a referendum on ratification there. The successful outcome of the Irish referendum allowed the SEA to be implemented throughout the Community on July 1, 1987.

The SEA's relatively weak institutional reforms disappointed many supporters of federalism and supranationalism in the Community.   Nevertheless they gave a huge boost to the **Commission's** morale and provided the means to implement the single market program, which in turn reinvigorated the movement for European integration. British Prime Minister **Margaret Thatcher's** reaction to the SEA best indicates its actual impact. At first Thatcher was scornful of the SEA, proclaiming that it would make little difference to the Community. Subsequently, as the Community grew stronger and the SEA triggered renewed interest in **European Monetary Union** (EMU), Thatcher denounced it as the root of all evil. As one British commentator remarked, to Thatcher's disgust the SEA could well be relabeled "The Nooks and Crannies (Enabling the Commission) Act."

SINGLE MARKET PROGRAM   The **European Community's** program to transform the economies of the **Twelve** into a single market of more than 340 million people originated in the early 1980s, partly in the vogue for deregulation that swept Europe from the U.S. and partly from the favorable outcome of collaboration between EC officials and European industrialists in the high-technology sector.   By 1985, when **Jacques Delors** became **Commission** president, there was a ground swell of support among European business people for completing the internal market, one of the **Community's** first, but still unaccomplished, objectives. Moreover, a number of landmark **Court of Justice** cases, notably **Cassis de Dijon**, established the principle of mutual recognition, thus making it unnecessary to harmonize the product standards of each member state.

Arthur Cockfield took responsibility for the internal market in Delors' Commission and immediately set about identifying the steps necessary to achieve a single market in which goods, capital, services, and people moved freely. In June 1985 Lord Cockfield produced the so-called "**White Paper**," a list of approximately 300 directives that the **Council of Ministers** would have to pass in order to complete the single market. These directives covered the remaining physical barriers that prevented free movement of people and goods in the EC, the differences in national technical standards that hindered the free movement of goods, and the differences in indirect tax rates between the member states that continued to inhibit trade.

To quantify the cost to the Community of maintaining a fragmented market, the Commission initiated a research program on "the cost of non-Europe." Based on data from the four largest member states, independent consultants assessed the costs and benefits of maintaining the status quo by analyzing the impact of market barriers and by comparing the Community with North America. Research began in 1986 and ended in early 1988 with a massive, sixteen-volume publication. A condensed version, entitled *The European Challenge: 1992* but popularly known as the "**Cecchini Report**," after its author, the Italian economist Paolo Cecchini, also appeared in 1988. The gist of the Cecchini Report was that existing physical, technical, and fiscal barriers to trade cost the Community 3% to 6% of GDP, or a total of $250 billion, annually.

Despite the member states' enthusiasm for the single market program, the initiative could not have succeeded without a reform of Community decision making. By the early 1980s about 800 Commission proposals were said to be stuck in the Council of Ministers because of member states' reluctance to use majority voting for fear of violating a real or supposed "vital national interest." If the single market program similarly fell victim to the "**Luxembourg Compromise**," no progress would ever be made. In any event, the member states already appreciated the need for institutional reform. Embarrassment about the Community's abysmal legislative record, fear of a deeper decision-making debacle after the impending third enlargement, and a desire to improve the Community's international competitiveness and standing caused the **Ten** to convene an intergovernmental conference in 1985.

The ensuing **Single European Act** (SEA) both set a target date for completion of the single market program and introduced qualified-majority voting for most of the program's proposals, thus guaranteeing their passage through the Council of Ministers. The SEA, which came into effect on July 1, 1987, declared that "the Community shall adopt measures with the aim of progressively establishing the internal market over a period expiring on December 31, 1992...The internal market shall comprise an area without frontiers in which the free movement of goods, persons and capital is ensured in accordance with the provisions of the **Treaty [of Rome]**."

Once launched, the "**1992**" program became spectacularly

successful, but not before the member states approved the
"**Delors I**" package of budgetary proposals to fund additional
financial transfers to the Community's poor member states
compensating them for the distortions of a single market. As
soon as the member states approved Delors I at the 1988
Brussels **Summit**, the 1992 program took off for a number of
reasons: Delors' commitment to it and his reappointment as
Commission president until the target date of December 31, 1992
(at the Lisbon Summit in June 1992, the heads of state and
government reappointed Delors for an unprecedented fifth two-
year term, until the end of 1994); the vigorous implementation of
competition policy in the Community, especially by Competition
Commissioner **Leon Brittan** (1985-   ); the obvious benefit to
European business of an open, freer market, resulting in business
peoples' continuing support for the program; and the
extraordinary popular appeal of the 1992 slogan.

By 1992, the final year of the program, the Council of Ministers
had adopted most of the important directives. Not surprisingly,
the outstanding proposals included the most controversial, for
instance, how to implement the free movement of people, plants,
and animals across borders, in view of terrorism, immigration, and
health concerns in the U.K. Apart from a small number of
proposals that remain unresolved by the Council of Ministers,
implementation of the directives at the national level is poor. In
most cases, however, this is due more to tardiness than to a
deliberate effort to sabotage aspects of the single market
program.

Apart from its expected impact on European business,
unintended side effects of the single market's success include the
general rejuvenation of the Community in the late 1980s, the rush
of applications by **European Free Trade Association** (EFTA)
member states, and a renewed interest in **European Monetary
Union** (EMU), culminating in the **European Council's** decision
first to request, and then to implement, the **Delors Plan**.
Another external manifestation of the single market program's
success has been U.S. business interest in it, giving rise initially to
fears of a "fortress Europe" and subsequently to an awareness of
the Community's relative openness to, and the enormous
potential for, American trade and investment in the EC.

The SIX   This refers to the six original member states of the
Community: France, Germany, Italy, Belgium, The Netherlands,
and Luxembourg.

The SNAKE In April 1972, following three years of unprecedented
currency fluctuations, the **Six** member states of the **European
Community** hatched the "snake," a regime to keep EC currency
fluctuations within a 2.5% margin inside the "tunnel" established
during the Smithsonian talks of December 1971 to repair the
damaged international monetary system. For the next three years
the **Community**'s currencies wiggled in and out of the snake, with
the deutsche mark, buoyed by Germany's low inflation and large
trade surplus, pushing through the top and the pound, franc, and
lira, weakened by their countries' high inflation and large trade
deficit, falling through the bottom. By the mid-1970s, however,
widely divergent inflation rates and economic performances in the
member states completely undermined the snake and ended the
EC's first experiment with **Economic and Monetary Union**.

SOAMES AFFAIR   The Soames Affair, a diplomatic incident
between France and Britain, takes its name from a meeting in
Paris, in February 1969, between Christopher Soames, the British
ambassador, and French President **Charles de Gaulle**. In the
meeting, de Gaulle spoke of possible British membership in a
broader and weaker **European Community**, directed by Britain,
France, Germany, and Italy, which would form the nucleus of an
association of Western European states independent of the U.S.
De Gaulle's vague proposal appeared to have been motivated by
recent foreign policy setbacks and by a belated realization of
Germany's growing economic and political power within the
Community.

According to the British record, de Gaulle suggested to Soames
that Britain and France pursue the proposal bilaterally before
consulting other countries. Furious over de Gaulle's two previous
vetoes of Britain's EC membership application, and suspecting a
French diplomatic trap, the British Foreign Office released a
record of the de Gaulle-Soames conversation to a number of
European posts, which in turn informed their host governments.
This incensed de Gaulle, who accused the British of indiscretion

and breach of trust. Whether or not de Gaulle had changed his mind about British membership of the Community, the Soames Affair ensured that enlargement was not an option as long as he remained in power.

SOCIAL CHARTER As a complementary initiative to the **single market program**, **Commission** President **Jacques Delors** promoted the idea of a Social Charter to ensure that workers in the **Community** would benefit as much as employers from a fully functioning internal market. In support of his position, Delors harked back to the preamble of the **Treaty of Rome**, which listed as one of the Community's objectives "the economic and social progress" of the member states and the "constant improvement of the living and working conditions of their peoples." In June 1988, at the Hanover **Summit**, the **European Council** emphasized the importance of the single market's social dimension. Based on contributions from the **European Parliament** and the **Economic and Social Committee**, in October 1989 the **Council of Ministers** completed a draft "Charter of Basic Social Rights of Workers."

The issue became extremely controversial because some politicians, especially British Prime Minister **Margaret Thatcher**, argued that the Social Charter would nullify the single market's gains by pushing up labor costs. Thatcher made her case at the Strasbourg Summit in December 1989, at which the other Community leaders adopted, in the form of a declaration, the text of the Council's Social Charter. The European Council noted that the Commission had formulated an "Action Program" and invited it to submit precise proposals for legislation.

The Action Program and the Social Charter covered such areas as pay; better living and working conditions; social security; freedom of association and collective bargaining; health protection and workplace safety; and, most controversial of all, information, consultation, and worker participation in managing a company. The Social Charter was not legally binding but indicated the eleven member states' intention to incorporate legislation on the areas covered by it as the single market program progressed.

At the **Maastricht Summit** in December 1991, **John Major**, Britain's new prime minister, maintained his predecessor's opposition to the Social Charter and succeeded in removing it entirely from the **Treaty on European Union.** Instead, in a protocol to the treaty, the other Eleven decided to use existing institutions and decision-making procedures to pursue social policy, but outside the Community's treaty framework.

SOLEMN DECLARATION ON EUROPEAN UNION At their **summit** in Stuttgart in June 1983, the heads of state and government adopted a "Solemn Declaration," in which they proclaimed the **Community's** international identity and the member states' determination to coordinate more closely in **European Political Cooperation** (EPC). Known also as the **Stuttgart Declaration,** the initiative grew out of the **Genscher-Colombo Proposals.** In November 1981 the **European Council** asked the **Ten** foreign ministers to consider and report back on German Foreign Minister **Hans-Dietrich Genscher's** and Italian Foreign Minister Colombo's proposals for EPC reform. The foreign ministers failed to agree on a way forward and could not concur on the relatively mild foreign and security policy suggestions contained in the Draft Act. Consequently, their report to the Stuttgart **European Council** was weak, as was the ensuing Solemn Declaration.

SPAAK, PAUL-HENRI (1899-1972) Paul-Henri Spaak's popular nickname, "Mr. Europe," attests to his leading role in the post-war movement for European integration. Before the war, Spaak had been prominent in Belgian politics, having served as a government minister since 1935, including a brief spell in 1938-39 as Belgium's first Socialist prime minister. While in government Spaak had championed Belgium's neutrality and sought to keep his country out of the coming conflagration. But Belgium's ignominious capitulation in May 1940, followed by four years of German occupation, which Spaak spent in exile in London, radically altered his international outlook. Thereafter Spaak was a firm believer in both international alliances and European integration.

In the immediate postwar years, Spaak was variously prime minister and foreign minister of Belgium, sometimes simultaneously. At the same time, he became increasingly prominent on the European scene, first as chairman of the newly founded **Organization for European Economic Cooperation**, then as president of the Consultative Assembly of the **Council of Europe**. He was also a leading supporter of the **Schuman Plan** and the Pleven Plan to establish the **European Defense Community** (EDC). Moreover, he presided over the attempt to establish a **European Political Community**, which came to grief when the French Assembly failed to ratify the proposed European Defense Community.

But Spaak's greatest contribution to the **Community** came when he chaired the intergovernmental conference, formed after the **Messina Conference** in June 1955, to draft plans for further European integration. Spaak was well suited, by reputation, temperament, and conviction, to direct the difficult negotiations. As chairman of the conference, which opened in Brussels on June 26, 1955, but began in earnest in the fall, Spaak steered the work of the various committees and subcommittees that drafted specific parts of the final proposal. Spaak's report, presented to his fellow foreign ministers at a meeting in Venice in May 1956, proposed that the two objectives of sectoral (atomic energy) integration and wider economic integration (a **common market**) be realized in separate organizations, with separate treaties. The Venice foreign ministers' meeting marked the first stage of a protracted process of intergovernmental negotiations, culminating in the signing of the **Treaties of Rome** in March 1957, establishing the **European Atomic Energy Community** and the **European Economic Community**.

Spaak continued to serve well into the 1960s as Belgian foreign minister, interrupted by a spell as secretary-general of the **North Atalantic Treaty Organization** (NATO) between 1957 and 1961. His later years as foreign minister and as a leading advocate of European integration were marred by a series of clashes with French President **Charles de Gaulle**, first over de Gaulle's veto of Britain's EC membership application in 1963, then over the **"Empty Chair Crisis"** of 1965-66. Dejected by de Gaulle's cavalier treatment of his EC partners, preoccupied in the early 1960s with Belgium's problems in the Congo, and increasingly distracted by his country's linguistic quarrels, Spaak left public office for the last time in 1966.

SPAAK REPORT The Spaak Report, presented by Belgian Prime Minister **Paul-Henri Spaak** to his fellow foreign ministers at a meeting in Venice in May 1956, outlined a plan to revive European integration after the setback of the **European Defense Community's** collapse. Spaak urged that the two contending objectives of sectoral (atomic energy) integration and wider economic integration (a **common market**) be realized in separate organizations, with separate treaties. The Venice foreign ministers' meeting marked the first stage of a protracted process of intergovernmental negotiations, culminating in the signing of the **Treaties of Rome** in March 1957, establishing the **European Atomic Energy Community** and the **European Economic Community**.

SPAIN Along with Portugal, Spain is the **Community's** newest member state. After almost twenty-five years of overtures to the Community, Spain became a full member in January 1986. Spain's early efforts to join the EC were unsuccessful, largely because of Francisco Franco's authoritarian regime, which governed Spain from 1939 until 1975. Even after Spain's post-Franco democratic reforms, French farming interests threatened by Spain's enormous agricultural production and fundamental intra-Community difficulties hampered negotiations between Spain and the Community and delayed Spain's road to full membership for several years. Only until member states put the EC budgetary house in order and paved the way for strengthening the Community through treaty revision was Spain's entry into the Community finally assured.

Since accession, Spain has been one of the Community's strongest advocates of deeper integration, signing the **Single European Act** (SEA) in one of its first moves as a full member, consistently supporting moves toward **Economic and Monetary Union** (EMU), and lobbying for the idea of European citizenship (incorporated into the **Maastricht Treaty**). In security issues, Spain has made similar "European" gestures, advocating an expansive role for the **Common Foreign and Security Policy** and supporting, along with France, the idea of a European defense identity outside the **North Atlantic Treaty Organization** (NATO) umbrella.

Spain has benefited from EC membership both politically and economically. EC membership helped to solidify Spain's transition to democracy. Still recovering from Franco's backward and oppressive regime, Spaniards looked to the EC as their hope for the future. And so it proved to be. The breakdown in trade barriers and surge in foreign investment that accompanied EC membership combined with other factors to help Spain enjoy an impressive economic boom in the first years of membership. Also, shortly after Spain's accession the Community decided to overhaul the make-up of its structural funds under "Delors I," a move that doubled the amount of money **Brussels** gives to the EC's less developed regions. Spain has since had a large slice of the structural funds pie.

In addition to championing European citizenship, whereby EC nationals are allowed to vote in local elections wherever they live in the Community, Spain has made other important contributions to the EC. Maintaining the special link with its former colonies, Spain added Latin America to the EC political agenda, introducing regular multilateral meetings and, in general, broadening the scope of **European Political Cooperation** (EPC). More recently, in a quiet coup of diplomacy Spain demanded and got the promise of a **cohesion** fund in the Maastricht Treaty, entitling Spain, along with the three other relatively poor member states (Greece, Ireland, and Portugal), to Community assistance on environmental and infrastructural projects. Moreover, throughout 1992 Spain insisted that agreement on "Delors II," the **Commission's** five-year budget package which includes massive expenditures for structural funds and the new cohesion fund, must precede any formal talks on enlargement.

Despite the obvious rewards the country has reaped from Community membership and the Maastricht promise of more money, Spanish perceptions of the EC are now largely shaped by the realization that the steps required to meet the so-called convergence criteria for EMU outlined at Maastricht will not be easy ones. If Spain intends to ride the first wave of EMU at the end of the decade, its inflation rate, interest rates, and budget deficit must all be at a prescribed level. That means fiscal discipline and tight credit--and the assumption that growth will continue apace. Reaching these goals will be a difficult task for a country with high unemployment, uneven development, and strike-prone trade unions.

SPINELLI, ALTIERO (1907-1986)   Altiero Spinelli, a former commissioner (1970-76) and MEP (1976-1986), was a leading advocate of European federalism.   His involvement in the movement for European integration began during World War II, when he was exiled to the Italian island of Ventotene for his antifascist activities.   There, in 1940 and 1941, Spinelli drafted a manifesto for a "free and united Europe."   Following his release after Mussolini's ouster in 1943, Spinelli founded the European Federalist Movement in Milan.   He then traveled secretly to Switzerland for a meeting of European resistance representatives. Out of that meeting, held in Geneva in June and July 1944, came the "Draft Declaration of the European Resistance," including a call for a "Federal Union among the European peoples."

In the postwar years, Spinelli became a leading figure in the **European movement**.   At home in Italy, he pursued a political career in the Italian Action Party, of which he was a founder member and secretary-general until 1962.   In the mid-1960s he founded and directed the prestigious Institute for International Affairs in Rome before becoming an adviser to the Italian foreign minister in the late 1960s.

In 1970 Spinelli became a commissioner but left unexpectedly to join the **European Parliament** as an independent Communist. Not only was his political affiliation surprising--Spinelli had broken with communism as early as 1937--but his decision to become an MEP in the then powerless Parliament surprised almost everyone.   But Spinelli was positioning himself to become an influential figure in the first directly elected Parliament. Spinelli interpreted the results of the first direct elections, in June 1979, as a mandate to launch a constitutional revision of the **Community**.   He and like-minded MEPs became known as the Crocodile Group, because of their habit of meeting in the expensive Crocodile restaurant during plenary meetings of the Parliament in **Strasbourg**.   The Crocodile Group pressed success-fully for the establishment in the Parliament of an Institutional Affairs Committee, which in turn drafted a treaty on **European Union**, which the whole house passed on February 14, 1984.

The **Draft Treaty on European Union** was Spinelli's final contribution to the Community. Although Spinelli tended to be unrealistic and farfetched, the Draft Treaty was a pragmatic document that sought to shame the member states into reviving the Community's flagging institutional framework. To a great extent, Spinelli's tactic worked. It coincided with a number of related developments--the **Genscher-Colombo Proposals**, the recent accession of Greece and the impending accession of Spain and Portugal, and growing interest in European business circles for the establishment of a single market--that together accounted for the Community's resuscitation in the mid-1980s. It is not unreasonable to say that the **Single European Act** was Spinelli's bequest to **Brussels**.

STRASBOURG Strasbourg is known as the home of the **European Parliament**, although the Parliament holds only its plenary sessions (lasting usually one week each month) there. In the late 1940s, the founding states of the **Council of Europe** decided to locate its Assembly in Strasbourg, a frequently fought-over city on the border between France and Germany. This was intended both to keep the Assembly away from a national capital and to symbolize European reconciliation. Later, the **Six** founding members of the **European Community** followed suit and placed its Parliament there also. As the European Community revived and flourished in the 1980s, many MEPs regretted the choice of Strasbourg, located over two hundred miles from the **Commission** and **Council of Ministers'** Secretariat in **Brussels**, as the Parliament's seat. For them, Strasbourg came to symbolize not Franco-German reconciliation but the obscurity and relative unimportance of their own institution.

STUTTGART DECLARATION   see **Solemn Declaration on European Union**

SUBSIDIARITY Subsidiarity became the latest **European Community** buzzword in the summer of 1992, during the **Maastricht Treaty** ratification crisis. Denmark's rejection of the Maastricht Treaty, in a referendum on June 2, and the narrow French vote in favor in the September 20 referendum signaled growing popular concern throughout the **Community** about the centralization of power in **Brussels**. Although exaggerated and generally unwarranted, these concerns sent shock waves through the member state governments and through the **Commission**.

The solution seemed to lie in the vague and wooly "principle" of subsidiarity: the idea that the Community should undertake and assume only those tasks and responsibilities that could be carried out better in common than by member states acting separately. Subsidiarity suddenly became the panacea for the Community's ills and the means by which the Maastricht Treaty might, after all, survive. Alarmed by growing Conservative back-bench opposition to Maastricht, the British government championed subsidiarity as the best way to curb the Commission's supposed encroachment into every "nook and cranny" of daily life. Norman Lamont, the Chancellor of the Exchequer, even went as far on BBC radio as to call subsidiarity "that very British idea that no one was interested in at first."

In fact, the need to distinguish between Community competence and member state responsibilities is as old as the Community itself. Moreover, the word "subsidiarity" first surfaced in the Community context in the late 1970s. The Preamble of the **European Parliament's** 1984 **Draft Treaty on European Union** referred specifically to the "principle of subsidiarity." Later in the 1980s, following implementation of the **Single European Act** and at the beginning of a renewed debate about institutional reform and Community competence, Commission President **Jacques Delors** embraced subsidiarity and referred frequently to it.

Yet Delors' understanding of subsidiarity is far different from what the British government now takes it to mean. For Delors, subsidiarity is an essential element of Euro-federalism. It would permit the Community to concentrate on key areas, such as monetary policy and foreign affairs, while leaving the member states to deal with lesser, more mundane issues. For opponents of Euro-federalism, by contrast, subsidiarity is a safeguard against creeping Community control over the traditional national prerogatives.

During the 1991 intergovernmental conference (IGC) on **Political Union**, pressure to include a reference to subsidiarity came mostly from Euro-federalists. In April 1991, the European

Parliament adopted a report by former French President **Valéry Giscard d'Estaing** calling on the IGC to focus explicitly on subsidiarity "in order to ensure the dynamic development of European integration and the best possible transparency in the repartition of competencies between the EC and the member states." As expected, the Maastricht Treaty included a specific and highly significant reference to subsidiarity. According to Article 3(B), "In areas which do not fall within its exclusive competence, the Community shall take action, in accordance with the principle of subsidiarity, only if and in so far as the objectives of the proposed action cannot be sufficiently achieved by the Member States and can therefore, by reason of the scale and of the effects of the proposed action, be better achieved by the Community." The *Financial Times* accurately called this concept "an intellectual jellyfish."

Reeling from the impact of popular hostility toward the Maastricht Treaty in the summer and fall of 1992, Delors began to implement the principle of subsidiarity. Without in any way abandoning his Euro-federalist ambition, Delors scaled back the Commission's involvement in policy areas that could best be left to the member states. Hoping especially to help the British government with its difficult task of treaty ratification, Delors scrapped some of the Commission's most intrusive procedures, notably in the area of environmental policy. To Delors' detractors this seemed like a retreat; for Delors himself, it was an opportunity to refocus the Commission on the urgent objective of European integration.

In the meantime, subsidiarity became all things to all men. Advocacy of subsidiarity allowed Euro-federalists to press ahead with their agenda, while permitting Euro-antifederalists to claim that the Commission's wings had been clipped. The emergency **European Council** in October 1992, called by British Prime Minister **John Major** to try to resolve the ratification problem, failed to deal with subsidiarity. Thus, the concept remains sufficiently elastic to satisfy all sides in the Community.

SUMMIT Meetings of the **Community's** heads of state and government and of the **Commission** president are known as summits. Summits take place at least twice a year under the

auspices of the **European Council** and in exceptional circumstances can be convened on short notice, as happened in
Birmingham in October 1992 to discuss the **Maastricht Treaty.**

-T-

The TEN   After the accession of Greece to the **European
Community** in 1981, the **Nine** member states became Ten. Thus
the Community was often referred to as "the Ten" between 1981
and 1986, when Spain and Portugal joined and the Ten became
Twelve.

THATCHER, MARGARET (1925-) Lady Thatcher, the former
British prime minister (1979-90), is famous--or infamous--for her
opposition to the **Maastricht Treaty** of February 1992. The
treaty's provisions for **Economic and Monetary Union** (EMU),
increased **Community** competence, and greater legislative power
for the **European Parliament** were anathema to her vision of
contemporary Europe and Britain's place alongside it. As the
newly elevated Baroness Thatcher of Kesteven, Thatcher seized
every opportunity in late 1992 to denounce the treaty and rally
Conservative opinion against its ratification in the U.K. To the
government she had led for eleven years she became an
embarrassment and an object of ridicule; to the average Euro-
phobic little-Englander, she remained a heroine.

Thatcher's forceful stand against Maastricht was the
culmination of a long-simmering political, philosophical, and
ideological dispute with **Brussels.** As a stout defender of national
sovereignty, Thatcher disliked the **European Commission's**
federalist agenda and the Community's supranational ambition.
She is often compared to French President **Charles de Gaulle:**
both were ardent nationalists and both resolutely opposed the
Community's increasing encroachment on their countries
sovereignty.

Yet there are obvious differences between them. The most
striking is their contrasting attitude and behavior toward the
United States. De Gaulle resented America's hegemony in the
alliance and did everything possible to assert French and

European independence of Washington. His attempt to bring about a "Europe of the States," in contradistinction to a divided continent under the wings of the two superpowers, and his break from the **North Atlantic Treaty Organization** (NATO) in 1966, are legendary. By contrast, Thatcher deliberately cultivated the Anglo-American "special relationship" and struck up a warm friendship with President Ronald Reagan. Thatcher formulated her policy toward Europe largely in relation to her policy toward the U.S. She strove to become Washington's most trusted ally and favored interlocutor on transatlantic economic, diplomatic, and military affairs.

The **European Community** played a prominent role in Thatcher's political career. In 1975 she made her maiden speech as leader of the Conservative opposition in the House of Commons on the then-burning issue of Britain's renegotiation of accession terms and referendum on continued membership. In typically strident tones, Thatcher argued against a constitutionally unprecedented referendum; in view of the Labour government's decision to hold a referendum in any case, she argued in favor of Britain remaining in the Community. Both positions appeared paradoxical in 1992, but only the first is. In 1992 Thatcher repudiated her earlier stand and called for a U.K. referendum on Maastricht. Yet she remains true to her original support for Community membership. What she objected to in 1992, as in the past, was not a Community of European states dedicated to implementing common economic policies but the federalism inherent in European integration, which received a big boost under Commission President **Jacques Delors'** leadership in the late 1980s.

The Labour government's 1975 renegotiation of Community membership was to have resolved the unsatisfactory issue of Britain's budgetary contribution to Brussels. Instead, the 1975 renegotiation was a cosmetic exercise intended to assuage British public opinion and hold the pro- and anti-EC sides of the Labour Party together. Moreover, Britain's favorable transition terms disguised the extent of its unfair budgetary situation. By the time Thatcher came to power in 1979, however, the enormity of the budgetary anomaly was glaring. Because, compared to other member states, Britain imported far more manufactured goods and agricultural produce from outside the Community, Britain paid more in import duties and agricultural levies into the Community's coffers. On the other hand, because Britain had a highly efficient agricultural sector, the country received little from the **Common Agricultural Policy** (CAP), which accounted for over 70% of Community expenditure.

Thatcher immediately seized on the "British Budgetary Question." Here was a cause that was just, easy to understand, and bound to win domestic support. Even her Community colleagues conceded the inequity of Britain's case. Yet the British Budgetary Question soon became the most heated and controversial issue in the Community. It lasted five years and dominated fifteen **European Councils** before being resolved at the **Fontainebleau Summit** in June 1984. Why did it preoccupy the Community to that extent?

The answer lies largely in Thatcher's temperament, outlook, and style. Her obduracy, intransigence, and complete disregard for diplomatic convention, let alone personal politeness, turned the other Eleven against her. Efforts by her own Foreign Office to mediate a settlement merely reinforced Thatcher's determination to grind the opposition down. In the end her strategy worked, but at enormous political cost. Thanks largely to French President **Francois Mitterrand**'s conciliation, and to German Chancellor **Helmut Kohl**'s eventual acquiescence, Thatcher got an extremely favorable financial settlement at Fontainebleau. In the long term, however, she ensured that, at least during her prime ministership, Britain would be no more than a bit player in Community affairs.

Yet indirectly Thatcher played a prominent part in the Community's revival in the mid-1980s. An unswerving champion of deregulation and economic liberalism, throughout the debilitating budgetary question she persistently advocated completion of the Community's long-awaited internal market. In 1985 she sent **Arthur Cockfield,** her former trade minister, to Brussels. As a Commission vice-president with responsibility for the internal market, Lord Cockfield produced the **"White Paper"** that launched the spectacularly successful **"1992"** program. In her remaining years in Number 10 Downing Street, Thatcher pushed hard for implementation of the White Paper's proposals.

Like almost everyone else at the time, Thatcher never expected the **single market program** to revive the movement for deeper European integration. She was lukewarm about the **Single European Act**--a constitutional change essential for completion of the single market--lest it strengthen the Commission's power and foster further supranationalism. She especially feared a renewal of interest in EMU, a logical corollary of a single market. That put her on a collision course with Delors, who enthusiastically espoused EMU not only because of its intrinsic merit, but also because of its potential for promoting European integration. Thatcher's opposition to Delors and all he represented culminated in her famous speech at the College of Europe in Bruges in September 1988. The Bruges speech was a brilliant harangue against an "identakit" Europe and a socialist, centralized Community.

In the late 1980s Thatcher found herself fighting a rear guard action in Brussels and London against the **Delors Plan** on EMU. The key issue became Britain's participation in the exchange rate mechanism (ERM) of the **European Monetary System** (EMS). Thatcher promised to join the ERM, but only at the most propitious moment for Britain. Her cabinet colleagues pressed for ERM participation in 1988 and 1989, both to strengthen the British pound and to signal the country's commitment to EMU. Combined with a bitter domestic dispute over the "Poll Tax" (a new method of taxation), controversy over ERM poisoned relations in the government. More arrogant and self-righteous than ever, Thatcher became increasingly unpopular and isolated. Once they realized that her continuing support for the hugely hated Poll Tax meant that the Conservative Party could not win another election under her leadership, Thatcher's senior cabinet ministers launched a palace revolution. In November 1990 she lost the party leadership and, consequently, the prime ministership.

Thatcher's opposition to EMU had contributed to her downfall. Deeper European integration was never popular in the U.K., but Thatcher's strident opposition to it, at a time of increasing domestic recession, began to alienate even her own supporters. **John Major,** her successor, distanced himself from Thatcher by striking a constructively critical note on Community affairs.

Major's performance at Maastricht won respect in the Community and secured safeguards for Britain on EMU and an opt-out on the **Social Charter**. At home, sulking on the backbenches of the House of Commons, Thatcher decried Major's sellout. During Britain's Community presidency in the second half of 1992, she continued her hectoring from the greater political distance of the House of Lords and reveled in the government's discomfiture during the Maastricht Treaty ratification crisis.

THORN, GASTON (1938-) Gaston Thorn succeeded **Roy Jenkins** as **Commission** president in 1981, serving for four years before handing over to **Jacques Delors** in January 1985. Before coming to **Brussels**, Thorn had been a government minister in Luxembourg since 1969, including a long period as prime minister between 1974 and 1979. Thus, from the perspective of the **Council of Ministers**, Thorn had a sound knowledge of how the **Community** worked. Moreover, between 1959 and 1969 he had been a member of the **European Parliament**.

Yet Thorn was a disappointment as Commission president. He failed to maintain the momentum Jenkins developed and was completely overshadowed by his successor, Jacques Delors. Even in his own Commission Thorn appeared to have less influence and ambition than **Etienne Davignon**, whose name, rather than Thorn's, is often used to identify the 1980-84 Commission. After his departure from Brussels, Thorn entered international banking.

TINDEMANS, LEO (1922-) As prime minister of Belgium between 1974 and 1978, Leo Tindemans was one of the most prominent politicians in the **Community** who sought to cure Euro-sclerosis and get the EC back on its feet. He is best known during that time for the Tindemans Report (1975), a set of recommendations for rekindling the Community, which, predictably, got nowhere. In the economic climate of the mid-1970s, the member states simply lacked the political will to take Tindemans' proposals seriously.

As foreign minister between 1981 and 1989, Tindemans played a part in the Community's eventual revival. He used Belgium's presidencies to promote the **single market program** and advance the **Single European Act**. In 1989 Tindemans was elected to the **European Parliament**, where he continues to espouse deeper European integration as a leading Christian Democratic member.

TREATIES OF ROME   The two treaties signed in Rome by representatives of France, Germany, Italy, Belgium, The Netherlands, and Luxembourg on March 25, 1957, establishing the **European Economic Community** and the **European Atomic Energy Community** (Euratom).

TREATY OF ROME   Although there are two Treaties of Rome, establishing the **European Economic Community** and the **European Atomic Energy Community** (Euratom), the Treaty of Rome generally refers to the former. It was signed in Rome on March 25, 1957, by representatives of France, Germany, Italy, Belgium, The Netherlands, and Luxembourg. The treaty outlined the **Community's** institutional framework and sphere of competence. It was amended twice: in 1986 by the **Single European Act** and in 1992 by the **Treaty on European Union**.

TREATY ON EUROPEAN UNION   The Treaty on European Union, also known as the **Maastricht Treaty**, was signed by **Community** foreign and finance ministers in the southern Dutch town of Maastricht on February 7, 1992. Two months previously, at the **European Council** in Maastricht, the heads of state and government had negotiated the treaty as the culmination of twelve months of intergovernmental conferences on **Economic and Monetary Union** and **European Political Union**. The treaty, and the subsequent controversy over its ratification, marked a decisive turning point in the Community's history.

The treaty established a **European Union**, consisting of three pillars: the **European Community**, a **Common Foreign and Security Policy**, and cooperation on justice and internal affairs. With the conspicuous exception of Britain, the member states also agreed to establish a **Social Charter** outside the European Union, but using Community institutions. The treaty extensively modified the European Community (the name by which the **European Economic Community** would henceforth officially be called) both institutionally and substantially. The most important reform was to set a precise timetable and strict criteria for monetary union and the creation of a common currency.

The Treaty on European Union was to have crowned the Community's development in the new post-**Cold War** era. Instead, it threatened to cause the Community's undoing. Danish rejection of the treaty, in a referendum in June 1992, imperiled its ratification throughout the Community and fueled popular resentment against **Brussels** in a number of member states. A backlash against Brussels' seeming insensitivity to citizens' concerns and remoteness from everyday life led to a ground swell of indignation about the Community's direction and ambition. French President **Francois Mitterrand** miscalculated the popular mood in France when he called for a referendum on Maastricht after the Danish "no" vote. On September 20, 1992, only a narrow majority (51%) of French voters approved the treaty. As a result, the future of the Treaty on European Union was by no means certain more than eight months after its signing in Maastricht.

The TWELVE Since the accession of Spain and Portugal in 1986, the EC is popularly known as the Twelve--the number of member states currently in the **Community**.

-U-

The UNITED KINGDOM (U.K.) The United Kingdom is the least enthusiastic **Community** member state. Most Britons are ambivalent about European integration--although **Roy Jenkins**, a successful **Commission** president, was British--and dislike especially the excessive centralization of Community decision making in **Brussels**. The British want to keep in London as much responsibility as possible for their own affairs. They oppose "federalism" in the Community because, in their view, federalism means the concentration of authority at the center. Paradoxically, according to that definition Britain, with one of the most highly centralized political systems in Europe, is a federal state.

Britain viewed Community membership in the 1950s as suitable for continental countries, with their history of incessant invasion and occupation, but unworthy of a country that had not been invaded for centuries, was cut off from the continent of Europe, and still considered itself a global power. By the early 1960s, however, the British government realized that in the radically changed circumstances of the postwar world, Britain could not afford to remain outside the Community--politically or economically. The United States, with which Britain apparently enjoyed a "special relationship," urged London to join. But Washington's prompting convinced French President **Charles de Gaulle**, who deeply disliked American hegemony in the **Atlantic Alliance** and sought to wrest Europe from superpower control, to keep Britain out. It was only after de Gaulle's resignation in 1969 that enlargement of the Community became politically possible. After intense accession negotiations, Britain (together with Denmark and Ireland) finally joined in 1973.

Like Roy Jenkins, **Edward Heath**, the British prime minister who brought his country into the Community, was a Euro-fanatic. Both Jenkins and Heath were exceptions in their respective Labour and Conservative parties. Most British politicians disliked the Community and resented having had to join. The question of Community membership split the Labour Party, which came to power in 1974. In an effort to keep the party together, **Harold Wilson**, the Labour leader and prime minister, renegotiated the terms of Britain's entry. Talks centered on the extent of Britain's budgetary contribution to Brussels and ended with a settlement politically acceptable to Wilson. However, the "British budgetary question" would resurface dramatically at the end of the decade, when Prime Minister **Margaret Thatcher** doggedly pursued a financially more favorable agreement.

Wilson's--and subsequently Thatcher's--emphasis on the material aspects of membership disappointed the U.K.'s partners, especially those small countries that looked to British membership as a possible means of weakening the Community's Franco-German axis. Admittedly the Community was in deep recession in the 1970s and early 1980s, when integration made little headway. But by the time the Community emerged from the political and economic darkness of the post-oil crisis period into the light of the **Single European Act** era, Britain had signaled its disinterest in playing a positive, constructive role. Certainly

Thatcher supported the **single market program**, but she resisted
every effort to move the Community in other directions, notably
toward **Economic and Monetary Union** (EMU) and **Political
Union**. Thatcher's famous 1988 Bruges speech was an anti-Euro-
federalist manifesto. It brilliantly argued the British case for
maintaining national sovereignty and against further integration.
   Thatcher's rhetoric was extreme, but her position was not
atypical in the U.K. **John Major**, her successor, steered a more
moderate course in the Community but still managed at the
Maastricht Summit to win a possible "opt-out" for Britain on
EMU and to remove the **Social Charter** entirely from the
European Union treaty. Denmark's rejection of the **Maastricht
Treaty** and a populist reaction throughout the Community against
centralization and bureaucratization triggered a Conservative
back-bench reaction that embarrassed Major politically and made
British ratification of Maastricht even more difficult. The
Community-wide ratification crisis showed that opinion in Britain
and elsewhere in the Community coincided on the need to close
the "democratic deficit" and promote "subsidiarity" but that a
huge gulf on the extent and inherent value of European
integration nevertheless remained.

URI, PIERRE (1911-   ) Pierre Uri, a French professor, public
   servant, and journalist, was a collaborator of **Jean Monnet** and
   Robert Marjolin in the early days of European integration.
   Between 1947 and 1952, as financial and economic adviser to the
   French Planning Commission, Uri contributed to the change in
   French policy toward Germany that gave rise to the **Schuman
   Declaration** and, subsequently, the **Coal and Steel Community**
   (ECSC). He served as a senior official in the ECSC from 1952
   to 1959 before leaving public service to become a writer,
   consultant, and academic.

URUGUAY ROUND   see **General Agreement on Tarrifs and
   Trade**

U.S.-EC DECLARATION On November 20, 1990, in Washington,
   D.C., U.S. President George Bush, President of the **Council of
   Ministers** Julio Andreotti, and **Commission** President **Jacques**

Delors signed a "Declaration on U.S.-EC Relations." The
declaration sought to put U.S.-EC relations on a new, more
equitable footing, especially in view of "the accelerating process
by which the **European Community** is acquiring its own identity
in economic and monetary matters, in foreign policy and in the
domain of security." Apart from its general significance for
transatlantic relations, the declaration's only tangible contribution
is a strengthened framework for regular consultations to enable
both sides to "inform and consult each other on important
matters of common interest, both political and economic, with a
view to bringing their positions as close as possible, without
prejudice to their respective independence." As a result, the
president of the U.S., the president of the Council of Ministers,
and the Commission president hold regular, biannual meetings.

-W-

WERNER PLAN The Werner Plan for **Economic and Monetary
Union** (EMU) emerged directly from the **Community** member
states' endorsement, at the December 1969 **Hague Summit**, of
"completion, deepening, enlargement." "Completion" meant
finalizing a financial provision for the **Common Agricultural
Policy**, "deepening" meant extending the Community's
competence, and "enlargement" meant admitting Britain and the
other applicant states. In an effort to deepen European
integration, the member states asked Pierre Werner, prime
minister of Luxembourg, to prepare a report on EMU.

In October 1970 Werner presented an ambitious seven-stage
plan to achieve EMU in the Community within ten years, by
means of institutional reform and closer political cooperation.
The plan glossed over contending French and German emphases
on monetary measures and economic policy coordination by
proposing parallel progress in both spheres. But differences
between Paris and Bonn soon emerged over the plan's scope and
the pace at which it should be implemented. Although a firm
supporter of monetary policy coordination, French President
Georges Pompidou was loath to take any measure likely to
advance supranationalism in the Community. German Chancellor

Willy Brandt and the other Community leaders, by contrast, saw the Werner Plan as an ideal opportunity to accelerate closer integration.

At their **Paris Summit** in October 1972, the heads of state and government called for EMU by 1980. Despite their optimism, the Werner Plan soon became a victim of the sclerosis that beset the Community in the 1970s. High inflation rates and growing economic divergence made nonsense of the 1980 target date and consigned the Werner Plan to the archives. It was only in the late 1980s that EMU resurfaced, this time under the radically different circumstances of the successful **single market program** and the push toward **Political Union.**

WESTERN EUROPEAN UNION (WEU) With the collapse of the **European Defense Community** in 1954 as a vehicle for German rearmament, Anthony Eden, the British prime minister, proposed instead that Germany sign the **Brussels Treaty** of 1948 and participate with Britain, France, Italy, Belgium, The Netherlands, and Luxembourg in the Western European Union (WEU). The 1954 protocols modifying the Brussels Treaty to establish the WEU enabled Germany to join the **Atlantic Alliance** and also stressed the WEU's role in promoting European integration.

For the next thirty years, the WEU was largely inactive. For instance, its Council of Ministers never met between 1973 and 1984. But in the early 1980s, in the context of the sudden deterioration in East-West relations, some EC member states sought to coordinate their positions on defense, security, and military issues. As such coordination was then beyond the EC's competence and because Ireland, Denmark, and Greece objected to bringing defense into the EC's purview, the other member states decided to reactivate the WEU, to which they all belonged. As a result, the WEU came back to life at a meeting of its foreign and defense ministers in Rome, in October 1984.

The 1987 WEU Platform on European Security emphasized the organization's commitment to European integration, especially in the context of the **Single European Act.** Spain's and Portugal's membership in the WEU in 1989 further reinforced the organization's link with the **Community.** In the late 1980s and early 1990s, the WEU became involved in a number of military operations outside the NATO area. These included minesweeping efforts in the Gulf in 1987 and imposition of the embargo against Iraq in 1990-91.

The December 1991 **Maastricht Summit** gave a huge boost to the WEU's fortunes, when the heads of state and government explicitly made the organization an integral part of the newly established **European Union**. The WEU's member states invited Ireland, Denmark, and Greece, the three EC countries not in the WEU, to join the organization or at least become observers. They also decided to move the WEU's secretariat to **Brussels**, close to the EC **Commission** and **North Atlantic Treaty Organization** (NATO) headquarters. Finally, the member states agreed to review the WEU's role and organization before the expiration of the Brussels Treaty in 1998. By that time, the WEU is likely to become the basis of a full-fledged EC military organization.

WHITE PAPER   The term "White Paper" refers to **Commission** Vice-President **Arthur Cockfield's** June 1985 document outlining the legislative steps necessary for the **Community** to achieve a single market by the end of 1992. Officially entitled *Completing the Internal Market*, the White Paper caught the attention of business people and politicians in the Community and generated enough momentum to get the **single market program** off the ground. It led directly to the **Single European Act** of 1986 and played a pivotal part in the Community's spectacular revival at the end of the 1980s.

WILSON, HAROLD (1916-   )   In 1967, as prime minister of Britain, Harold Wilson presented his country's second application for **European Community** membership. In 1975, again as prime minister (after an interlude during which **Edward Heath**, the Conservative Party leader, brought Britain into the **Community**), Wilson called a referendum on whether or not Britain should stay in the Community, based on his renegotiation of Heath's entry terms. The result was a vote in favor of continued membership, but the conduct of the renegotiation, and of the referendum itself, perpetuated ambivalence in Britain about Community membership, an ambivalence Wilson personified.

In 1967 Wilson was equivocal about joining the Community but, like **Harold Macmillan** in the early 1960s, saw no feasible alternative. If anything, Britain's declining political and economic links with the Commonwealth and growing commercial contacts with the Community increased the urgency of accession. Nevertheless the issue split the Labour Party and pitted a pro-Europe wing on the center and right against the anti-Marketeers on the left. Wilson had to warn his cabinet colleagues, under pain of dismissal, to maintain unity and adhere to the principle of collective responsibility while the government again explored the option of membership.

In any event, French President **Charles de Gaulle** vetoed Britain's membership, just as he had done four years previously. Four days after Wilson submitted Britain's second application, in May 1967, de Gaulle called a press conference to explain why he thought Britain was not yet ready to join. Although the status of Britain's application was uncertain, it became clear to the other member states that negotiations would not go anywhere. Accordingly, on December 20, 1967, the Foreign Office announced that, in effect, Britain would shelve its membership request.

Wilson lost the 1970 general election. By the time he returned to office in 1974, the Conservative government had successfully brought Britain into the Community the previous year. But the Labour Party had been deeply divided over the entry negotiations. Wilson himself had initially equivocated and turned to open opposition as the talks unfolded, bringing the bulk of Labour with him. Whether motivated by conviction or opportunism, Wilson denounced Heath's accession terms and declared that a Labour government would renegotiate Britain's membership in the Community. **Roy Jenkins**, a future **Commission** president, led an increasingly isolated pro-EC group on the right wing of the party and eventually resigned from the party's Front Bench.

Having won the election in 1974, Wilson and James Callaghan, his foreign secretary, duly pursued their pledge to renegotiate with the other member states. French President **Valéry Giscard d'Estaing** strongly opposed any renegotiation and doubted that more favorable terms would end British dissatisfaction with the

Community. Only German Chancellor **Helmut Schmidt,** a fellow socialist, sympathized with Wilson's predicament. Ultimately, Schmidt brokered the dispute between Giscard and Wilson and helped to get the talks off the ground.

Wilson's main point was that under the present system Britain made a disproportionately high contribution to the Community's budget. Other demands included reform of the **Common Agricultural Policy,** retention of Parliamentary sovereignty, freedom to control capital movements, protection of Commonwealth interests, no harmonization of value-added tax, and no tying of the pound to a fixed parity. As the negotiations progressed, changing circumstances made many of these points either superfluous or counterproductive. By the end of 1974, only the budgetary and Commonwealth demands remained active on Britain's agenda. Community leaders thrashed both issues out at a **summit** in Dublin, in March 1975. Resolution of the budget dispute was based on a "correcting mechanism," proposed by the Commission, to prevent Britain, or any other member state, from paying too much into the Community.

In the meantime, Wilson had successfully contested the October 1974 general election, the second in less than a year, largely on the renegotiation issue. During the campaign, Wilson pledged either another general election or a referendum to validate the renegotiation result. Labour's election victory kept the question of continued Community membership at the top of the political agenda and caused Wilson to call for referendum after the Dublin Summit on Britain's continued membership in the Community. With the leadership of the two main parties, and also of the Liberal Party, advocating a positive result, the outcome of the referendum was hardly in doubt. On June 5, 1975, of the 64% of the electorate who voted, 67% cast their ballots for, and 33% against, staying in the Community.

Renegotiation of Britain's membership terms had lasted eleven months, dominated two Community summits, and driven Britain's partners to distraction. Domestically, the renegotiation and referendum had further divided the Labour Party. The entire episode hardly reflected well on Wilson, who remained prime minister until 1976, when he handed over leadership of the Labour Party and of the country to James Callaghan.

-Y-

YEAR OF EUROPE In order to overcome recent strains in U.S.-
EC trade relations and to influence the development of **European
Political Cooperation** in America's favor, Henry Kissinger,
President Richard Nixon's national security adviser, decided to
designate 1973 the "Year of Europe." While unveiling his
grandiose scheme, which included a call for a "New Atlantic
Charter," Kissinger appealed for closer cooperation on trade,
defense, and foreign policy issues. Most Europeans responded
unfavorably, seeing in Kissinger's initiative a bid to reassert
American superiority under the cloak of a better transatlantic
bargain. Kissinger's distinction between Europe's regional role
and America's global responsibilities seemed especially con-
descending. Far from reassuring European opinion, Kissinger
further antagonized relations with the **Community,** and the much-
vaunted Year of Europe came to nothing. However, it deepened
suspicion in the U.S. about the nature of European integration
and deepened suspicion in the EC about U.S. policy toward
Europe.

BIBLIOGRAPHY

I. *Official Documents*

(This is a selected list of EC official documentation, published mostly by the Community's Office for Official Publications in Luxembourg.)

Bulletin of the European Communities, official monthly record of events and policy actions for all institutions, published by the Commission.

Bulletin of the European Communities (Supplement), selected legislative or consultative documents, published at irregular intervals by the Commission.

COM Documents, proposals and amendments issued by the Commission (approximately 80% are published in the "C" series of the *Official Journal of the European Communities*).

Common Positions of the Council of Ministers (announced in the "C" series of the *Official Journal of the European Communities*).

Completing the Internal Market: Current Status Reports, updates on the 1992 legislative program, published twice a year.

Directory of Community Legislation in Force, published every June and December.

European Documentation, series of explanatory publications on EC policies published approximately five to seven times a year.

European Economy, published four times a year by the Commission's Directorate-General for Economic and Financial Affairs.

European File, series of small pamphlets outlining various aspects

of EC development and policies, titles published approximately
twenty times a year.

European Perspectives, academic monographs on EC-related subjects,
published occasionally.

European Political Cooperation Documentation Bulletin, reproduces
texts of the statements issued under EPC.

*Fact Sheets on the European Parliament and the Activities of the
European Communities,* outlines Community polices, legislation,
and activities, published by the Parliament and updated
periodically.

General Report on the Activities of the European Communities,
published annually by the Commission.   Works published
annually as addenda to the *General Report*:
   The Agricultural Situation in the Community
   Report on Social Developments
   Report on Competition Policy

Official Journal of the European Communities, legislation and other
official acts of the EC, divided into four parts:
   - Legislation ("L") series, for regulations, directives, and other
     binding acts.
   - Communications ("C") series, for nonbinding decisions,
     resolutions, and notices.
   - Supplement ("S") series, for public works and supply
     contracts.
   - Annex, for plenary sessions of the European Parliament.

*Opinions and Information Reports of the Economic and Social
Committee* (published in the "C" section of the *Official Journal of
the European Communities*).

Panorama of EC Industry, describes over 150 sectors of
manufacturing and service industries in the EC, published
annually by the Commission.

Protocols, full texts of agreements between the EC and third
countries, published by the Council.

Reports of Cases Before the Court, published by the Court of Justice
in annual series, parts appearing at irregular intervals throughout
the year.

Reports, Opinions, and Debates of the European Parliament (opinions are published in the "C" section of the *Official Journal of the European Communities*; EP debates are published in the Annex of the *Official Journal*).

Research on the Cost of "Non-Europe": Basic Findings (1988), a sixteen-volume study of the cost to the Community of not completing the single market program.

Review of the Council's Work, published annually by the Council of Ministers.

SCAD Bulletin, bibliographic guide published weekly by the Commission, lists wide range of EC documentation and articles from non-EC periodicals.

Statistical Office of the European Communities (Eurostat), produces various statistical publications arranged according to themes, including general statistics, economy and finance, foreign trade, and environment, among others.

Treaties Establishing the European Communities and Documents Concerning the Accessions to the European Communities, 2 vols. (1987), also includes text of the Single European Act and various resolutions and declarations.

Treaty on European Union (1992), reproduces text of the Maastricht Treaty.

II. *Reference*

Arbuthnott, Hugh; Edwards, Geoffrey. *A Common Man's Guide to the Common Market*. London: Macmillan, 1979.

Bliss, Howard. *The Political Development of the EC: A Documentary Collection*. Waltham, MA: Blaisdell, 1970.

Colchester, N.; Buchan, D. *Europower: The Essential Guide to Europe's Transformation in 1992*. London: Times Books, 1990.

Cook, Chris; Francis, Mary. *The First Elections: A Handbook and Guide*. London: Macmillan, 1979.

Cox, Andrew; Furlong, Paul. *A Modern Companion to the European Community: A Guide to Key Facts, Institutions and Terms*. Cheltenham, England: Edward Elgar, 1992.

Crampton, Stephen. *1992 Eurospeak Explained*. Brussels: European Bookshop Ltd., 1990.

European Access: The Current Awareness Bulletin to the Politics and Activities of the European Community, comprehensive guide to current policies and activities in the EC, published six times a year by Chadwyck-Healey in association with the United Kingdom Offices of the European Commission.

Hopkins, M. *Political Formation in the EC: A Bibliographical Guide to Community Documentation, 1958-1978*. London: Mansell, 1981.

Hudson, Raymond; Rhind, David; Mounsey, Helen. *An Atlas of EC Affairs*. London: Methuen, 1984.

Jacobs, F. G.; Durand, A. *References to the European Community: Practice and Procedures*. London: Butterworths, 1975.

Jacobs, F. G., ed. *Yearbook of European Law*. Oxford: Clarendon Press, 1987.

Jeffries, John. *A Guide to the Official Publications of the EC*. 2nd ed. London: Mansell, 1981.

Jones, Peter. *International Yearbook of Foreign Policy Analysis*. London: Croom Helm, 1975.

Kujath, Karl. *Bibliography on European Integration*. Bonn: Europa Union Verlag, 1977.

Morris, Brian; Crane, Peggy; Boehm, Klaus. *The European Community: A Guide for Business and Government*. Bloomington, IN: Indiana University Press, 1981.

Palmer, Doris M., ed. *Sources of Information on the European Community*. London: Mansell, 1979.

Political and Economic Encyclopedia of Western Europe. Brussels: European Bookshop Ltd., 1990.

Rosenberg, Jerry. *The New Europe: An A to Z Compendium on the*

European Community. Washington, DC: Bureau of National Affairs, 1991.

Roy, Jean-Louis. *1992: A Guide to the European Economic Community Charter.* New York: Collier Books, 1992.

Sampson, Anthony. *The New Europeans: A Guide to the Workings, Institutions and Character of Contemporary Western Europe.* London: Hodder & Stoughton, 1968.

Thomson, Ian. *The Documentation of the European Communities: A Guide.* London: Mansell, 1989.

Warnecke, Steven J., ed. *The EC Research Resources.* New York: Council on European Studies, 1978.

Winter, Audrey. *Europe Without Frontiers: A Lawyer's Guide.* Washington, DC: Bureau of National Affairs, 1989.

III. *Overview*

Alting von Geusau, Frans. *Beyond the EC.* Leiden, The Netherlands: A. W. Sijthoff, 1969.

Amin, A.; Dietrich, M., eds. *Towards a New Europe: Structural Change in the European Community.* Brookfield, VT: Edward Elgar, 1991.

Armand, Louis; Drancourt, Michael. *The European Challenge.* New York: Atheneum, 1970.

Benoit, Emile. *Europe at Sixes and Sevens.* New York: Columbia University Press, 1961.

Broad, Roger; Jarrett, Bob. *Community Europe Today.* 2nd ed. London: Oswald Wolff, 1973.

Burstein, Daniel. *Euroquake: Europe's Explosive Economic Challenge Will Change the World.* New York: Simon & Schuster, 1991.

Calleo, David. *Europe's Future: The Grand Alternatives.* New York: Horizon, 1965.

Coffey, Peter. *Europe and Money*. London: Macmillan, 1977.

Cooney, John. *EEC in Crisis*. Dublin: Dublin University Press, 1979.

Cromwell, William, ed. *The Dynamics of European Integration*. London: Pinter, 1990.

Crouch, Colin; Marquand, David. *The Politics of 1992: Beyond the Single European Market*. Cambridge, MA: Basil Blackwell, 1990.

Curtis, Michael. *Western European Integration*. New York: Harper & Row, 1965.

Cutler, Tony. *1992 and the Struggle for Europe: A Critical Evaluation of the European Community*. Oxford: Berg, 1989.

Dagtoglou, P. D. *Basic Problems of the EC*. Oxford: Basil Blackwell, 1975.

Delors, Jacques. *Le Nouveau Concert Européen*. Paris: Editions Odile Jacob, 1992.

Delors, Jacques. *Our Europe: The Commmunity and National Development*. London: Verso, 1992.

Deniau, Jean Francois. *The Common Market*. London: Barrie & Rockliff, 1967.

Deutsch, Karl. *France, Germany and the Western Alliance: A Study of Elite Attitudes on European Integration and World Politics*. New York: Scribner's Sons, 1967.

Edwards, Geoffrey; Regelsberger, Elfriede. *Europe's Global Links: The EC and Inter-Regional Cooperation*. New York: St. Martin's, 1990.

Edwards, Geoffrey; Wallace, William. *A Wider EC? Issues and Problems of Further Enlargement*. London: Federal Trust for Education and Research, 1976.

Galtung, J. *The EC: A Superpower in the Making*. New York: Allen & Unwin, 1973.

Galtung, J. *Europe in the Making*. New York: Crane Russak, 1989.

Gazzo, Marina, ed. *Towards European Union*. 2 vols. Brussels: Agence Europe, 1985 and 1986.

George, Stephen. *Politics and Policy in the EC*. 2nd ed. Oxford: Clarendon Press, 1991.

Goodman, S. F. *The European Community*. New York: St. Martin's, 1990.

Guerrieri, P.; Padoan, P. *The Political Economy of European Integration: States, Markets and Institutions*. Savage, MD: Barnes & Noble, 1989.

Harrop, Jeffrey. *The Political Economy of Integration in the European Community*. 2nd ed. Aldershot, England: Edward Elgar, 1992.

Hodges, Michael. *European Integration*. Harmondsworth, England: Penguin, 1972.

Howell, Patton R. *War's End: The Revolution of Consciousness in the European Community*. San Francisco: Saybrook, 1989.

Hurwitz, Leon. *The EC and the Management of International Cooperation*. New York: Greenwood, 1987.

Hurwitz, Leon; Lequesne, Christian, eds. *The State of the European Community: Policies, Institutions, and Debates in the Transition Years*. Boulder, CO: Lynne Rienner, 1991.

Hurwitz, Leon, ed. *Contemporary Perspectives on European Integration*. Westport, CT: Greenwood, 1980.

Ionescu, Ghita. *The New Politics of European Integration*. London: Macmillan, 1972.

Ionescu, Ghita, ed. *The European Alternatives*. Alphen aan den Rijn, The Netherlands: Sijthoff & Noordhoff, 1979.

Kaiser, Karl, ed. *The European Community: Progress or Decline?* London: RIIA, 1983.

Keohane, Robert O.; Hoffmann, Stanley, eds. *The New European Community: Decision-making and Institutional Change*. Boulder, CO: Westview, 1991.

Kerr, J. C. *The Common Market and How It Works*. Oxford: Pergamon, 1977.

Kitzinger, Uwe. *The Challenge of the Common Market*. Oxford: Oxford University Press, 1961.

Kitzinger, Uwe. *The European Common Market and Community*. New York: Barnes & Noble, 1967.

Lane, Jan-Erik; Ersson, Evante O. *Politics and Society in Western Europe*. 2nd ed. Newbury Park, CA: Sage, 1991.

Lankowski, Carl. *Europe's Emerging Identity: Regional Integration and Opposition Movements in the European Community*. Boulder, CO: Lynne Rienner, 1992.

Lee, J. J., ed. *Europe in Transition: Political, Economic and Security Prospects in the 1990s*. Austin, TX: Lyndon Johnson School of Public Affairs, 1991.

Lintner, Valerio; Mazey, Sonia. *The European Community: Economic and Political Aspects*. Brussels: European Bookshop Ltd., 1991.

Lodge, Juliet, ed. *The European Community and the Challenge of the Future*. London: Pinter, 1989.

Lodge, Juliet, ed. *European Union: The European Community in Search of a Future*. London: Macmillan, 1986.

Ludlow, Peter. *The Making of the European Monetary System*. London: Butterworths, 1982.

Mackay, R. W. G. *Towards a United States of Europe*. Westport, CT: Greenwood, 1976.

Mayne, Richard. *The Community of Europe: Past, Present and Future*. New York: Norton, 1962.

Meade, James Edward, ed. *Case Studies in European Integration: The Mechanics of Integration*. Oxford: Oxford University Press, 1962.

Mendes, Pierre. *Une Vision du Monde 1974-82*. Paris: Gallimard, 1991.

Miljan, Toivo. *The Reluctant Europeans*. London: Hurst & Co., 1977.

Nelson, Brian; Roberts, David; Veit, Walter, eds. *The Idea of Europe: Problems of National and Transnational Identity*. Oxford: Berg, 1992.

Nicoll, William; Salmon, Trevor. *Understanding the European Communities*. London: Philip Allen, 1990.

Nugent, N. *The Government and Politics of the EC*. 2nd ed. Durham, NC: Duke University Press, 1992.

Nutting, Anthony. *Europe Will Not Wait*. London: Hollis & Carter, 1960.

Olson, Mancur. *The Rise and Decline of Nations*. New Haven, CT: Yale University Press, 1987.

Pijpers, Alfred. *The European Community at the Crossroads*. Dordrecht, The Netherlands: Martinus Nijhoff, 1992.

Pinder, John. *European Community: The Building of a Union*. Oxford: Oxford University Press, 1991.

Pryce, Roy. *The Politics of the EC*. London: Butterworths, 1973.

Pryce, Roy, ed. *The Dynamics of European Union*. London: Croom Helm, 1987.

Puchala, Donald J. *Fiscal Harmonization in the European Communities: National Politics and International Cooperation*. London: Pinter, 1984.

Puissochet, J. P. *The Enlargement of the European Communities*. Leiden, The Netherlands : A. W. Sijthoff, 1975.

Shonfield, Andrew. *Europe: Journey to an Unknown Destination*. London: Allan Lane, 1973.

Spinelli, Altiero. *The European Adventure: Tasks for the Enlarged Community*. London: Charles Knight, 1972.

Steinberg, Michael, ed. *The Technical Challenge and Opportunities of a United Europe*. Savage, MD: Barnes & Noble, 1990.

Strauss, Franz-Josef. *Challenge and Response: A Program for Europe.* New York: Atheneum, 1970.

Taylor, Paul. *The Limits of European Integration.* London: Croom Helm, 1983.

Treverton, Gregory, ed. *The Shape of the New Europe.* New York: Council on Foreign Relations, 1991.

Wallace, Helen. *Widening and Deepening: the European Community and the New European Agenda.* London: RIIA, 1989.

Wallace, William. *The Transformation of Western Europe.* London: RIIA, 1990.

Wallace, William; Wallace, Helen; Webb, Carole. *Policy-Making in the European Community.* 2nd ed. New York: Wiley, 1983.

Wallace, William, ed. *The Dynamics of European Integration.* London: Pinter, 1990.

Warnecke, Steven Joshua, ed. *The European Community in the 1970s.* New York: Praeger, 1972.

Willis, Roy. *European Integration.* New York: New Viewpoints, 1975.

IV. *External Relations*

Allen, David; Pijpers, Alfred. *European Foreign Policy Making and the Arab-Israeli Conflict.* The Hague: Martinus Nijhoff, 1984.

Allen, David; Rummel, Reinhardt; Wessels, Wolfgang. *European Political Cooperation: Towards a Foreign Policy for Western Europe?* London: Butterworth, 1982.

Alting von Geusau, Frans, ed. *The External Relations of the EC: Perspectives, Policies and Responses.* Lexington, MA: Lexington Books, 1974.

Alting von Geusau, Frans, ed. *The Lomé Convention and a New International Economic Order.* Leiden, The Netherlands: A.W. Sijthoff, 1977.

Andren, Nils; Biernbaum, Karl. *Beyond Détente: Prospects for East-West Cooperation and Security*. Leiden, The Netherlands: A. W. Sijthoff, 1976.

Angarita, C.; Coffey, P. *Europe and the Andean Countries: A Comparison of Economic Policies & Institutions*. London: Pinter, 1988.

Baldwin, R.; Hamilton, C.; Sapir, Andre, eds. *Issues in US-EC Trade Relations*. Chicago: University of Chicago Press, 1988.

Barfield, Claude E.; Perlman, Mark. *Industry, Services, and Agriculture in the 1990s: The United States Faces a New Europe*. Washington, DC: American Enterprise Institute, 1992.

Bethlen, Steven; Volgyer, Ivan, eds. *Europe and the Superpowers: Political, Economic, and Military Policies in the 1980s*. Boulder, CO: Westview, 1985.

Birnbaum, Karl. *The Politics of East-West Communication in Europe*. Farnborough, England: Saxon House, 1979.

Birrenbach, Kurt. *The Future Atlantic Community: Toward European-American Partnerships*. New York: Praeger, 1963.

Brandon, Henry, ed. *In Search of a New World Order: The Future of U.S.-European Relations*. Washington, DC: Brookings Institution, 1992.

Camps, Miriam. *The European Common Market and American Policy*. Princeton: Center of International Studies, Princeton University, 1956.

Chare, J.; Ravenal, E., eds. *Atlantis Lost: US-European Relations After the Cold-War*. New York: New York University Press, 1976.

Coffey, Peter. *The External Relations of the EEC*. London: Macmillan, 1976.

Coffey, Peter; Correa de Lago, L., eds. *The EEC and Brazil*. London: Pinter, 1988.

Coffey, Peter; Wionczek, M., eds. *The EEC and Mexico*. Dordrecht, The Netherlands: Martinus Nijhoff, 1987.

Cohen, Stephen D. *The EC and the GATT.* Washington, DC: EC Information Service, 1975.

Collins, Michael. *Western European Integration: Implications for US Policy and Strategy.* New York: Praeger, 1992.

Cooney, Stephen. *NAM Report on Developments in the European Community's Internal Market Program and the Effects on the US Manufacturers.* Annual Series. Washington, DC: National Association of Manufacturers, 1989.

Cosgrove, Carol; Twitchett, Kenneth. *The New International Actors: The UN and the EEC.* London: Macmillan, 1970.

Cromwell, William C. *The United States and the Atlantic Pillar: The Strained Alliance.* New York: St. Martin's, 1992.

Curzon, Victoria. *The Essentials of European Integration: Lessons from the EFTA Experience.* London: Macmillan, 1974.

Dahrendorf, Ralf; Sorensen, Theodore C.; Pierre, Andrew, eds. *A Widening Atlantic? Domestic Change and Foreign Policy.* New York: Council on Foreign Relations, 1986.

Davidson, Paul; Kregel, J. A., eds. *Economic Problems of the 1990s: Europe, the Developing Countries and the United States.* Brookfield, VT: Edward Elgar, 1991.

De Porte, Anton. *Europe Between the Superpowers: The Enduring Balance.* New Haven, CT: Yale University Press, 1979.

Dean, Vera Micheles. *Europe and the United States.* New York: Knopf, 1950.

Dyson, Kenneth, ed. *European Détente: Case Studies of the Politics of East-West Relations.* London: Pinter, 1986.

Edwards, Geoffrey; Regelsberger, Elfriede. *Europe's Global Links: The EC and Inter-Regional Cooperation.* New York: St. Martin's, 1990.

Evans, John. *The Kennedy Round in American Trade Policy: The Twilight of the GATT.* Cambridge, MA: Harvard University Press, 1971.

Everts, Philip. *The EC in the World*. Rotterdam: Rotterdam University Press, 1973.

Federal Trust Study Group. *The EC and the Developing Countries: A Policy for the Future*. London: Federal Trust, 1988.

Feld, Werner. *The European Community in World Affairs: Economic Power and Political Influence*. New York: Alfred, 1976.

Feld, Werner, ed. *The Foreign Policies of West European Socialist Parties*. New York: Praeger, 1978.

Freney, Michael; Hartley, Rebecca. *United Germany and the United States*. Washington, DC: National Planning Association, 1991.

Gautron, Jean-Claude, ed. *Les Relations Communauté Européenne: Europe de l'Est*. Paris: Economica, 1991.

Geiger, Theodore. *The Fortunes of the West*. Bloomington, IN: Indiana University Press, 1973.

Gianaris, Nicholas V. *The European Community and the United States: Economic Relations*. New York: Praeger, 1991.

Goodman, Elliott R. *The Fate of the Atlantic Community*. New York: Praeger, 1975.

Gordon, Colin, ed. *The Atlantic Alliance: A Bibliography*. London: Pinter, 1978.

Graubard, Stephen R., ed. *Eastern Europe-Central Europe-Europe*. Boulder, CO: Westview, 1991.

Griffith, William E. *Central and Eastern Europe: The Opening Curtain?* Boulder, CO: Westview, 1989.

Hanrieder, Wolfram. *Germany, America, Europe: Forty Years of German Foreign Policy*. New Haven, CT: Yale University Press, 1989.

Hill, Christopher, ed. *National Foreign Policies and EPC*. London: Allen & Unwin, 1983.

Hinshaw, R. *The EC and American Trade*. New York: Praeger, 1964.

Holland, Martin, ed. *The Future of European Political Cooperation.* New York: St. Martin's, 1991.

Hufbauer, Gary Clyde, ed. *Europe 1992: An American Perspective.* Washington, DC: Brookings Institution, 1990.

Ifestos, Panayiotis. *European Political Cooperation: Towards a Framework for Supranational Diplomacy.* Aldershot, England: Avebury, 1987.

Joffe, Josef. *The Limited Partnership: Europe, the United States and the Burdens of Alliance.* Cambridge, MA: Ballinger, 1987.

John, Ieuan G., ed. *EEC Policy Towards Eastern Europe.* Farnborough, England: Saxon House, 1975.

Jordan, Robert, ed. *Europe and the Superpowers: Perceptions of European International Politics.* Boston: Allyn & Bacon, 1971.

Kaiser, Karl; Schwartz, Hans-Peter, eds. *America and Western Europe: Problems and Prospects.* Lexington, MA: Lexington Books, 1979.

Kaser, Michael. *Comecon: Integration Problems of the Planned Economies.* 2nd ed. Oxford: Oxford University Press, 1967.

Kissinger, Henry A. *The Troubled Partnership.* New York: McGraw-Hill, 1965.

Kitzinger, Uwe. *The Politics and Economics of European Economic Integration: Britain, Europe and the United States.* New York: Praeger, 1963.

Kleiman, Robert. *Atlantic Crisis: American Diplomacy Confronts a Resurgent Europe.* New York: Norton, 1964.

Kohnstamm, Max; Hager, Wolfgang, eds. *A Nation Writ Large: Foreign Affairs Problems Before the EC.* New York: Wiley, 1973.

Laird, Robbin. *The Europeanization of the Alliance.* Boulder, CO: Westview, 1991.

Landes, David. *Western Europe: The Trials of Partnership.* Lexington, MA: Lexington Books, 1977.

Levine, Robert A., ed. *Transition and Turmoil in the Atlantic Alliance*. New York: Crane Russak, 1991.

Lippmann, Walter. *Western Unity and the Common Market*. Boston: Little, Brown & Co., 1962.

Lister, Marjorie. *The European Community and the Developing World: The Role of the Lomé Convention*. Aldershot, England: Avebury, 1988.

Ludlow, Peter. *Beyond 1992: Europe and Its World Partners*. Brussels: Center for European Policy Studies, 1989.

Mally, Gerhard. *The New Europe and the US*. Lexington, MA: Lexington Books, 1976.

Marjolin, Robert. *Europe and the US in the World Economy*. Durham, NC: Duke University Press, 1953.

Mennes, L. B. M.; Kol, Jacob. *European Trade Policies and the Developing World*. London: Croom Helm, 1988.

Merlini, Cesare. *The Community and the Emerging Democracies: A Government Policy Report*. London: RIIA, 1991.

Miljan, Toivo. *The Reluctant Europeans: The Attitudes of the Nordic Countries Towards European Integration*. Montreal: McGill University Press, 1977.

Moss, Joanna. *The Lomé Conventions and Their Implications for the US*. Boulder, CO: Westview, 1982.

Neustadt, Richard. *Alliance Politics*. New York: Columbia University Press, 1970.

Nuttall, Simon. *European Political Cooperation*. Oxford: Clarendon Press, 1992.

Palankai, Tibor. *The EC and Central European Integration: The Hungarian Case*. Boulder, CO: Westview, 1991.

Perle, Richard. *Reshaping Western Security: The United States Faces a United Europe*. Lanham, MD: University Press of America, 1991.

Peterson, John. *Europe and America in the 1990s: Prospects for Partnership*. Brookfield, VT: Edward Elgar, 1992.

Pijpers, Alfred; Regelsberger, Elfriede; Wessels, Wolfgang, eds. *European Political Cooperation in the 1980s: A Common Foreign Policy for Western Europe?* Dordrecht, The Netherlands: Martinus Nijhoff, 1989.

Pinder, John. *The European Community and Eastern Europe*. London: RIIA, 1991.

Pinder, John; Pinder, Pauline. *The EC Policy Towards Eastern Europe*. London: Chatham House, 1975.

Pomfret, Richard. *Mediterranean Policy of the EC: A Study of Discrimination in Trade*. London: Macmillan, 1986.

Porter, Michael. *The Competitive Advantage of Nations*. New York: The Free Press, 1990.

Portes, Richard. *The EC and Eastern Europe After 1992*. London: Center for European Policy Research, 1990.

Ransom, Charles. *The EC and Eastern Europe*. London: Butterworths, 1973.

Ravenhill, John. *Collective Clientelism: The Lomé Councils and North-South Relations*. New York: Columbia University Press, 1985.

Ruyt, Jean de. *European Political Cooperation: Toward a Unified European Foreign Policy*. Washington, DC: Atlantic Council of the United States, 1989.

Sandalow, Terrance; Stein, Eric. *Courts and Free Markets: Perspectives from the United States and Europe*. New York: Oxford University Press, 1982.

Schneider, Heinrich. *Austria and the EC*. London: RIIA, 1989.

Schoutheete, Phillippe de. *La Cooperation Politique Européenne*. Paris: Nathan, 1980.

Schwok, Rene. *U.S.-EC Relations in the Post-Cold War Era: Conflict or Partnership?* Boulder, CO: Westview, 1991.

Serfaty, Simon. *Fading Partnership: America and Europe After Thirty Years*. New York: Praeger, 1979.

Servan-Schreiber, J. J. *The American Challenge*. New York: Atheneum, 1968.

Shlaim, A.; Yannopoulos, G., eds. *The EEC and Eastern Europe*. New York: Columbia University Press, 1978.

Shlaim, A.; Yannopoulos, G., eds. *The EEC and the Mediterranean Countries*. Cambridge: Cambridge University Press, 1986.

Sjostedh, Gunner. *The External Role of the EC*. Farnborough, England: Saxon House, 1977.

Steenbergen, Jacques; Clercq, Guido de; Foque, René. *Change and Adjustment: External Relations and Industrial Policy in the EC*. Boston: Kluwer Law and Taxation, 1983.

Szita, Janos. *Perspectives for All-European Economic Integration*. Leiden, The Netherlands: A. W. Sijthoff, 1977.

Tovias, Alfred. *The European Community's Single Market: The Challenge of 1992 for Sub-Saharan Africa*. Washington, DC: The World Bank, 1990.

Tovias, Alfred. *Foreign Economic Relations of the European Community: The Impact of Spain and Portugal*. Boulder, CO: Lynne Rienner, 1990.

Treverton, Gregory. *America, Germany and the Future of Europe*. New York: Council on Foreign Relations, 1992.

Treverton, Gregory, ed. *Europe and America Beyond 2000*. London: RIIA, 1989.

Tsoukalis, Loukas. *Europe, America and the World Economy*. Oxford: Basil Blackwell, 1986.

Tulloch, Peter. *The Politics of Preferences*. London: Croom Helm, 1975.

Twitchett, Carol Cosgrove. *Europe and Africa: From Association to Partnership*. Farnborough, England: Teakfield, 1978.

Twitchett, Carol Cosgrove. *A Framework for Development: The EEC and the ACP*. London: Allen & Unwin, 1981.

Twitchett, Kenneth, ed. *Europe and the World: The External Relations of the Common Market*. London: Europa, 1976.

Tykkylainen, Markku, ed. *Development Issues and Strategies in the New Europe*. Brookfield, VT: Dartmouth, 1992.

United States Congress, House Committee on Foreign Affairs. *Europe and the United States: Competition and Cooperation in the 1990s*. Washington, DC: Government Printing Office, 1992.

United States International Trade Commission. *1992: The Effects of Greater Economic Integration Within the European Community on the United States*. Initial report and series of follow-up reports. Washington, DC: USITC, 1989.

Vree, Johan K. de; Coffey, Peter; Lauwaars, R. H.; Jensen, Max; Pijppers, Alfred; Volker, Edmond. *Towards a European Foreign Policy: Legal, Economic and Political Dimensions*. Boston: Martinus Nijhoff, 1987.

Wall, Irwin M. *The United States and the Making of Postwar France, 1945-54*. New York: Cambridge University Press, 1991.

Wallace, Helen; Wessels, Wolfgang. *Towards a New Partnership: The EC and EFTA in the Wider Western Europe*. Geneva: EFTA, 1990.

Wallace, Helen, ed. *The Wider Western Europe: Reshaping the EC/EFTA Relationship*. London: RIIA, 1991.

Wallace, William; Clarke, Roger A. *Comecon, Trade and the West*. London: Pinter, 1986.

Wasserman, M. J.; Hultman, C.; Moore, R. *The Common Market and American Business*. New York: Simmons-Boardman, 1964.

Williams, Phil. *US Troops in Europe*. London: Routledge & Kegan Paul for RIIA, 1984.

Woolcock, Stephen. *Trading Partners or Trading Blows? Market Access Issues in EC-US Relations*. London: RIIA, 1991.

Woolcock, Stephen; Hart, Jeffrey A.; Van der Ven, Hans.

Interdependence in the Post-Multilateral World: Trends in US-European Trade Relations. Cambridge, MA: Center for International Affairs, Harvard University, 1985.

Yannopoulos, George, ed. *Europe and America: 1992.* New York: Manchester University Press, 1991.

Zartman, William, ed. *Europe and Africa: The New Phase.* Boulder, CO: Lynne Rienner, 1992.

V. *History*

Acheson, Dean. *Present at the Creation: My Years in the State Department.* New York: Norton, 1969.

Acheson, Dean. *Sketches from Life of Men I Have Known.* New York: Harper, 1961.

Adenauer, Konrad. *Memoirs, 1945-1953.* Chicago: Regnery, 1966.

Aron, Raymond; Lerner, Daniel, eds. *France Defeats the European Defense Community.* New York: Praeger, 1957.

Ball, George W. *The Past Has Another Pattern.* New York: Norton, 1982.

Beloff, Max. *The United States and the Unity of Europe.* Washington, DC: Brookings Institution, 1963.

Beloff, Nora. *The General Says No.* London: Penguin, 1963.

Benn, Anthony. *Diaries, 1968-1972.* London: Hutchinson, 1988.

Bidault, G. *Resistance: The Political Biography of Georges Bidault.* New York: Praeger, 1967.

Bodenheimer, Susanne J. *Political Union: A Microcosm of European Politics, 1960-1966.* Leiden, The Netherlands: A. W. Sijthoff, 1967.

Bohlen, C. E. *Witness to History, 1929-1969.* New York: Norton, 1973.

Brandt, Willy. *People and Politics: The Years 1960-1975*. Boston: Little, Brown & Co., 1978.

Brinkley, Douglas; Hackett, Clifford, eds. *Jean Monnet: The Path to European Unity*. New York: St. Martin's, 1991.

Bromberger, Merry; Bromberger, Serge. *Jean Monnet and the United States of Europe*. New York: Coward-McCann, 1969.

Bullen, Roger; Pelly, M. E. *The Schuman Plan, the Council of Europe and Western European Integration*. London: HMSO, 1986.

Bullock, Alan. *Ernest Bevin: Foreign Secretary, 1948-1951*. London: Heinemann, 1983.

Burgess, Michael. *Federalism and European Union: Political Ideas, Influences and Strategies in the European Community, 1972-1987*. London: Routledge, 1989.

Butler, Michael. *Europe: More Than a Continent*. London: Heinemann, 1986.

Butler, Richard Austen. *The Art of the Possible: The Memoirs of Lord Butler*. Boston: Gambit, 1972.

Byrnes, James Francis. *Speaking Frankly*. New York: Harper, 1947.

Callaghan, James. *Time and Change*. London: Collins, 1987.

Campbell, John. *Roy Jenkins: A Biography*. London: Weidenfeld & Nicolson, 1983.

Camps, Miriam. *The European Common Market and the Free Trade Area*. Princeton: Center for International Studies, Princeton University, 1957.

Camps, Miriam. *European Unification in the Sixties: From the Veto to the Crisis*. New York: McGraw-Hill, 1966.

Camps, Miriam. *What Kind of Europe? The Community Since de Gaulle's Veto*. Oxford: Oxford University Press, 1966.

Couve de Murville, Maurice. *Une Politique Etrangère, 1958-1969*. Paris: Plon, 1971.

De Gaulle, Charles. *Memoirs of Hope: Renewal and Endeavor*. New York: Simon & Schuster, 1971.

De Menil, Lois Pattison. *Who Speaks for Europe? The Vision of Charles de Gaulle*. London: Weidenfeld & Nicolson, 1977.

Destler, Irving M. *Political Union in Europe: 1960-1962*. Princeton: Woodrow Wilson School of Public and International Affairs, 1967.

Fursdon, Edward. *The European Defence Community: A History*. London: Macmillan, 1980.

Giles, Frank. *The Locust Years*. New York: Secker & Warburg, 1991.

Gillingham, John. *Coal, Steel and the Rebirth of Europe, 1945-1955*. Cambridge: Cambridge University Press, 1991.

Gimbel, John. *The Origins of the Marshall Plan*. Stanford: Stanford University Press, 1968.

Gorley, James L. *The Collapse of the Grand Alliance, 1945-48*. Baton Rouge, LA: Louisiana State University Press, 1987.

Griffith, Richard; Milward, Alan. *The Beyen Plan and the European Political Community*. Florence: European University Institute, 1985.

Grosser, Alfred. *The Foreign Policy of the Fifth Republic*. Boston: Little, Brown & Co., 1967.

Grosser, Alfred. *Les Occidentaux*. Paris: Fayard, 1978.

Grosser, Alfred. *The Western Alliance: European-American Relations Since 1945*. New York: Vintage, 1982.

Hallstein, Walter. *Europe in the Making*. London: Allen & Unwin, 1972.

Hanrieder, Wolfram. *Germany, America, Europe: Forty Years of German Foreign Policy*. New Haven, CT: Yale University Press, 1989.

Healey, Denis. *The Time of My Life*. London: Joseph, 1989.

Heller, Francis H.; Gillingham, John. *NATO: The Founding of the*

Atlantic Alliance and the Integration of Europe. New York: St. Martin's, 1992.

Henderson, William Otto. *The Genesis of the Common Market*. Chicago: Quadrangle, 1962.

Hoffmann, Stanley; Maier, Charles, eds. *The Marshall Plan: A Retrospective*. Boulder, CO: Westview, 1984.

Hogan, Michael. *The Marshall Plan: America, Britain and the Reconstruction of Western Europe, 1947-1952*. Cambridge: Cambridge University Press, 1987.

Horne, Alistair. *Harold Macmillan, 1957-1986*. New York: Penguin, 1989.

Howard, Anthony. *Rab: The Life of R. A. Butler*. London: Cape, 1987.

Jansen, Max. *A History of European Integration, 1945-1975*. Amsterdam: Europa Institut, 1975.

Jenkins, Roy. *European Diary, 1977-1981*. London: Collins, 1989.

Jenkins, Roy. *Life at the Center*. London: Macmillan, 1991.

Jensen, Finn B. *The Common Market: Economic Integration in Europe*. Philadelphia: Lippincott, 1965.

Kennan, George. *Memoirs, 1925-1950*. Boston: Little, Brown & Co., 1967.

Kissinger, Henry. *White House Years*. Boston: Little, Brown & Co., 1979.

Kramer, Alan. *The West German Economy, 1945-55*. Manchester: Manchester University Press, 1991.

Lacouture, Jean. *De Gaulle: The Ruler, 1945-1970*. London: Collins Harvill, 1991.

Laqueur, Walter. *Europe Since Hitler: The Rebirth of Europe*. Revised ed. New York: Penguin, 1982.

Levi, Lucio, ed. *Altiero Spinelli and Federalism in Europe and the*

World. London: Lothian Foundation, 1991.

Lipgens, Walter. *History of European Integration*. 2 vols. London: Oxford University Press, 1981 and 1986.

Ludlow, Peter. *The Making of the European Monetary System*. London: Butterworths, 1982.

Machlop, Fritz. *A History of Thought on Economic Integration*. London: Macmillan, 1977.

Macmillan, Harold. *At the End of the Day, 1961-1963*. New York: Harper & Row, 1973.

Macmillan, Harold. *Pointing the Way, 1959-1961*. New York: Harper & Row, 1972.

Macmillan, Harold. *Riding the Storm, 1956-1959*. New York: Harper & Row, 1971.

Macridis, Roy C. *De Gaulle: Implacable Ally*. New York: Harper & Row, 1966.

Macridis, Roy C. *French Politics in Transition: The Years After de Gaulle*. Cambridge, MA: Winthrop, 1975.

Maier, Charles S., ed. *The Cold War in Europe: Era of a Divided Continent*. New York: Markus Wiener, 1991.

Margairaz, Michel. *L'Etat, les finances et l'économie: Histoire d'une conversion 1932-52*. Paris: Ministère de L'Economie, des finances et du budget, 1992.

Marjolin, Robert. *Architect of European Union: Memoirs, 1911-1986*. London: Weidenfeld & Nicolson, 1989.

Mayne, Richard. *Federal Union: The Pioneers*. London: Macmillan, 1990.

Mayne, Richard. *Postwar: The Dawn of Today's Europe*. New York: Schocken, 1983.

Mayne, Richard. *The Recovery of Europe: From Devastation to Unity*. London: Weidenfeld & Nicolson, 1970.

McGhee, George. *At the Creation of a New Germany: From Adenauer to Brandt: An Ambassador's Account.* New Haven, CT: Yale University Press, 1989.

Meade, James Edward. *Negotiations for Benelux: An Annotated Chronicle 1943-56.* Princeton: Princeton University Press, 1957.

Milward, Alan. *The Reconstruction of Western Europe, 1945-51.* London: Methuen, 1983.

Monnet, Jean. *Memoirs.* Garden City: Doubleday, 1978.

Morgan, Annette. *From Summit to Council: Evolution of the EC.* European Series. London: Chatham House, 1976.

Morgan, Roger. *West European Politics Since 1945: The Shaping of the European Community.* London: Batsford, 1972.

Morse, Edward L. *Foreign Policy and Interdependence in Gaullist France.* Princeton: Princeton University Press, 1973.

Mowat, R. C. *Creating the European Community.* New York: Harper & Row, 1973.

Newhouse, John. *Collision in Brussels: The Common Market Crisis of 30 June 1965.* New York: Norton, 1967.

Newhouse, John. *De Gaulle and the Anglo-Saxons.* London: Deutsch, 1970.

Nicholson, F.; East, R. *From the Six to the Twelve: The Enlargement of the European Communities.* Harlow, England: Longman, 1987.

Ovendale, Richard. *Foreign Policy of the British Labour Government, 1945-1951.* London: Pinter, 1984.

Pickles, Dorothy. *The Uneasy Entente: French Foreign Policy and Franco-British Misunderstandings.* Chatham House Essays. New York: Oxford University Press, 1966.

Pinder, John; Pryce, Roy. *Europe After de Gaulle: Towards a United States of Europe.* London: Penguin, 1969.

Pogue, Forrest. *George C. Marshall: Statesman, 1945-1959.* New York: Viking Press, 1987.

Poidevin, Raymond. *Robert Schuman: Homme d'Etat, 1866-1963*. Paris: Imprimerie Nationale, 1986.

Poidevin, Raymond, ed. *Origins of European Integration: March 1948-May 1950*. Brussels: Bruylant, 1986.

Pollard, Robert A. *Economic Security and the Origins of the Cold War, 1945-50*. New York: Columbia University Press, 1985.

Pollard, Sidney. *European Economic Integration, 1815-1970*. London: Thames & Hudson, 1974.

Pompidou, Georges. *To Reestablish a Truth*. Paris: Flammarion, 1982.

Ransome, Patrick, ed. *Towards the United States of Europe: Studies in the Making of the European Community*. London: Lothian Foundation, 1991.

Rassieri, Ruggiero. *Italy and the Schuman Plan Negotiations*. Florence: European University Institute, 1986.

Ridley, Nicholas. *My Style of Government: The Thatcher Years*. London: Hutchinson, 1991.

Rosenthal, Glenda. *The Men Behind the Decisions*. Farnborough, England: Teakfield for Lexington Books, 1975.

Rothwell, Victor. *Anthony Eden: A Political Biography, 1931-1957*. Manchester: Manchester University Press, 1992.

Schlesinger, Arthur. *A Thousand Days: John F. Kennedy in the White House*. Boston: Houghton Mifflin, 1965.

Schmidt, Hans A. *European Union: From Hitler to de Gaulle*. New York: Reinhold, 1969.

Schmidt, Helmut. *The Path to European Union: From the Marshall Plan to the Common Market*. Baton Rouge, LA: Louisiana State University Press, 1962.

Schwartz, Thomas A. *America's Germany: John J. McCloy and the Federal Republic of Germany*. Cambridge, MA: Harvard University Press, 1991.

Serfaty, Simon. *France, de Gaulle and Europe: The Policy of the Fourth and Fifth Republics Toward the Continent.* Baltimore: Johns Hopkins University Press, 1968.

Simonian, Haig. *The Privileged Partnership: Franco-German Relations and the European Community, 1969-1984.* Oxford: Clarendon Press, 1985.

Spinelli, Altiero. *The Eurocrats: Conflict and Crisis in the European Community.* Baltimore: Johns Hopkins University Press, 1966.

Stirk, Peter M. R. *European Unity in Context: The Interwar Period.* New York: Pinter, 1989.

Stirk, Peter; Willis, David, eds. *Shaping Postwar Europe: European Unity and Diversity, 1945-1957.* New York: St. Martin's, 1991.

Tsoukalis, Loukas. *The Politics and Economics of European Monetary Integration.* London: Allen & Unwin, 1977.

Tugendhat, Christopher. *Making Sense of Europe.* New York: Penguin, 1986.

Urwin, Derek W. *The Community of Europe: A History of European Integration Since 1945.* New York: Longman, 1991.

Van der Beugel, E. H. *From Marshall Aid to Atlantic Partnership: European Integration as a Concern of American Foreign Policy.* Amsterdam: Elsevier, 1966.

Vaughan, Richard. *Post-War Integration in Europe.* London: Edward Arnold, 1976.

Von der Groeben, Hans. *The European Community: The Formative Years: The Struggle to Establish the Common Market and the Political Union (1958-1966).* European Perspectives Series. Luxembourg: Office for Official Publications of the European Communities, 1987.

Wexler, Imanuel. *The Marshall Plan Revisited.* Westport, CT: Greenwood, 1983.

White, Theodore H. *Fire in the Ashes: Europe in Mid-Century.* New York: Sloan, 1953.

Williams, Philip. *Hugh Gaitskell: A Political Biography*. London: Cape, 1979.

Willis, Roy. *European Integration*. New York: New Viewpoints, 1975.

Willis, Roy. *France, Germany and the New Europe*. 2nd ed. Stanford: Stanford University Press, 1968.

Wilson, Harold. *The Labour Government*. London: Weidenfeld & Nicolson, 1971.

Wilson, Harold. *A Personal Record: The Labour Government, 1964-1970*. Boston: Little, Brown & Co., 1971.

Young, John W. *Britain, France and the Unity of Europe, 1945-1951*. Leicester, England: Leicester University Press, 1984.

Zurcher, Arnold. *The Struggle to Unite Europe, 1940-1958*. New York: New York University Press, 1958.

VI. *Institutions and Decision Making*

Bieber, Roland; Jacque, Jean-Paul; Weiler, Joseph, eds. *An Ever Closer Union: A Critical Analysis of the Draft Treaty on European Union*. European Perspective Series. Luxembourg: Office for Official Publications of the European Communities, 1985.

Brown, Neville L.; Jacobs, Francis G. *The Court of Justice of the European Communities*. London: Sweet & Maxwell, 1977.

Bulmer, Simon; Wessels, Wolfgang. *The European Council: Decision-Making in European Politics*. London: Macmillan, 1987.

Cahan, Alfred. *The WEU and NATO: Strengthening the Second Pillar of the Alliance*. Washington, DC: Atlantic Council, 1990.

Capotorti, Francesco; Hils, Meinhardt; Jacobs, Francis; Jacque, Jean-Paul, eds., *The European Union Treaty: Commentary on the Draft Adopted by the European Parliament on 14 February 1984*. Oxford: Clarendon Press, 1986.

Coombes, David. *Politics and Bureaucracy in the European*

Communities. London: Allen & Unwin, 1970.

Coombes, David. *The Power of the Purse: The Role of the European Parliament in Budgetary Decisions.* London: Allen & Unwin, 1976.

De Bassompierre, Guy. *Changing the Guard in Brussels: An Insider's View of the EC Presidency.* New York: Praeger, 1988.

Edwards, Geoffrey; Wallace, Helen. *The Council of Ministers of the EC and the President in Office.* London: Federal Trust, 1977.

Fraser, Robert. *Western European Economic Organizations.* Brussels: European Bookshop Ltd., 1991.

Harrop, Jeffrey. *The Political Economy of Integration in the European Community.* 2nd ed. Aldershot, England: Edward Elgar, 1992.

Henig, Stanley. *Power and Decision in Europe: The Political Institutions of the EC.* London: Europotentials, 1980.

Hoscheit, Jean-Marc; Wessels, Wolfgang. *The European Council 1974-86: Evaluation and Prospects.* Maastricht: European Institute of Public Administration, 1988.

Jacobs, F.; Corbett, R. *The European Parliament.* Boulder, CO: Westview, 1990.

Jamar, J.; Wessels, W., eds. *Community Bureaucracy at the Crossroads.* Bruges: College of Europe, 1985.

Jouve, Edmond. *Le Général de Gaulle et la Construction de l'Europe (1940-1966).* Paris: Librarie Général de Droit, 1967.

Kirchner, Emil. *Decision-Making in the European Community: The Council Presidency and European Integration.* New York: St. Martin's, 1992.

Lehne, Stefan. *The Vienna Meeting of the CSCE, 1986-89.* Boulder, CO: Westview, 1991.

Locourt, Robert. *L'Europe des Juges.* Brussels: Bruylant, 1976.

Lodge, Juliet. *Direct Elections to the European Parliament, 1984.* London: Macmillan, 1986.

Lodge, Juliet; Herman, Valentine. *Direct Elections to the European Parliament: A Community Perspective*. London: Macmillan, 1982.

Lodge, Juliet, ed. *European Union: The European Community in Search of a Future*. London: Macmillan, 1986.

Lodge, Juliet, ed. *The 1989 Elections to the European Parliament*. London: Macmillan, 1990.

Ludlow, Peter. "The European Commission." In Robert O. Keohane and Stanley Hoffmann, eds., *The New European Community: Decision-making and Institutional Change*. Boulder, CO: Westview, 1991.

Marquand, David. *Parliament for Europe*. London: Cape, 1979.

Morgan, Annette. *From Summit to Council: Evolution in the EEC*. London: RIIA, 1976.

Noël, Emile. *Working Together: The Institutions of the EC*. Luxembourg: Office for Official Publications of the European Communities, 1988.

O'Nuallain, Colin. *The President of the European Council of Ministers: Impacts and Implications for National Governments*. London: Croom Helm, 1985.

Palmer, Michael. *The European Parliament*. New York: Pergamon, 1981.

Plumb, Lord. *Building A Democratic Community: The Role of the European Parliament*. London: Lothian Foundation, 1991.

Pridham, Geoffrey; Pridham, Pippa. *Transnational Party Groups in the European Parliament and European Integration: The Process Towards Direct Elections*. London: Allen & Unwin, 1981.

Sasse, Christopher. *Decision-Making in the EC*. New York: Praeger, 1977.

Sbragia, Alberta, ed. *Euro-Politics: Institutions and Policymaking in the "New" European Community*. Washington, DC: Brookings Institution, 1992.

Wallace, Helen. *National Governments and the European*

Bibliography

Community. London: RIIA, 1973.

Werts, Jan. *The European Council.* Amsterdam: North Holland, 1992.

Wilke, Marc; Wallace, Helen. *Subsidiarity: Approaches to Power-Sharing in the EC.* London: RIIA, 1990.

Wood, Alan; Wood, David. *The Times Guide to the European Parliament, June 1984.* London: Times Books, 1985.

VII. *Member States, Politics, and Political Movements*

Barnouin, Barbara. *The European Labor Movement and European Integration.* London: Pinter, 1986.

The British Application for Membership in the EC, 1963-1968. Paris: Western European Union, 1968.

Bruneau, Thomas C.; Da Rosa, Victor; Macleod, Alexandre. *Portugal in Development: Emigration, Industrialization, and the European Community.* Ottawa: University of Ottawa Press, 1991.

Brunt, Barry. *The Republic of Ireland.* London: Clapman, 1988.

Buckley, M.; Anderson, M. *Women, Equality and Europe.* London: Macmillan, 1988.

Bulmer, Simon. *The Domestic Structure of EC Policy-Making in West Germany.* New York: Garland, 1986.

Bulmer, Simon; Patterson, Willie. *The Federal Republic of Germany and the EC.* London: Allen & Unwin, 1987.

Butler, David; Marquand, David. *European Elections and British Politics.* London: Longman, 1981.

Campbell, Edwina S. *Germany's Past and Europe's Future: The Challenge of West Germany's Foreign Policy.* Washington, DC: Pergamon-Brassey's, 1989.

Camps, Miriam. *Britain and the European Community.* Princeton:

Princeton University Press, 1964.

Carrilo, Santiago. *Europeanism and the State.* London: Lawrence & Wishart, 1977.

Clarke, Michael. *British External Policy-Making in the 1990s.* Washington, DC: Brookings Institution, 1992.

Clogg, Richard, ed. *Greece in the 1980s.* London: Macmillan, 1983.

Crouch, Colin; Marquand, David. *The New Centrism: Britain out of Step in Europe?* Oxford: Blackwell, 1989.

Featherstone, K. *Socialist Parties and European Integration.* Manchester: Manchester University Press, 1988.

Featherstone, K.; Katsoudas, D., eds. *Political Change in Greece, Before and After the Colonels.* London: Croom Helm, 1987.

Feld, Werner. *West Germany and the EC: Changing Interests and Competing Policy Options.* New York: Praeger, 1981.

Fitzmaurice, John. *Party Groups in the European Parliament.* Lexington, MA: Lexington Books, 1975.

Franklin, Michael. *Britain's Future in Europe.* London: RIIA, 1990.

Franklin, Michael; Wilke, Marc. *Britain in the EC.* London: RIIA, 1991.

Freney, Michael; Hartley, Rebecca. *United Germany and the United States.* Washington, DC: National Planning Association, 1991.

Fritsch-Bournazel, Renata. *Europe and German Reunification.* Oxford: Berg, 1991.

Gatzke, H.W. *Germany and the US: "A Special Relationship?"* Cambridge: Harvard University Press, 1980.

George, Stephen. *An Awkward Partner: Britain in the European Community.* Oxford: Clarendon Press, 1990.

George, Stephen, ed. *Britain and the European Community: The Politics of Semi-Detachment.* Oxford: Clarendon Press, 1992.

Gregory, Francis Edward Coulton. *Dilemmas of Government: Britain and the EC*. Cambridge, MA: Basil Blackwell, 1983.

Hall, Peter A.; Haywards, Jack; Machin, Howard, eds. *Developments in French Politics*. New York: St. Martin's, 1990.

Harrison, Michael. *The Reluctant Ally: France and Atlantic Security*. Baltimore: Johns Hopkins University Press, 1981.

Heath, Edward. *Old World, New Horizons: Britain, the Common Market and the Atlantic Alliance*. Cambridge: Cambridge University Press, 1970.

Henig, Stanley; Pinder, John. *European Political Parties*. London: Allen & Unwin, 1970.

Henig, Stanley, ed. *Political Parties in the European Community*. London: Allen & Unwin, 1979.

Hood, Christopher. *Beyond the Bureaucratic State: Public Administration in the 1990s*. London: London School Of Economics, 1990.

Kindersly, Richard, ed. *In Search of Eurocommunism*. London: Macmillan, 1981.

Kirchner, Emil; Sperling, James, eds. *The Federal Republic of Germany and NATO*. New York: St. Martin's, 1992.

Kohl, Wilfred L.; Basevi, Giorgio. *West Germany: A European and Global Power*. Lexington, MA: Lexington Books, 1980.

Kolinsky, Martin; Peterson, William, eds. *Social and Political Movements in Western Europe*. New York: St. Martin's, 1976.

Lange, Peter; Vannicelli, Maurizio. *The Communist Parties of Italy, France and Spain: Postwar Change and Continuity, A Casebook*. London: Allen & Unwin, 1981.

Langgutt, Gerd. *Berlin and the German Question*. Boulder, CO: Westview, 1989.

Leaman, Jeremy. *The Political Economy of West Germany, 1945-85: An Introduction*. London: Macmillan, 1987.

Loriause, Michael. *France After Hegemony: International Change and Financial Reform.* Ithaca, NY: Cornell University Press, 1992.

Maxwell, Kenneth, ed. *Spanish Foreign and Defense Policy.* San Francisco: Westview, 1991.

Mazery, Sonia; Newman, Michael. *Mitterrand's France.* London: Croom Helm, 1987.

Moncrieff, Anthony, ed. *Britain and the Common Market, 1967.* London: BBC Publications, 1967.

Moreton, Edwina, ed. *Germany Between East and West.* Cambridge: Cambridge University Press, 1987.

Morgan, Roger; Bray, Caroline, eds. *Partners and Rivals in Western Europe: Britain, France, Germany.* Aldershot, England: Gower, 1986.

O'Neill, Francis. *The French Radical Party and European Integration.* New York: St. Martin's, 1981.

Oudenhove, Guy van. *The Political Parties in the European Community.* Leiden, The Netherlands: A. W. Sijthoff, 1965.

Paterson, William. *The SPD and European Integration.* Lexington, MA: Lexington Books, 1974.

Pinder, John. *The Economies of Europe: What the Common Market Means to Britain.* London: Knight, 1971.

Pollack, Benny. *The Paradox of Spanish Foreign Policy: Spain's International Relations from Francoism to Democracy.* London: Pinter, 1987.

Pridham, Geoffrey; Pridham, Pippa. *Transnational Party Groups in the European Parliament and European Integration: The Process Towards Direct Elections.* London: Allen & Unwin, 1981.

Richardson, James L. *Germany and the Atlantic Alliance: The Interaction of Strategy and Politics.* Cambridge, MA: Harvard University Press, 1966.

Ross, George; Hoffmann, Stanley; Malzacher, Sylvia. *The Mitterrand Experiment: Continuity and Change in Modern France.*

Cambridge, England: Polity, 1987.

Rotfield, Adam D.; Stutzle, Walter, eds. *Germany and Europe in Transition*. Oxford: Oxford University Press, 1991.

Sharp, Paul. *Irish Foreign Policy and the European Community*. Aldershot, England: Gower, 1990.

Smyser, W. R. *The Economy of United Germany: Colossus at the Crossroads*. New York: St. Martin's, 1992.

Sowden, John Kenneth. *The German Question, 1945-73: Continuity in Change*. New York: St. Martin's, 1975.

Stares, Paul B., ed. *New Germany and the New Europe*. Washington, DC: Brookings Institution, 1992.

Treverton, Gregory. *America, Germany and the Future of Europe*. New York: Council on Foreign Relations, 1992.

Tsoukalis, Loukas. *The EC and Its Mediterranean Enlargement*. London: Allen & Unwin, 1981.

Twitchett, Kenneth; Twitchett, Carol, eds. *Building Europe: Britain's Partners in the EC*. London: Europa Publications, 1981.

Tykkylainen, Markku, ed. *Development Issues and Strategies in the New Europe*. Brookfield, VT: Dartmouth, 1992.

Vallance, E.; Davies, E. *Women of Europe: Women MEPs and Equality Policy*. New York: Columbia University Press, 1986.

Wallace, William. *Britain's Bilateral Links Within Western Europe*. London: Routledge & Kegan Paul, for RIIA, 1984.

Wallace, William, ed. *Britain in Europe*. London: Heinemann, 1980.

Windsor, Philip. *Germany and the Management of Détente*. New York: Praeger, 1971.

Woolcock, Steven; Hodges, Michael; Schreiber, Kristin. *Britain, Germany and 1992: The Limits of Deregulation*. London: RIIA, 1991.

VIII. *Policies and Programs*

Agnew, J. *Competition Law*. London: Allen & Unwin, 1985.

Audretsch, H.R.H. *Supervision in EC Law*. Amsterdam: North Holland, 1978.

Bakhoven, A.E. *The Completion of the Common Market in 1992*. The Hague: Martinus Nijhoff, 1989.

Barounos D.; Hall, D. F.; Jones, J.R. *EEC Antitrust Law*. London: Butterworths, 1975.

Barzanti, Sergio. *The Underdeveloped Areas Within the Common Market*. Princeton: Princeton University Press, 1965.

Beije, Paul R., ed. *A Competitive Future for Europe? Towards a New European Industrial Policy*. London: Croom Helm, 1987.

Bellamy, Christopher. *Common Market Law of Competition*. 3rd ed. London: Sweet & Maxwell, 1987.

Bliss, Christopher; Macedo, Jorge de. *Unity and Diversity in the European Economy*. London: Center for European Policy Research, 1990.

Brealey, Mark; Quigley, Conor. *Completing the Internal Market of the EC: 1992 Handbook*. Dordrecht, The Netherlands: Klewer, 1992.

Brebner & Co. *Setting Up a Company in the European Community: A Country by Country Guide*. Phoenix, AZ: Oryx Press, 1989.

Bredimas, Anna. *Methods of Interpretation and Community Law*. Amsterdam: North Holland, 1978.

Burrows, F. *Free Movement in EC Law*. Oxford: Clarendon Press, 1987.

Cahen, Alfred. *The Western European Union (WEU) and NATO: Strengthening the Second Pillar of the Alliance*. Washington, DC: Atlantic Council of the United States, 1990.

Calingaert, Michael. *The 1992 Challenge from Europe: Development of the European Community's Internal Market*. Washington, DC:

National Planning Association, 1988.

Cecchini, Paolo. *The European Challenge 1992: The Benefits of a Single Market*. Aldershot, England: Wildwood House, 1988.

Coffey, Peter, ed. *Main Economic Policy Areas of the EEC Toward 1992*. 3rd ed. Dordrecht, The Netherlands: Kluwer, 1990.

Creasey, Pauline; May, Simon, eds. *The European Armaments Industry and Procurement Cooperation*. London: Macmillan, 1988.

Daiffill, John; Beber, Massimo, eds. *A Currency for Europe*. London: Lothian Foundation, 1991.

Daltrop, Anne. *Politics and the EC*. 2nd ed. New York: Longman, 1987.

Danspeckgruber, Wolfgang, ed. *Emerging Dimensions of European Security Policy*. Boulder, CO: Westview, 1991.

De Cecco, Marcello; Giovannini, Alberto, eds. *A European Central Bank: Perspectives on Moving Unification After Ten Years of EMS*. London: Center for European Policy Research, 1989.

Diebold, William. *The Schuman Plan: A Study in Economic Cooperation, 1950-1959*. New York: Praeger, 1959.

Drury, Robert; Xuereb, Peter, eds. *European Community Laws: A Comparative Approach*. Brookfield, VT: Dartmouth, 1990.

Duchene, Francois; Szczepanik, Edward; Legg, Wilfrid. *New Limits on European Agriculture: Politics and the Common Agricultural Policy*. London: Croom Helm, 1985.

Easson, Alexander James. *Tax Law and Policy in the EEC*. London: Sweet & Maxwell, 1980.

Emerson, Michael. *The Economics of 1992*. Oxford: Oxford University Press, 1988.

Erdmenger, J. *EC Transport Policy*. Aldershot, England: Gower Press, 1983.

Euromonitor Publications Limited. *The Single Market Handbook*. London: Euromonitor Publications Ltd., 1990.

Farrell, John; Elles, James. *In Search of a Common Fisheries Policy.* Aldershot, England: Gower, 1984.

Fennell, Rosemary. *The Common Agricultural Policy of the European Community.* London: Granada, 1979.

Folsom, Ralph H. *European Community Law.* St. Paul, MN: West, 1991.

Fonseca-Wollheim, H. *Ten Years of EPC.* Brussels: EC Commission, 1981.

Fratianni, Michele; Peeters, Theo. *One Money for Europe.* London: Macmillan, 1978.

Fratianni, Michele; Von Hagen, Juergen. *The EMS and EMU.* Boulder, CO: Westview, 1991.

Freeman, Christopher; Sharp, Margaret; Walker, William. *Technology and the Future of Europe: Global Competition and the Environment in the 1990.* London: Pinter, 1991.

George, Kenneth Desmond; Joll, Caroline. *Competition Policy in the UK and the EEC.* New York: Columbia University Press, 1975.

Giavazzi, Francesco; Micossi, Stefano; Miller, Marcus, eds. *The European Monetary System.* Cambridge: Cambridge University Press, 1988.

Ginsberg, Roy. *Foreign Policy Actions of the European Community: The Politics of Scale.* Boulder, CO: Lynne Rienner, 1989.

Giovanni, Alberto; Mayer, Colin. *European Financial Integration.* London: Center for European Policy Research, 1991.

Goodman, John B. *Monetary Sovereignty: The Politics of Central Banking in Western Europe.* Ithaca, NY: Cornell University Press, 1992.

Gowland, David; James, Stephen, eds. *Economic Policy After 1992.* Brookfield, VT: Dartmouth, 1991.

Green, Nicholas; Hartley, Trevor; Usher, John. *The Legal Foundations of the Single European Market.* Oxford: Oxford University Press, 1991.

Hagland, David G. *Alliance Within the Alliance? Franco-German Cooperation and the European Pillar of Defense.* Boulder, CO: Westview, 1991.

Hall, Graham, ed. *European Industrial Policy.* London: Croom Helm, 1986.

Hathaway, Dale E. *Agriculture and the GATT: Rewriting the Rules.* Washington, DC: Institute for International Economics, 1987.

Haughwont Folson, Ralph. *Corporate Competition Law in the EC.* Lexington, MA: Heath, 1978.

Hewstone, Malcolm. *Understanding the Attitudes of European Integration.* Cambridge: Cambridge University Press, 1986.

Hill, Brian E. *The Common Agricultural Policy: Past, Present and Future.* London: Methuen, 1984.

Hine, R.C. *The Political Economy of European Trade: An Introduction to the Trade Policies of the EEC.* New York: St. Martin's, 1985.

Hufbauer, Gary Clyde. *The New Europe in the World Economy.* Washington, DC: Institute for International Economics, 1992.

Hyde-Price, Adrian. *European Security Beyond the Cold War.* London: RIIA, 1991.

Jackson, Robert. *The Powers of the European Parliament.* London: The Conservative Group for Europe, 1977.

Jacobs, F. G., ed. *Yearbook of European Law.* Oxford: Clarendon Press, 1987.

Joffe, Josef. *The Limited Partnership: Europe, the United States and the Burdens of Alliance.* Cambridge, MA: Ballinger, 1987.

Johnson, Peter, ed. *The Structure of European Industry.* Brookfield, VT: Edward Elgar, 1992.

Johnson, Stanley P.; Corcelli, Guy. *The Environmental Policy of the EC.* London: Graham & Trotman, 1991.

Jopp, Mathias; Rummel, Reinhardt; Schmidt, Peter, eds. *Integration and Security in Western Europe: Inside the European Pillar.* Boulder, CO: Westview, 1991.

Jovanovic, Miroslav N. *International Economic Integration.* New York: Routledge, 1992.

Keating, Michael; Jones, Barry, eds. *Regions in the EC.* Oxford: Oxford University Press, 1985.

Keatinge, Patrick, ed. *Political Union.* Studies in European Union. Dublin: Institute of European Affairs, 1991.

Keeble, D.; Wever, E. *New Firms and Regional Development in Europe.* London: Croom Helm, 1986.

Kennedy, Ellen. *The Bundesbank: Germany's Central Bank in the International Monetary System.* London: RIIA, 1991.

Kent, Penelope. *European Community Law.* London: Pitman, 1992.

Keohane, Robert O. *After Hegemony: Cooperation and Discord in the World Political Economy.* Princeton: Princeton University Press, 1984.

King, Kenneth. *US Monetary Policy and European Responses in the 1980s.* London: RIIA, 1982.

Kirby, Stephen; McNeill, Terry; Harris, Sally. *Europe After the Gulf War: Reassessing Security Options.* Cheltenham, England: Edward Elgar, 1992.

Kirschen, E.; Bloch, H.; Bassett, W. *Financial Integration in Western Europe.* New York: Columbia University Press, 1969.

Klein, M. W.; Welfens, P. J. J., eds. *Multinationals in the New Europe and Global Trade.* Berlin: Springer-Verlag, 1992.

Knore, Francis. *The Common Market World Agriculture: Trade Patterns in Temperate-Zone Foodstuffs.* New York: Praeger, 1972.

Kruse, D. C. *Monetary Integration in Western Europe: EMU, EMS and Beyond.* London: Butterworths, 1980.

Leebaert, Derek. *European Security: Prospects for the 1980s.* Lexington, MA: Lexington Books, 1979.

Leigh, Michael. *European Integration and the Common Fisheries Policy*. London: Croom Helm, 1983.

Levich, Richard; Sommariva, Andrea. *The ECU Market: Current Developments and Future Prospects of the European Currency Unit*. Lexington, MA: Lexington Books, 1987.

Lodge, Juliet. *Political Union in Europe: The Crisis of Political Authority in the EC*. Cheltenham, England: Edward Elgar, 1992.

Louis, Jean-Victor. *The Community Legal Order*. 2nd ed. European Perspectives Series. Brussels: EC Commission, 1980.

Louis, Jean-Victor. *From EMS to Monetary Union*. Luxembourg: Office for Official Publications of the European Communities, 1990.

Lucas, N. J. D. *Energy and the EC*. London: Europa Publications, 1977.

Mackenzie, Stewart; Alexander, John. *The European Commmunity and the Rule of Law*. London: Stevens & Sons, 1977.

Macmillan, Malcolm. *European Integration and Industry*. Tilburg, The Netherlands: Tilburg University Press, 1987.

Marjolin, Robert. *Europe in Search of Its Identity*. New York: Council on Foreign Relations, 1981.

Marsden, David, ed. *Pay and Employment in the New Europe*. Brookfield, VT: Edward Elgar, 1992.

Marsh, J. S.; Swanney, P. J. *Agriculture and the EC*. London: Allen & Unwin, 1980.

Masera, R. S.; Triffin, R. *Europe's Money: Problems of European Monetary Coordination and Integration*. Oxford: Clarendon Press, 1984.

Mathijsen, P. *A Guide to European Community Law*. London: Sweet & Maxwell, 1985.

Matthew, Alan. *The Common Agricultural Policy and the Less Developed Regions*. Dublin: Gill & Macmillan, 1985.

Mendes, A. J. Marques. *Economic Integration and Growth in Europe.* London: Croom Helm, 1987.

Miller, Debra L. *EC 1992: A Commerce Department Analysis of European Community Directives.* Washington, DC: US Department of Commerce, 1989.

Molle, Willem. *The Economics of European Integration.* Brookfield, VT: Dartmouth, 1990.

Molle, Willem; Cappellin, Ricardo. *Regional Impact of Community Policies.* Brookfield, VT: Avebury, 1988.

Montagnon, Peter, ed. *European Competition Policy.* London: RIIA, 1991.

Morgan, Roger. *High Politics and Low Politics: Towards a Foreign Policy for Western Europe.* Beverly Hills: Sage, 1973.

Mottola, Kari. *Ten Years After Helsinki: The Making of the European Security Regime.* Boulder, CO: Westview, 1986.

Neuhold, Hans P. *The European Neutrals in the 1990s.* Boulder, CO: Westview, 1991.

Neville-Rolfe, Edmund. *The Politics of Agriculture in the EC.* London: European Center for Policy Studies, 1984.

Padoa-Schioppa, Tommaso. *Efficiency, Stability and Equity: A Strategy for the Evolution of the Economic System of the European Community.* Oxford: Oxford University Press, 1987.

Pearce, Joan. *The Common Agricultural Policy: Prospects for Change.* London: Routledge & Kegan Paul, 1981.

Pearce, Joan; Sutton, John. *Protectionism and Industrial Policy in Europe.* London: RIIA, 1986.

Pelkmans, Jacques. *Market Integration in the EC.* The Hague: Martinus Nijhoff, 1984.

Pelkmans, Jacques; Winters, Alan. *Europe's Domestic Market.* London: RIIA, 1988.

Pierre, Andrew J.; Press, Frank, eds. *A High Technology Gap?*

Europe, America and Japan. New York: Council on Foreign Relations, 1987.

Plender, Richard. *A Practical Introduction to EC Law.* London: Sweet & Maxwell, 1980.

Plender, Richard; Usher, John. *Cases and Materials on the Law of the EC.* London: Macmillan, 1980.

Quelch, John A.; Buzzell, Robert D.; Salama, Eric R. *The Marketing Challenge of 1992.* Reading, MA: Addison-Wesley, 1989.

Rasmussen, Hjalte. *On Law and Policy in the European Court of Justice.* Dordrecht, The Netherlands: Martinus Nijhoff, 1986.

Reed, Lawrence. *Europe in a Shrinking World: A Technological Perspective.* London: Oldbourne, 1967.

Richardson, J. J., ed. *Policy Styles in Western Europe.* London: Allen & Unwin, 1982.

Rummel, Reinhardt, ed. *The Evolution of an International Actor: Western Europe's New Assertiveness.* Boulder, CO: Westview, 1990.

Rummel, Reinhardt, ed. *Western European Security Policy: Asserting European Priorities.* Boulder, CO: Westview, 1989.

Rusi, Alpo M. *After the Cold War: Europe's New Political Architecture.* New York: St. Martin's, 1991.

Ruyt, Jean de. *L'Acte Unique Européen.* Brussels: Editions de l'Université de Bruxelles, 1987.

Sandholtz, Wayne. *High-Tech Europe: The Politics of European Cooperation.* Berkeley, CA: University of California Press, 1991.

Schott, Jeffrey J., ed. *Completing the Uruguay Round: A Results-Oriented Approach to the GATT Trade Negotiations.* Washington, DC: Institute for International Economics, 1990.

Schuknecht, Ludger. *Trade Protection in the EC.* Philadelphia: Harwood, 1992.

Shackleton, Michael. *Financing the EC.* London: Pinter, 1990.

Shanks, Michael. *European Social Policy: Today and Tomorrow*. Oxford: Pergamon, 1977.

Sharp, Margaret. *Europe and the New Technologies: Six Core Studies in Innovation and Adjustment*. Ithaca, NY: Cornell University Press, 1986.

Sharp, Margaret; Shearman, Claire. *European Technological Collaboration*. London: RIIA, 1987.

Siebert, Horst. *The Completion of the Internal Market: Symposium 1989*. Boulder, CO: Westview, 1990.

Siedentopf, Heinrich; Ziller, Jacques, eds. *Making European Policy Work*. London: Sage for the European Institute of Public Administration, 1988.

Smit, Hans; Herzog, Peter. *The Law of the EEC*. New York: Bender for the Columbia Law School, 1977.

Snyder, Francis. *Law of the CAP*. London: Sweet & Maxwell, 1985.

Springer, Beverly. *The Social Dimension of 1992: Europe Faces a New EC*. New York: Greenwood, 1992.

Stanley, Andrew. *Agriculture and the Common Market*. Ames, IA: Iowa State University Press, 1973.

Steenbergen, Jacques; Clercq, Guido de; Foque, René. *Change and Adjustment: External Relations and Industrial Policy in the EC*. Boston: Kluwer Law and Taxation, 1983.

Stein, George. *Benelux Security Cooperation: A New European Defense Community?* Boulder, CO: Westview, 1990.

Strasser, Daniel. *The Finances of Europe*. New York: Praeger, 1977.

Swann, Dennis. *Competition and Industrial Policy in the EC*. London: Methuen, 1983.

Swann, Dennis. *The Economics of the Common Market*. 5th ed. Harmondsworth, England: Penguin, 1984.

Talbot, Ross. *The EC's Regional Fund*. Oxford: Pergamon, 1977.

Taylor, Trevor. *European Defense Cooperation*. London: Routledge & Kegan Paul for RIIA, 1984.

Trezise, Philip. *The EMS: Its Promise and Prospects*. Washington, DC: Brookings Institution, 1979.

Tsoukalis, Loukas. *The New European Economy: The Politics and Economics of Integration*. Oxford: Oxford University Press, 1991.

Tsoukalis, Loukas. *The Politics and Economics of Euromonetary Integration*. London: Allen & Unwin, 1977.

Van Ypersele, Jacques. *The European Monetary System: Origins, Operation and Outlook*. Chicago: St. James, 1985.

Wallace, Helen. *Budgetary Politics: The Finances of the European Communities*. London: Allen & Unwin, 1980.

Wallace, William; Hodges, Michael, eds. *Economic Divergence in the EC*. London: Allen & Unwin, 1981.

Wallace, William; Paterson, William, eds. *Foreign Policy Making in Western Europe*. New York: Praeger, 1978.

Warnecke, Steven Joshua; Suleiman, Ezra N. *Industrial Policy in Western Europe*. New York: Praeger, 1975.

Weyman-Jones, T. *Energy in Europe: Issues and Policies*. London: Methuen, 1986.

Williams, Geoffrey Lee; Williams, Alan Lee. *Crisis in European Defense*. London: Charles Knight, 1974.

Williams, Phil. *US Troops in Europe*. London: Routledge & Kegan Paul for RIIA, 1984.

Winters, Alan L.; Venables, Anthony. *European Integration: Trade and Industry*. London: Center for European Policy Research, 1991.

Wise, Michael. *The Common Fisheries Policy of the EC*. London: Methuen, 1984.

Woods, Stanley. *Western Europe: Technology and the Future*. London: Croom Helm, 1987.

Worthey, B. A., ed. *The Law of the Common Market*. Dobbs Ferry, NY: Manchester University Press and Oceana Publications, 1974.

Yuill, Douglas; Allen, Kevin; Hull, C., eds. *Regional Policy in the EC: The Role of Regional Incentives*. London: Croom Helm, 1980.

Appendix I

CHRONOLOGY

1950

May 9   French Foreign Minister **Robert Schuman**, in a historic declaration at the Foreign Ministry in Paris, calls for the pooling of Franco-German coal and steel production in a new supranational organization open to all European countries.

June 20   France convenes an intergovernmental conference, held in Paris and chaired by **Jean Monnet**, to implement the **Schuman Plan** and organize the proposed **European Coal and Steel Community** (ECSC).

October 24   French Prime Minister René Pleven announces a plan for German remilitarization under the aegis of a **European Defense Community** (EDC).

1951

April 18   Treaty establishing the **European Coal and Steel Community** (ECSC) is signed in Paris by representatives of France, Germany, Italy, Belgium, The Netherlands, and Luxembourg (henceforth called the **Six**).

1952

May 27	The **Six** sign the Paris Treaty establishing the EDC, which includes an article calling for a supranational political authority to direct the Defense Community.
August 10	The ECSC begins operation in **Luxembourg**.
September 10	The ECSC Common Assembly holds its first sitting in **Strasbourg**.

1954

August 30	The French National Assembly refuses to ratify the EDC Treaty.
October 23	The 1948 **Brussels Treaty** is amended to establish the **Western European Union** (WEU).

1955

May 5	Germany joins the **North Atlantic Treaty Organization** through the WEU.
June 1 and 2	At the **Messina Conference**, foreign ministers of the **Six** ask Belgian Foreign Minister **Paul-Henri Spaak** to form a committee and prepare a report on future options for European integration.
June 26	**Paul-Henri Spaak** convenes an intergovernmental conference in **Brussels** to discuss the Messina proposals.

1956

May 29   At a meeting of foreign ministers of the **Six** in Venice, **Paul-Henri Spaak** presents a report proposing that the dual objectives of sectoral (atomic energy) integration and wider economic integration (a **common market**) be realized in separate organizations, with separate treaties.

1957

March 25   Treaties establishing the **European Economic Community** (EEC) and the **European Atomic Energy Community** (Euratom) are signed at the Capitol in Rome.

1958

January 1   The EEC and Euratom are launched.

January 7   **Walter Hallstein** becomes the first president of the **EEC Commission**.

July 3 to 11   A conference in Stressa lays the foundations for the the **Common Agricultural Policy** (CAP).

1959

January 1   First steps are taken in the progressive elimination of customs duties and quotas in the EEC.

1960

December 19 and 20   The **Council of Ministers** approves the basic principles governing the CAP.

1961

July/August   Ireland (July 31), the United Kingdom (August 9), and Denmark (August 10) apply to join the EEC.

November 2   The French government submits a draft treaty establishing a **Political Union** of the **Six** (known as the **Fouchet Plan**).

1962

January 1   The **Community** begins the second stage in the establishment of a **common market**.

April 17   The **Fouchet Plan** collapses at a meeting of foreign ministers, primarily over disagreement about Britain's role.

April 30   Norway applies for membership in the **Community**.

May 15   The **Six** decide a second time to speed up establishment of the **common market**.

1963

January 14   At a press conference, French President **Charles de Gaulle** effectively vetoes British membership by declaring that the United Kingdom is not ready to join the EEC.

January 22   France and Germany sign a Treaty of Friendship and Cooperation in Paris (the **Elysée Treaty**).

January 29   Accession negotiations with the United Kingdom end at the insistence of the French government; negotiations with the other applicant countries are also suspended.

July 20   Association Convention between the EEC and
                     seventeen African states and Madagascar is signed
                     in Yaoundé, Cameroon.

1964

June 1   Yaoundé Convention enters into force.

July 1   The CAP's Guidance and Guarantee Fund
                     (EAGGF) enters into force.

1965

April 8   The **Six** sign the **Merger Treaty**, fusing the
                     executives of the EEC, the ECSC, and Euratom,
                     thereby establishing a single **Council** and a single
                     Commission of the **European Communities**.

July 1   Beginning of the **"Empty Chair Crisis."**

1966

January 1   The EEC enters the third and final stage of the
                     common market transitional period.

January 28   Resuming its special meeting in **Luxembourg**, the
and 29   **Council** agrees on the **"Luxembourg Compromise,"**
                     ending the **"Empty Chair Crisis."**

1967

May   The governments of the United Kingdom (May
                     10), Ireland (May 10), and Denmark (May 11)
                     submit new applications to join the Communities.

July 1   **Merger Treaty** enters into force.

July 6   The new, nine-member joint **Commission** of the **European Communities** takes office, with **Jean Rey** as president.

July 25   Norway makes a second application to join the Communities.

November 27   French President **Charles de Gaulle** again vetoes Britain's membership application by restating that the United Kingdom is not ready to join the Community.

December 19   The **Council** fails to reach agreement on new negotiations with the applicant countries.

1968

July 1   The customs union is completed eighteen months ahead of the schedule prescribed by the **Treaty of Rome**: customs duties between member states are removed, and the common customs tariff replaces national customs duties in trade with the rest of the world.

1969

July 23   Following French President **Charles de Gaulle's** resignation in April 1969, the **Council** resumes examination of the membership applications from the United Kingdom, Ireland, Denmark, and Norway.

December 1   Conference of the heads of state and government
and 2   at The Hague (the **Hague Summit**).

December 31   The twelve-year transitional period provided for in the EEC Treaty for the establishment of the **common market** ends.

1970

June 30   Negotiations with the four applicant countries formally open in **Luxembourg**.

July 2   A new **Commission**, composed of nine members and presided over by **Franco Malfatti**, takes office.

October 7 and 8   A committee chaired by Luxembourg Prime Minister Pierre Werner presents a report (the **Werner Plan**) on **Economic and Monetary Union** (EMU).

October 27   Foreign ministers of the **Six**, meeting in **Luxembourg**, adopt the **Davignon Report** on **European Political Cooperation** (EPC).

November 19   First meeting of foreign ministers in EPC.

1971

January 1   The second Yaoundé Convention and Arusha Agreement enter into force.

1972

January 22   Treaty and related documents concerning the accession to the EC of Denmark, Ireland, Norway, and the United Kingdom are signed in **Brussels**.

March 21   Introduction of the currency **"snake."**

September 25   In referendum in Norway on EC membership, a

majority votes against. The Norwegian government asks the **Community** for a free-trade agreement instead of accession.

October 19   The **Nine** heads of state and government of the en-
to 21   larged **Community** hold a conference in Paris
                  (the **Paris Summit**).

1973

January 1   Denmark, Ireland, and the United Kingdom join
                  the **European Communities.**

July 3 to 7   The **Conference on Security and Cooperation in
                  Europe** (CSCE) opens in Helsinki.

October 6   Following the Yom Kippur War, Arab oil-producing
to 27   countries announce that oil exports to certain
                  Western countries will be cut or stopped. The
                  Organization of Petroleum Exporting Countries
                  (OPEC) decides to raise oil prices substantially.

December 14   The heads of state and government of the member
and 15   states confer in Copenhagen (the **Copenhagen
                  Summit**).

1974

April 1   The new Labour government in Britain asks for a
                  "renegotiation" of the United Kingdom's member-
                  ship terms.

July 31   The Euro-Arab Dialogue opens in Paris.

September 14   At the invitation of French President **Valéry
                  Giscard d'Estaing**, the heads of state and
                  government of the **Nine** and the president of the

Commission meet for informal talks at the Elyseé and decide to launch the **European Council.**

December 9 and 10	The Nine heads of state and government hold a **summit** conference in Paris.

1975

March 10 and 11	The **European Council** holds its inaugural meeting in Dublin and ends Britain's renegotiation.
June 5	In a referendum in the U.K., a large majority vote in favor of remaining in the **Community**.
June 12	Greece applies to join the **European Community**.
July 22	A treaty strengthening the budgetary powers of the **European Parliament** and setting up a Court of Auditors is signed in **Brussels**.
August 1	In Helsinki, the Final Act of the **Conference on Security and Cooperation in Europe** is signed by the thirty-five states taking part.
December 29	Belgian Prime Minister **Leo Tindemans** submits his report on **European Union**.

1976

April 1	A convention between the EEC and forty-six African, Caribbean, and Pacific (ACP) states, signed at Lomé on 28 February 1975, enters into force.

1977

March 28	Portugal applies for **Community** membership.

July 1   A **customs union** is achieved in the enlarged **Community**.

July 28   Spain applies for **Community** membership.

1978

July 6 and 7   At the **Bremen Summit**, the **European Council** approves a Franco-German plan to set up a **European Monetary System** (EMS).

December 4 and 5 The **European Council**, meeting in **Brussels**, agrees to set up the EMS based on a European currency unit (ECU). The EMS comprises an exchange and intervention mechanism, credit mechanisms, and a mechanism for the transfer of resources to less prosperous Community countries. Eight member states decide to participate fully in the EMS. The United Kingdom opts to remain outside the exchange rate mechanism (ERM) of the EMS.

1979

May 28   Treaty and related documents concerning Greece's accession to the Communities are signed in Athens.

June 7 to 10   First direct elections to the **European Parliament**.

October 31   The second ACP-EEC Convention governing cooperation between the **Community** and fifty-eight African, Caribbean, and Pacific countries is signed in Lomé.

November 29   At the Dublin **European Council**, the new British government asks for resolution of the British budgetary question, thus provoking a five-year-long crisis in the Community.

1980

October 1   Cooperation Agreement between the EEC and the Association of Southeast Asian Nations (ASEAN) comes into operation.

1981

January 1   Greece becomes the tenth member of the Community. The second ACP-EEC Convention, signed in Lomé on 31 October 1979, comes into operation.

July 7 to 9   On the initiative of **Altiero Spinelli**, the **European Parliament** decides to set up an institutional affairs committee to draft amendments to the existing treaties.

November 6 and 12   The German and Italian governments submit to the other member states, to the **European Parliament**, and to the **Commission** a "Draft European Act" (the **Genscher-Colombo Proposals**).

1982

June 30   The presidents of **Parliament**, the **Council**, and the **Commission** sign a joint declaration on improving the budgetary procedure.

1983

January 25   After six years of negotiations, agreement is reached on a common fisheries policy.

June 17 to 19   At the **European Council** in Stuttgart the heads of
state and government sign the "**Solemn Declaration
on European Union.**"

1984

February 14   By a large majority, the **European Parliament**
adopts the "Draft Treaty on European Union,"
prepared by its Committee on Institutional Affairs.

February 28   The **Council** adopts a decision that sets out a
European strategic program for research and
development in information technology (ESPRIT).

June 25   At the **Fontainebleau Summit**, the heads of state
and 26   and government resolve the British budgetary
question and agree to reform the CAP. They also
decide to set up an ad hoc committee on
institutional affairs, chaired by former Irish Foreign
Minister Jim Dooge, to consider amending the
Treaty of Rome (the **Dooge Committee**).

December 8   The third ACP-EEC Convention on cooperation
between the **Community** and sixty-five African,
Caribbean, and Pacific countries is signed in Lomé.

1985

February 1   Greenland leaves the **Community** but remains
associated with it as an overseas territory.

March 9   The **Dooge Committee** recommends that the
member states convene an intergovernmental
conference to negotiate reform of the **Treaty of
Rome.**

June 12   Instruments of accession of Spain and Portugal are signed.

June 14   The **Commission** publishes its **"White Paper"** on completing the internal market, which details the measures necessary to remove all physical, technical, and tax barriers between the member states by the end of 1992.

June 28   The **European Council**, meeting in Milan, decides
and 29   to convene an intergovernmental conference to draft revisions to the **Treaty of Rome**.

December 2   Based on the work of the intergovernmental con-
and 3   ference, the **European Council**, meeting in **Luxembourg**, agrees on reform of the **Community's** institutions designed to improve their efficiency, extend the Community's competence, and provide a legal framework for cooperation on foreign policy.

December 16   EC foreign ministers encapsulate proposed reforms in the **Single European Act** (SEA).

1986

January 1   Spain and Portugal join the **Community**.

January 17   Representatives of the governments of the **Twelve**
and 18   member states sign the SEA.

May 1   The third ACP-EEC Convention comes into operation.

September 15   In Punta del Este, Uruguay, ministers of ninety-two
to 20   countries agree to a new round of multilateral trade negotiations.

1987

February 15   In a communication entitled "The Single Act: A New Frontier for Europe," the **Commission** sets out the conditions for attaining the objectives of the **Single European Act**, including proposals to complete CAP reform and double the "structural funds" to promote **cohesion** in the **Community** (known as the **Delors I** budgetary package).

April 14   Turkey applies for EC membership.

May 26   A referendum in Ireland approves a constitutional amendment that clears the way for ratification of the SEA.

July 1   The **Single European Act** enters into force.

September 12   At an informal meeting in Nyborg, Denmark, EC finance ministers adopt measures to strengthen the EMS.

1988

February 11 to 13   The **European Council**, meeting in **Brussels**, ends nearly a year of budgetary wrangling and approves **Delors I**.

June 27 and 28   The **European Council**, meeting in Hanover, reappoints **Jacques Delors** as **Commission** president, and appoints a committee, to be chaired by Delors, to look into and propose specific steps that would lead to EMU.

September 20   In a speech at the College of Europe in Bruges, British Prime Minister **Margaret Thatcher** sharply criticizes the accelerating pace of European integration, attacks the **Brussels** bureaucracy, and condemns moves toward EMU.

December 8   Representatives of the governments of the member states appoint a new **Commission.**

1989

April 12   The Delors Committee presents its report on EMU (the **Delors Plan**).

June 26 and 27   The **European Council**, meeting in Madrid, unanimously adopts the **Delors Plan.**

July 17   Austria applies for EC membership.

December 8 and 9   At a **European Council** meeting in **Strasbourg**, the heads of state and government call for an intergovernmental conference to draw up the necessary amendments to the **Treaty of Rome** for implementation of EMU. The Council also adopts the Community Charter of Fundamental Social Rights of Workers (the **Social Charter**) and reaffirms the **Community's** international role, especially in relation to developments in Central and Eastern Europe.

December 15   The fourth ACP-EEC Convention is signed in Lomé by the **Community**, its member states, and the African, Caribbean, and Pacific countries.

December 19   Representatives of the **Community** and the **European Free Trade Association** (EFTA) agree to start formal negotiations to concluding a general agreement on closer cooperation between both organizations.

1990

February 8   The **Commission** sets up an emergency committee
                  to deal with imminent German unification and the
                  absorption of East Germany into the EC.

February 27   The U.S. and the EC agree to formalize relations
                  by holding regular meetings between both sides'
                  presidents.

March 23   German Chancellor **Helmut Kohl** visits **Brussels**
                  for discussions with **Commission** President **Jacques
                  Delors** on the EC and German unification.

April 19   In a letter to Irish Prime Minister and **European
                  Council** President Charles Haughey, French
                  President **Francois · Mitterrand** and German
                  Chancellor **Helmut Kohl** launch an initiative to
                  achieve **Political Union** and EMU by 1993.

April 28   The **European Council**, meeting in a special
                  summit in Dublin, instructs EC foreign ministers to
                  produce proposals on **European Political Union
                  (EPU)** for the next European Council in June.

May 29   The Charter for the **European Bank of Recon-
                  struction and Development** is signed in Paris.

June 19   The **Schengen Agreement**, which calls for the
                  eventual removal of border controls between the
                  signatory states, is signed by the **Benelux** countries,
                  Germany, and France.

June 25   The **European Council**, meeting in Dublin, agrees
and 26   to convene an intergovernmental conference (IGC)
                  on EPU to parallel the planned IGC on EMU.

July 4   Cyprus applies for EC membership.

July 16	Malta applies for EC membership.
October 3	Germany unifies. The U.K. joins the exchange rate mechanism of the EMS.
October 27 and 28	At a special **European Council** in Rome, member states (except Britain) commit themselves to launch the second stage of EMU on January 1, 1994.
November 19 to 21	At a special summit in Paris, the thirty-four members of the **Conference on Security and Cooperation in Europe** (CSCE) sign the Charter of Paris.
November 20	The United States and EC sign the **U.S.-EC Declaration**.
December 14 and 15	The **European Council**, meeting in Rome, formally launches the IGCs on EPU and EMU.
December 20	Foreign ministers from the EC and the Rio Group of Latin American countries sign the Declaration of Rome to develop closer economic and political links.

1991

March 13	The **Commission** adopts a **Community** support framework for structural assistance to the five new German Länder and eastern Berlin.
April 15	The **European Bank for Reconstruction and Development** begins operating in London.
June 28 and 29	The **European Council**, meeting in **Luxembourg**, approves the draft treaty prepared by the Luxembourg presidency.

July 1   Sweden applies for EC membership.

September 7   The EC-sponsored peace conference on Yugoslavia opens in The Hague.

October 21   The **Council** agrees on the establishment of a **European Economic Area** (EEA).

December 9 and 10   The **European Council**, meeting in Maastricht, settles on a draft **Treaty on European Union** (the **Maastricht Treaty**).

December 16   The EC signs "**European Agreements**" with Poland, Hungary, and Czechoslovakia.

1992

January 15   The EC recognizes the independence of Slovenia and Croatia.

February 7   Representatives of the **Twelve** EC member states sign the **Treaty on European Union** in Maastricht (the **Maastricht Treaty**).

February 12   In a communication entitled "From the Single Act to Maastricht and Beyond: The Means to Match Our Ambitions," the **Commission** introduces a new five-year budget package (**Delors II**).

May 2   The EC and the EFTA member states sign a treaty establishing the **European Economic Area** (EEA).

May 21   Agriculture ministers agree to reform the CAP by moving away from price supports toward more direct farm subsidies; cereal prices are cut immediately.

June 2   In a referendum on **European Union**, the Danish electorate rejects the **Maastricht Treaty** by a margin of less than 2%, throwing the treaty's future into doubt.

June 27 and 28   At the **European Council** meeting in Lisbon, the heads of state and government reappoint **Commission** President **Jacques Delors** to an unprecedented fifth two-year term but fail to reach agreement on the **Delors II** budgetary package.

September 16   Facing one of its worst financial crises since World War II, Britain responds to sterling's plummeting value on the world markets by suspending its participation in the exchange rate mechanism (ERM) of the EMS, a move that precipitates a major currency crisis among the EC member states. Italy withdraws the lira from the ERM the same day.

September 20   In a national referendum, French voters approve the **Maastricht Treaty** by a slim majority (51.05%).

October 16   An extraordinary meeting of the **European Council** is held in Birmingham, England, to discuss the **Maastricht Treaty** ratification crisis and the recent EMS crisis, but the **summit** is overshadowed by domestic political events in the U.K.

Appendix II

TABLES AND GRAPHS

The Commissioners and their Portfolios[1]

Jacques Delors *France*	President; Secretariat General; Monetary Affairs; Forward Studies Unit; Joint Interpreting and Conference Service; Security Office; Spokesman's Service
Frans Andriessen *The Netherlands*	Vice-President; External Relations; Commercial Policy; Cooperation with other European Countries
Henning Christopherson *Denmark*	Economic and Financial Affairs; Coordination of Structural Policies; Statistical Office
Manuel Marín *Spain*	Vice-President; Cooperation and Development; Fisheries
Filippo Maria Pandolfi *Italy*	Science, Research, and Development; Telecommunications, Information Industries, and Innovation; Joint Research Center
Martin Bangemann *Germany*	Internal Market and Industrial Affairs; Relations with the European Parliament

273

Sir Leon Brittan *United Kingdom*	Competition; Financial Institutions and Company Law
Carlo Ripa di Meana *Italy*	Environment and Nuclear Safety; Civil Protection
Antonio Cardoso E Cunha *Portugal*	Personnel and Administration; Energy; Enterprise Policy, Trade Tourism, and Social Economy
Abel Matutes *Spain*	Mediterranean Policy; Relations with Latin-America and Asia; North-South Relations
Peter Schmidhuber *Germany*	Budgets; Financial Control
Christiane Scrivener *France*	Customs Union and Indirect Taxation
Bruce Millan *United Kingdom*	Regional Policy
Jean Dondelinger *Luxembourg*	Information, Communication, and Culture
Ray MacSharry *Ireland*	Agriculture; Rural Development
Karel Van Miert *Belgium*	Transport; Credit and Investments; Consumer Policy Service
Vasso Papandreou *Greece*	Employment, Industrial Relations, and Social Affairs; Relations with Economic and Social Committee; Human Resources, Education, and Training

[1]Distributed by President Jacques Delors to his second Commission (1989-1992) in December 1988.

The Commission's Directorates-General (DGs)

    I. External Relations

   II. Economic and Financial Affairs

  III. Internal Market and Industrial Affairs

  IV. Competition

   V. Employment, Industrial Relations, and Social Affairs

  VI. Agriculture

 VII. Transport

VIII. Development

  IX. Personnel and Administration

   X. Information, Communication, and Culture

  XI. Environment, Nuclear Safety and Civil Protection

 XII. Science, Research and Education

XIII. Telecommunications, Information Industries, and Innovation

XIV. Fisheries

 XV. Financial Institutions and Company Law

XVI. Regional Policy

XVII. Energy Policy

XVIII. Credit and Investments

XIX. Budgets

XX. Financial Control

XXI. Customs Union and Indirect Taxation

XXII. Coordination of Structural Policy

XXIII. Enterprise Policy, Trade, Tourism, and Social Economy

Commission Presidents

Name (Years Served)	Member State	Highest Position Held in National Government[1]	Type of Leadership
Walter Hallstein (1958-67)	Germany	State Secretary, German Foreign Office	active
Jean Rey (1967-70)	Belgium	Minister of Economic Affairs	passive
Franco Malfatti (1970-72)	Italy	Minister for Posts and Telecommunications	passive
Sicco Mansholt (1972)	The Netherlands	Minister of Agriculture	passive
Francois-Xavier Ortoli (1973-77)	France	Minister of Finance	passive
Roy Jenkins (1977-81)	United Kingdom	Chancellor of the Exchequer	active
Gaston Thorn (1981-85)	Luxembourg	Prime Minister	passive
Jacques Delors (1985-)	France	Minister for the Economy, Finance, and Budget	active

[1]Before assuming the Commission presidency.

Commissioners per Member State

Dates	Number of Member States	Member States (Number of Commissioners)	Total Number of Commissioners
1967[a]-1972	6	France, Germany, and Italy (2 each); Belgium, The Netherlands, and Luxembourg (1 each)	9
1973-1980	9	France, Germany, Italy, and the UK (2 each); Belgium, The Netherlands, Luxembourg, **Denmark**, and **Ireland** (1 each)	13
1981-1985	10	France, Germany, Italy, and the UK (2 each); Belgium, The Netherlands, Luxembourg, Denmark, Ireland, and **Greece** (1 each)	14
1986-	12	France, Germany, Italy, the UK, and **Spain** (2 each); Belgium, The Netherlands, Luxembourg, Denmark, Ireland, Greece, and **Portugal** (1 each)	17

[a]Under the terms of the Merger Treaty, which came into effect on July 1, 1967, the ECSC High Authority combined with the Commissions of the EEC and Euratom to form the Commission of the European Communities.

REPRESENTATION IN EC INSTITUTIONS

COUNTRY	VOTES IN EC COUNCIL OF MINISTERS	NUMBER OF COMMISSIONERS	SEATS IN EUROPEAN PARLIAMENT	JUDGES IN COURT OF JUSTICE	DATES OF EC COUNCIL PRESIDENCY
BELGIUM	5	1	24	1	JUL-DEC 1993
DENMARK	3	1	16	1	JAN-JUN 1993
FRANCE	10	2	81	1	JAN-JUN 1995
GERMANY	10	2	81	1	JUL-DEC 1994
GREECE	5	1	24	1	JAN-JUN 1994
IRELAND	3	1	15	1	JUL-DEC 1996
ITALY	10	2	81	1	JAN-JUN 1996
LUXEMBOURG	2	1	6	1	JUL-DEC 1997
NETHERLANDS	5	1	25	1	JAN-JUN 1997
PORTUGAL	5	1	24	1	JUL-DEC 1998
SPAIN	8	2	60	1	JUL-DEC 1995
UK	10	2	81	1	JAN-JUN 1998
TOTAL	76	17	518	13[a]	

a. To prevent judicial gridlock, the governments of the member states appoint a thirteenth judge by common accord. The post has traditionally gone to one of the larger member states.

A Chronology of Referenda
Results from Member States and Applicant Countries

Country	Date	Issue	% of Electorate	% Yes	% No
France	April 23, 1972	enlargement	60	61	32[a]
Ireland	May 11, 1972	membership	70	83	17
Norway	September 25, 1972	membership	75	46.5	53.5
Denmark	October 2, 1972	membership	89.9	63.3	36.7
UK	June 5, 1975	continued membership	75	67.2	32.8
Denmark	February 27, 1986	Single European Act	74.8	56.2	43.8
Ireland	May 26, 1987	Single European Act	44.1	69.9	30.1
Denmark	June 2, 1992	Maastricht Treaty	82.9	49.3	50.7
Ireland	June 18, 1992	Maastricht Treaty	57	69	31
France	September 20, 1992	Maastricht Treaty	70	51.05	48.95

[a]Seven percent of the French electorate spoiled their ballots.

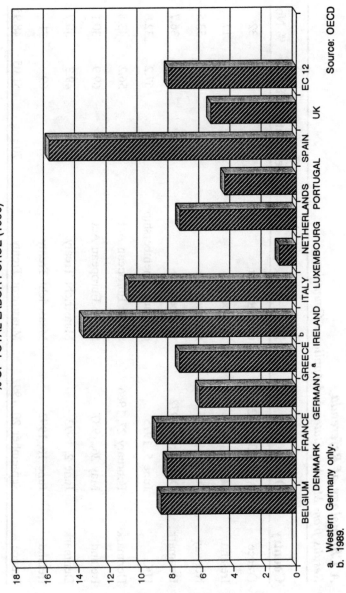

UNEMPLOYMENT RATES
% OF TOTAL LABOR FORCE (1990)

BELGIUM   DENMARK   FRANCE   GERMANY a   GREECE b   IRELAND   ITALY   LUXEMBOURG   NETHERLANDS   PORTUGAL   SPAIN   UK   EC 12

a. Western Germany only.
b. 1989.

Source: OECD

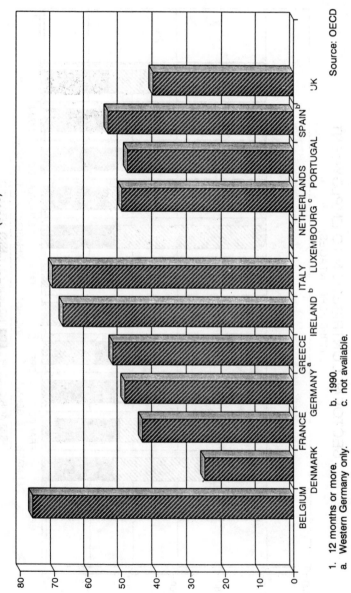

LONG-TERM UNEMPLOYMENT[1]
% OF TOTAL UNEMPLOYMENT (1989)

BELGIUM DENMARK FRANCE GERMANY[a] GREECE IRELAND[b] ITALY LUXEMBOURG[c] NETHERLANDS PORTUGAL SPAIN[b] UK

1. 12 months or more.   b. 1990.
a. Western Germany only.   c. not available.

Source: OECD

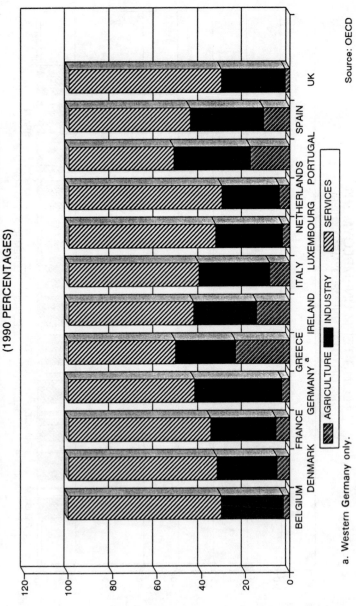

SECTORAL CONTRIBUTION TO EMPLOYMENT
(1990 PERCENTAGES)

AGRICULTURE ▨   INDUSTRY ■   SERVICES ▨

a. Western Germany only.

Source: OECD

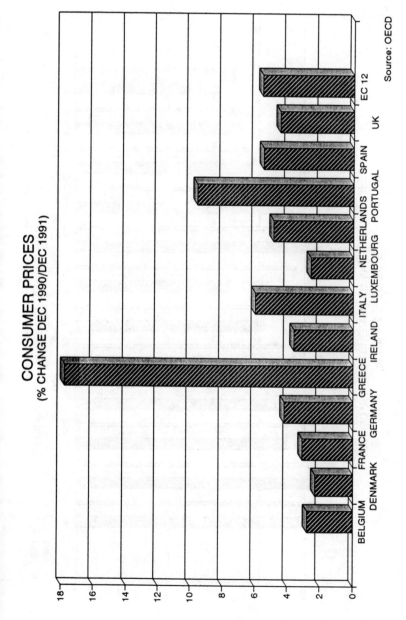

CONSUMER PRICES
(% CHANGE DEC 1990/DEC 1991)

Source: OECD

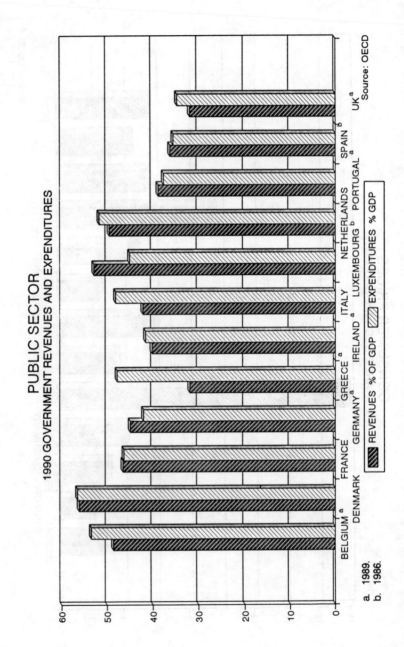

PUBLIC SECTOR
1990 GOVERNMENT REVENUES AND EXPENDITURES

BELGIUM a DENMARK FRANCE GERMANY a GREECE a IRELAND a ITALY LUXEMBOURG b NETHERLANDS PORTUGAL a SPAIN b UK a

REVENUES % OF GDP   EXPENDITURES % GDP

a. 1989.
b. 1986.

Source: OECD

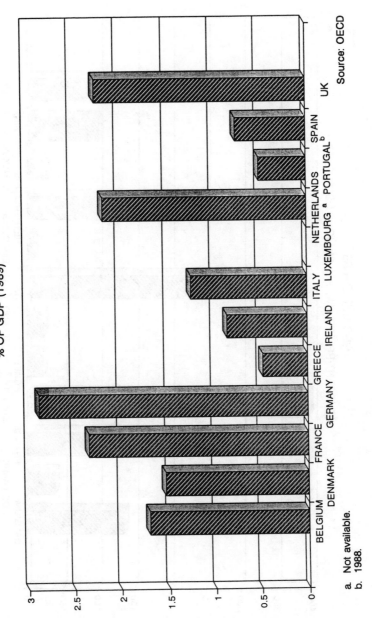

GROSS DOMESTIC EXPENDITURE ON R & D
% OF GDP (1989)

a. Not available.
b. 1988.

Source: OECD

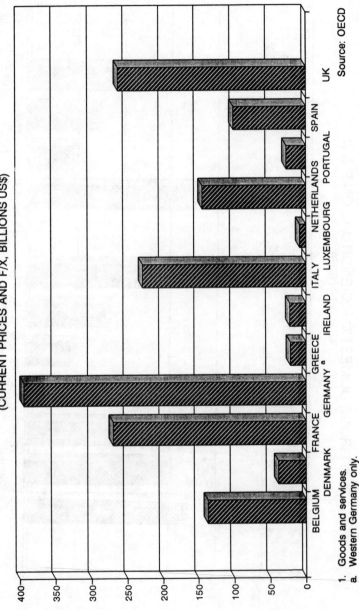

1990 IMPORTS[1]
(CURRENT PRICES AND F/X, BILLIONS US$)

1. Goods and services.
a. Western Germany only.

Source: OECD

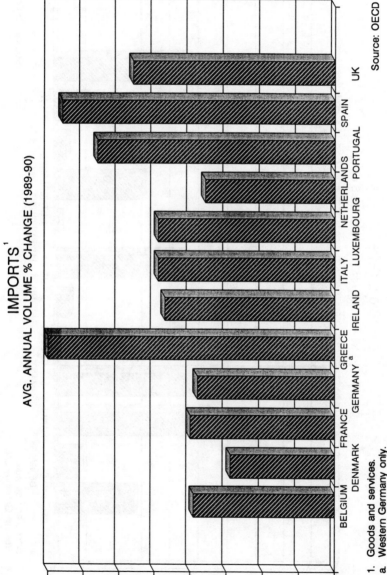

IMPORTS[1]
AVG. ANNUAL VOLUME % CHANGE (1989-90)

BELGIUM DENMARK FRANCE GERMANY[a] GREECE IRELAND ITALY LUXEMBOURG NETHERLANDS PORTUGAL SPAIN UK

1. Goods and services.
a. Western Germany only.

Source: OECD

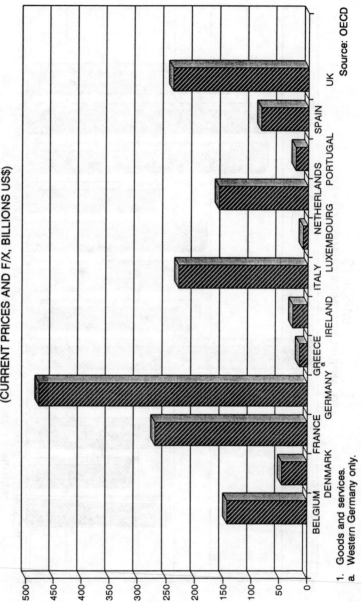

1990 EXPORTS[1]
(CURRENT PRICES AND F/X, BILLIONS US$)

BELGIUM   DENMARK   FRANCE   GERMANY[a]   GREECE   IRELAND   ITALY   LUXEMBOURG   NETHERLANDS   PORTUGAL   SPAIN   UK

1. Goods and services.
a. Western Germany only.

Source: OECD

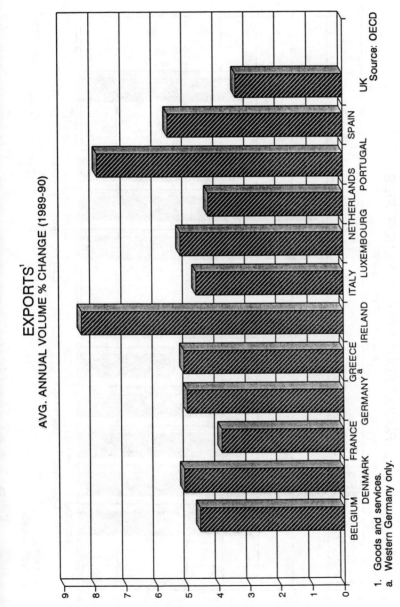

EXPORTS[1]
AVG. ANNUAL VOLUME % CHANGE (1989-90)

1. Goods and services.
a. Western Germany only.

Source: OECD

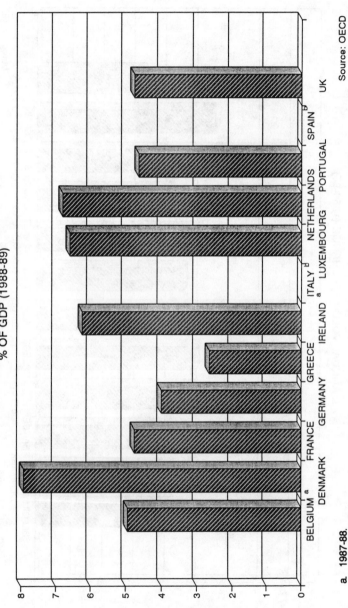

PUBLIC EDUCATION EXPENDITURES
% OF GDP (1988-89)

Source: OECD

a. 1987-88.
b. Not available.

ABOUT THE AUTHOR

Desmond Dinan is Director of the Center for European Community Studies and an Associate Professor of History at George Mason University in Fairfax, Virginia. A native of Ireland, he received his B.A. in European Studies from the National Institute for Higher Education, Limerick, his M.A. in International Politics from Georgetown University, Washington, D.C., and his Ph.D. from University College, Cork. Dr. Dinan has written extensively on Anglo-French diplomatic relations, Irish foreign policy, and the history and politics of European integration. He is currently working on a political and institutional analysis of the European Community, for publication in early 1994.